Change-Oriented Therapy
with Adolescents and Young Adults

Change-Oriented Therapy
with Adolescents and Young Adults

The Next Generation of Respectful
Processes and Practices

Bob Bertolino

W.W. Norton & Company
New York • London

For information about permission to reproduce
selections from this book, write to
Permissions, W. W. Norton & Company, Inc.,
500 Fifth Avenue, New York, NY 10110

Production Manager: Leeann Graham
Manufacturing by Haddon Craftsmen, Inc.

Library of Congress Cataloging-in-Publication Data

Bertolino, Bob, 1965–
Change-oriented therapy with adolescents and young adults : the next
generation of respectful processes and practices / Bob Bertolino.
p.   cm.
"A Norton professional book."
Includes bibliographical references and index.
ISBN: 0-393-70409-2
1. Adolescent psychotherapy.   I. Title.

RJ503.B475   2003
616.89'14035—dc21   2003059746

W. W. Norton & Company, Inc., 500 Fifth Avenue, New York, N.Y. 10110
www.wwnorton.com

W. W. Norton & Company Ltd., Castle House, 75/76 Wells St.,
London W1T 3QT

1 3 5 7 9 0 8 6 4 2

To Morgan—

Please don't grow up too fast.
I love you.

Contents

Preface

This is the eighth book that I have authored or coauthored. I've also written over 100 songs. At first glance these two mediums may seem very different—one more scientific, the other more artistic. But regardless of whether individuals are writing articles, poems, books, or songs—or creating some other form of art or science—they are always exposing themselves to the world. What follows may be scrutiny, acceptance, or a host of other responses from colleagues, the public, and so on. Yet I'm compelled to put my words down on paper and share them with the world. My writing process is akin to that of one of my favorite musical performers, Bono, from the band U2. In an article in *The Los Angeles Times*, the pop star commented about writing music:

> I wake up with a melody in my head in the morning and I have to write it down. I don't have to write it down because I think we need another song for a record. I write it down because I'm excited by the idea of making music.... But there is the feeling that once you have the songs, you want people to hear them. You don't want them to just sit in a closet. Take the R.E.M. album. "Reveal" has some truly beautiful songs on it, but they didn't get out there and fight for it, so people make the mistake of thinking they didn't believe in it. (Bono, "Joy Makes a Return," *The Los Angeles Times*, Robert Hilburn, Sunday, November 16, 2001)

Like Bono, I am passionate about my ideas. It's not enough for me to get them down on paper—I feel compelled to share them with the rest of the world too. To "spread the word," I've taught workshops throughout the United Stated, Australia, Canada, France, Germany, and the United Kingdom. Through these journeys I experienced many wonders of the world. More importantly, I had the privilege of meeting numerous wonderful people who made contributions to my life and work. This book represents my passion and that of others. I am hopeful that this passion will come alive on each and every page.

It is important to note that the ideas offered throughout this book serve a purpose other than helping adolescents, young adults, and families. It is my belief that these ideas reflect life. Further, I've witnessed their ability to counter burnout and extend the lives of mental health professionals. They promote hope and the possibility of change. On a more practical level, the ideas in this book simply make sense. They are useful and respectful. Because most people operate in "real life" settings, it is essential that ideas are applicable and "doable" in a variety of contexts.

HOW THIS BOOK IS ARRANGED

The book begins with an introduction that explores the rich history of therapeutic traditions in working with young people and families. It does this by delving briefly into the significant research movements in the fields of psychology, psychotherapy, and family therapy. It concludes with a discussion about the necessity of a new direction and describes how a change-oriented perspective can provide that new path.

Chapter 1 explores the foundational ideas of a change-oriented approach and emphasizes the importance of interplay between research and clinical practice. It discussed how we as practitioners can increase our effectiveness with young people and others through collaborative, client-informed processes. Each of the ideas offered in this chapter is discussed in depth to foster a better understanding of how a change-oriented philosophy translates into a clear, sound foundation that informs all practices.

Chapter 2 investigates the importance of collaborating with young people and others *prior to* the beginning of therapy and during initial interactions. The chapter offers ten specific ways of collaborating with those involved to strengthen the therapeutic relationship and alliance and to learn about young people and others' ideas about how to approach therapy.

Chapter 3 explores multiple ways of strengthening the therapeutic relationship and alliance. It teaches readers how to allow young people's and others' relational and conversational preferences guide therapy, and discusses how small changes in language can create openings for possibilities and change.

In Chapter 4, both formal and informal assessment processes are explored. Ways of learning about the concerns and problems, as well as strengths and resources, of young people and others are offered. The importance of establishing direction in therapy is also discussed. This chapter includes clear, practical ways of collaborating with those involved to learn about their goals and preferred futures.

Chapter 5 focuses on learning how young people's and other's orientations to change can guide therapy. This includes ways of evoking clients' ideas about the influences of context, their theories of change, and how they position themselves in relation to their concerns and problems. Numerous case examples illustrate possibilities for helping young people and others to achieve positive change.

The final chapter explores various ways of approaching subsequent sessions. This includes identifying and amplifying change, negotiating therapeutic impasses, and helping to transition young people and others involved out of therapy.

For the purposes of clarity, throughout this book, the terms *adolescents* and *young adults,* refer to people aged 10–18. The term *young people* is used to refer to people between the ages of 19 and 21. The terms *therapist, clinician, practitioner,* and *mental health professional* are used to refer to people who work with adolescents and others involved in their therapy.

ACKNOWLEDGMENTS

Thank you to Adrian Blow, Connie Burnett, Tom Conran, Mari Doyle, Barry Duncan, Michelle Gorman, Kelley Hartnett, Bill Heusler, Nancy Morrison, Scott Miller, Bill O'Hanlon, Steffanie O'Hanlon, Laura Harrison, Chris Turner, Beliuda and Don Willis, Wob, and my family. Additional thanks to the staff at Youth In Need, Inc., my supervisees, and my students in the departments of counseling and family therapy and social services at Saint Louis University and rehabilitation counseling at Maryville University.

A special thank you to Deborah Malmud, Michael McGandy, and the staff at W.W. Norton: Your efforts, patience, and enthusiasm are very much appreciated.

Bob Bertolino
February, 2003

For additional information, contact:
Therapeutic Collaborations
   Consultation & Training
P.O. Box 1175
St. Charles, MO 63302
(314) 983-9861
www.tcctinc.com
bertolinob@cs.com

Change-Oriented Therapy
with Adolescents and Young Adults

Introduction

In Search of Respectful and Effective Therapy

THERE ARE FEW POPULATIONS AS CHALLENGING AS ADOLESCENTS AND those transitioning out of adolescence and into young adulthood. To meet this challenge, be effective, and avoid personal insanity, therapists must be flexible and creative. Many practitioners also face an additional challenge: meeting the conditions of an everchanging climate in the field of mental health. Health maintenance organizations (HMOs), third-party payers, and federal, state, local, and other funding sources require that mental health practitioners be accountable. The situation is further complicated by the expectation that therapy remain relatively brief, and thus results-driven and outcome-oriented. Clinicians are required to solve the equation of how to work efficiently with adolescents and families without compromising effectiveness—a task that binds art and science, creativity and rationale.

Numerous books offer methods for working with adolescents and young adults. Perusing the shelves at the local bookseller, one finds volumes filled with ideas for working with "explosive," "defiant," "out-of-control," "violent," or just about any other "type" of "disordered" youth. Many of these approaches include steps, maneuvers, and recipes that prove enticing to clinicians in search of methods for increasing their therapeutic effectiveness. Reaching the goal of becoming more effective and ultimately improving outcomes with adolescents and young adults is paramount. It must continue to be a primary focus of clinicians and researchers. Accordingly, logic suggests that the more approaches and techniques from which clinicians have to choose, the more flexible, and hence effective, they can be in their helping relationships.

But if we already have a myriad of models at our disposal we must ask: Why another approach? Why another book? We've long known that logic is not always consistent with human experience. If you have worked with adolescents and young adults you know this all too well. Young people routinely defy logic and theory. In accordance, logic has led us astray by contributing to the misperception that methods, models, and techniques are what make therapy work. In spite of the promises that usually accompany the arrival of new treatment approaches, research conducted over the last 40 years has not found any one model, method, or package of techniques to be reliably superior— this is true even of the much-championed cognitive and biological (e.g., psychotropic medication) "revolutions" in mental health (Elkin, 1994; Lambert & Bergin, 1994; Lambert, Shapiro, & Bergin, 1986; Project Match Research Group, 1997; Smith, Glass, & Miller, 1980; Wampold et al., 1997).

Researcher Alan Kazdin (2000) has addressed this issue. Referring to the current state of research regarding children and adolescents, he stated:

> Research on child psychotherapy is floundering. When considering the ultimate question (what treatments to apply to whom under what conditions) or the reformulated research agenda (efforts to understand how therapy works), very little can be said about the accomplishments of child and adolescent psychotherapy research in the past 5 years versus the 5 years before those years. Moreover, given the focus of therapy research, there is no reason to believe that the next few years will see the leap in knowledge we need. (p. 14)

Kazdin's remarks reflect a conundrum that has plagued the fields of psychology, psychotherapy, and family therapy. That is, focus has remained on attempting to understand how therapy models (and associated methods and techniques) are the primary causal agents of change. This research movement has continued to garner major support with regard to children, adolescents, and young adults (see Carr, 2000; Fonagy, Target, Cottrell, Phillips, & Kurtz, 2002; Kazdin, 2000) despite growing evidence indicating that methods, models, and techniques account for little of the variance in therapeutic outcomes. The countless influx of books depicting new and improved therapy models is but one indication of the strength of this trend.

Contrary to the hopes of those in support of the model-based research movement, empirical findings and, more importantly, client feedback continue to demonstrate that positive outcomes have more to do with *general effects*, common factors, and incidental aspects[1] than methods, models, or what researchers refer to as *specific effects* or *ingredients* (Duncan & Miller, 2000; Hubble, Miller, & Duncan, 1999; Lambert, 1992; Miller, Duncan, & Hubble, 1997; Wampold, 2001). The term *general effects* refers to the benefits produced by incidental aspects—those not theoretically central (e.g., client contributions and differences, relationship factors)—whereas the term *specific effects* or *ingredients* refers to the benefits of specific actions (e.g., techniques, methods, models) considered necessary for the success of treatment (Wampold, 2001). Said differently, when positive change occurs, the majority of that change can be traced to general or non-theory-based effects as opposed to treatment models themselves.

Despite the lackluster evidence, emphasis has remained not only on researching, but also on teaching and promoting models. It is clear that the preponderance of literature purporting the superiority of models is simply unfounded. Nonetheless, psychotherapy theories are sold to mental health professionals, not clients. And understandably, it is certainly not as glamorous for clinicians to refer to their approaches as based on "common factors," "general effects," or "incidental aspects" as it is to use a catchy acronym (e.g., CBT, SFBT, DBT, EMDR, TFT). To this end, while therapists seek the comfort and protection of brand name theories, clients seek change—relief from pain and suffering.

This book takes a new direction by acknowledging the role of general effects and their contribution to treatment outcomes. In doing so, two specific areas are explored:

1.   Identifying and amplifying the influences and contributors to successful outcomes (regardless of the model being used); and
2.   Learning how clients initiate change and make therapy work.

Foremost, this book fills a void by offering an emerging, client-informed, outcome-oriented foundation for clinical practice with adolescents, young adults, and families—a foundation based solidly on empirical data and client feedback. Emphasis is on enhancing change-effecting influences and creating possibilities for achieving desired change through ideas and practices that are collaborative, respectful, and effective. The book explores a myriad of creative, flexible ways of working that yield the utmost respect to all participants and simultaneously promote accountability and positive change. Because clients are the engineers of

---

[1]For the remainder of this book the terms *common factors, general effects,* and *incidental aspects* will be used interchangeably to refer to non-theory-based contributions to psychotherapy outcome.

change, emphasis will be on collaborating with them in ways that encourage and facilitate growth. It is hoped that the practical ideas offered throughout this book will encourage you to think about your current work with adolescents, young adults, and families in new ways, allowing you to build on what you are already doing in a way that is both respectful and effective.

Following is an exploration of the research and theoretical movements that have both indicated the need for a new direction and influenced the development of a change-oriented perspective for adolescents and young adults. These include *the three waves of psychotherapy, empirically supported treatments, technical eclecticism and theoretical integration,* and *common factors.*

RESEARCH AND THEORETICAL INFLUENCES ON A CHANGE-ORIENTED APPROACH TO THERAPY

The Three Waves of Psychotherapy

Since its inception in the early 1900s, the field of psychotherapy has grown dramatically. A number of new therapeutic models have been created in an effort to determine more efficacious and effective practices. Currently there are in excess of 250 models, an increase of nearly 400 percent from the 1960s (Garfield, 1982; Herink, 1980; Kazdin, 1986). Nearly all of these approaches already have been or may be utilized with adolescents and young adults (Bailey, 2000; Kazdin, 2000; Prout & Brown, 1999). Furthermore, a relatively infinite number of techniques (e.g., role playing, behavioral charting, thought sampling, the empty chair) are either aligned with these approaches or considered as separate entities altogether. Whether designed for use with adults, children, adolescents, couples, families, or some other variation, each approach can be classified within or between three different "waves" of psychotherapy (Bertolino & O'Hanlon, 2002; O'Hanlon, 1994, 1999).

The First Wave

The first wave began with Freud's psychoanalysis and was characterized by intrapsychic approaches, defining mental illness as being within the individual. There was a search for underlying pathology that could be uncovered by experts delving deeply into the "patient's" past to identify repressed material that existed in the unconscious. Therapy was understood to be a process whereby patients revisited the past to discover, reexperience, and relive traumatic or painful events in order to process repressed material. This cathartic approach would lead to symptom amelioration. Today many of Freud's original ideas remain in tact, while others have been refined or disregarded altogether.

It is common for clinicians who work with adolescents and young adults and maintain analytic or psychodynamic ties to focus primarily on early childhood experiences, relationships, and attachment. For younger youth, there may also be emphasis placed on addressing risk factors, vulnerabilities, and in facilitating the development of mental capacities (Fonagy & Target, 1996). It is noteworthy that language and terminology (e.g., narcissistic, borderline, depression) most commonly associated with the *DSM* is a product of the first wave.

It was also during the first wave that behaviorism gained prominence and challenged the premises of analytic thinking. Behaviorists downplayed psychological processes and viewed change as resulting from the expertise of therapists who identified maladaptive behaviors and the contingencies of those behaviors. Because of their emphasis on specific goals, techniques, and attention to structure, behavioral approaches remain popular with those working with adolescents and young adults.

The Second Wave

The second wave, which began in the 1950s, brought about a shift in focus. Instead of attending to pathology located in the past, second-wave theorists concurred with behaviorists and placed emphasis on the present or "here and now." Problem-focused approaches were developed and family therapy ideas brought to light new ways of conceptualizing and approaching problems. For family therapists, the term intrapsychic was replaced with *interactional*—the study of relational systems. Systemic thinking defined problems as being within small systems and between people as opposed to within individuals. Family therapists hypothesized that the problematic behavior of children, adolescents, and young adults was due to dysfunction within relationships and could be understood by studying elements such as family structure, hierarchy, rules, roles, and boundaries (Haley, 1987; Hoffman, 1981; Minuchin, 1974). Clinicians also took responsibility for initiating change by designing interventions that would alter, interrupt, and ultimately change patterns of action and interaction, thereby alleviating symptoms.

Theories based on the family life cycle (Carter & McGoldrick, 1989, 1998) and family systems theory gained enormous popularity in the 1970s and offered new ways of explainations of the behavior of adolescents and young adults as well as new ways of working with that population. A handbook was even developed in an attempt to diagnostically categorize family and relational difficulties (Kaslow, 1996). Systems theory also brought with it a shift in language. It introduced therapists to terms such as *intergenerational, coalition,* and *enmeshment,* which for many brought about an alternative to first-wave, *DSM*-related language.

The Third Wave

The third wave began with a time of reexamination. In the late 1970s and early 1980s, mental health practitioners, particularly family therapists, began to take notice of their biases and blinders. Therapists were finding holes in their theories and prejudices (e.g., sexism and cultural biases) that had gone unacknowledged and unchallenged for years. The theories that began to emerge during this time shared a common thread— a competency base. O'Hanlon remarked, "We believed that the focus on problems often obscures the resources and solutions residing within clients. . . . We no longer saw the therapists as the source of the solution— the solutions rested in people and their social networks" (1994, p. 23).

With an emphasis on strengths, abilities, and resources, therapists no longer had to accept what their theories were saying—that clients were in some way damaged goods or incapable of positive change. For many practitioners the third wave opened the door to work with clients in ways that were more collaborative and hopeful. It also ushered in a host of new approaches for working with adolescents and young adults. These included solution-focused, solution-oriented, and narrative therapies, collaborative approaches, and reflecting teams (see Hoyt 1994, 1996, 1998). It was also during this time that the influence of constructivism and social constructionism gained prominence.

Constructivists purported that there are multiple, subjective realities and ways of viewing the world (Maturana, 1978; von Foerster, 1984; von Glasersfeld, 1984; Watzlawick, 1984). No subjective reality is considered more true or correct than another. Social constructionists emphasized the role of language and interaction in the creation of meaning (Berger & Luckmann, 1966; Gergen, 1982, 1985, 1994; Shotter, 1993). Although there is a physical reality, social realities are continually created and recreated through language and interaction. Bertolino and O'Hanlon (2002) remarked:

> Constructivist and social constructionist philosophies brought to light the role of language as the primary vehicle for creating meaning and change. Therapists learned that each therapeutic dialogue or interaction leads to the creation or recreation of something

new—a *reauthoring* or *rewriting* of a new story for the client. This shift to focusing on the role of language in therapeutic processes was significant because it was the first time that theorists thoroughly studied the implications of language on the construction and resolution of problems. (p. 5)

The major theoretical trends are each represented in the three waves of psychotherapy. Models ranging from psychoanalysis to cognitive therapy to strategic family therapy to solution-focused therapy all have roots in at least one of these movements. These approaches also have rich histories in terms of their applications to adolescents, young adults, and families (Bailey, 2000; Prout & Brown, 1999).

Regardless of whether it is inspired by first-, second-, or third-wave theories, psychotherapy clearly works. Numerous clinical studies have supported its effectiveness (Barker, Funk, & Houston, 1988; Lambert & Bergin, 1994; Lambert, Shapiro, & Bergin, 1986; Lipsey & Wilson, 1993; Prioleau, Murdock, & Brody, 1983; Seligman, 1995; Shapiro & Shapiro, 1982; VandenBos & Pino, 1980). In fact, research has indicated that the average person treated with therapy is better off than 80% of those who have not received treatment (Asay & Lambert, 1999; Lambert & Bergin, 1994; Smith, Glass, & Miller, 1980).

Studies have also demonstrated the viability of psychotherapy with adolescents and young adults (Casey & Berman, 1985; Prout & DeMartino, 1986; Tramontana, 1980; Weisz, Weiss, Alicke, & Klotz, 1987; Weisz, Weiss, & Donenberg, 1992; Weisz, Weiss, Han, Granger, & Morton, 1995). Specifically, meta-analytic studies involving children, adolescents, and young adults (ages 2 to 18) have produced effect sizes ranging from .71 to .88 (Casey & Berman, 1985; Kazdin, Bass, Ayers, & Rodgers, 1990; Weisz et al., 1987; Weisz et al., 1995). These effect sizes are considered moderate to large (Cohen, 1988), indicating that approximately eight out of ten children, adolescents, and young adults who received treatment were better off than those in control group conditions.

While a significant amount of empirical evidence has demonstrated that psychotherapy works, there has been a lack of sufficient data explaining what about it works. Therefore, two major yet quite divergent research movements have developed. The first is to identify models that are considered most efficacious[2] when paired with disorders. The second is to answer the question "What works in therapy?" Proponents of the latter movement have attempted to understand more

---

[2] *Efficacy* studies are laboratory-based experimental trials conducted in research settings. *Effectiveness* studies test the impact of treatment in naturalistic or "real life" clinical settings.

about what constitutes effective therapy, regardless of the model being practiced. This relates to identifying factors that contribute to successful outcomes. Next is a discussion of these two movements and their role in the development of therapeutic approaches with adolescents and young adults.

Movement 1: Empirically Supported Treatments, Technical Eclecticism, and Theoretical Integration

Perhaps the most debated movement in psychology and psychotherapy circles has been one to delineate what researchers refer to as *empirically supported treatments, empirically validated treatments, evidence-based treatment, evidence-based practice,* and *treatments that work* (Kazdin, 2000). The criteria for the variations within this movement tend to differ, albeit slightly, eliminating the ability to use the terms interchangeably. Nevertheless, as part of an overall direction in research, each thread has attempted to answer the same question, posed many years earlier: "What treatment, by whom, is most effective for this individual with that specific problem, under which set of circumstances?" (Paul, 1967, p. 111). Because of this shared direction within this research movement and for the purposes of discussion, this book will use the most common of the aforementioned terms: *empirically supported treatments* (ESTs).

There have been two ongoing efforts to identify ESTs. The first was born out of Division 12 of the American Psychological Association (APA). The Task Force on Promotion and Dissemination of Psychological Procedures (TFPP) (1995; Chambless & Hollon, 1998; Chambless, 1996) was created to identify, through stringent, clinically based, empirical studies, specific treatment approaches for specific mental health disorders. The TFPP hoped to "consider methods for educating clinical psychologists, third-party payers, and the public about effective psychotherapies" (p. 3). The task force was designed to identify superior treatment approaches primarily for adults, although work groups were established to determine psychosocial interventions for children and adolescents diagnosed with depression, anxiety disorders, conduct disorders, attention-deficit/hyperactivity disorder, and autism.

The second effort made to identify ESTs evolved in a slightly different way than the TFPP. According to Nathan and Gorman, the purpose of this effort was to determine "what treatments have been scientifically validated, what treatments are felt by a large number of experts to be valuable but have not been properly scientifically examined, and what treatments are known to be of little value" (1998, p. x). As with the APA research, this effort also focused primarily on pairing treatment models with disorders of adulthood, although some disorders of childhood and adolescence were also covered (Kazdin, 2000).

With the number of psychotherapy models exceeding 250, all could not possibly be studied in depth. Furthermore, it is arguable that not all models are worthy of study. Yet the two significant efforts to identify specific treatments paired with specific disorders has resulted in few models receiving attention at all. The researched approaches have been those consistent with the first wave (Bertolino & O'Hanlon, 2002; O'Hanlon, 1994, 1999) and the psychological paradigm (Cottone, 1992), focusing either largely or primarily on disorders of individuals. Moreover, the majority of treatments researched have been cognitive and behaviorally oriented therapies (see Duncan & Miller, 2000; Durlak, Wells, Cotten, & Johnson, 1995; Kazdin et al., 1990). These were also approaches most likely to be practiced in settings that support research endeavors and are able to secure funding. Not surprisingly, approximately 80% of the treatment approaches that both efforts have deemed "empirically supported" to date for adults, children, and adolescents are from within the cognitive and behavioral theoretical schools (Duncan & Miller, 2000; Kazdin, 2000; Nathan & Gorman, 1998).

According to the criteria of both research efforts, an "empirically supported" approach need only demonstrate superiority in two independent studies. Furthermore, superiority over a placebo condition (or no-treatment alternative for the TFPP) is sufficient to demonstrate efficacy. It is important to note that just about *any* treatment may be better than no treatment. Demonstrating efficacy over a placebo condition is not the same as demonstrating efficacy over other treatment approaches. It says very little about an approach except that it is better than the status quo. Therefore a minimal level of empirical data could "prove" the efficacy of a model and validate it with an EST version of the Good Housekeeping Seal of Approval (Lebow, 2001).

The results are also clear for the few EST-related studies that have compared one theory to another. For example, of the 300 EST-related studies of disorders of adulthood comparing cognitive-behavioral therapy to other models, only 15, or 5%, demonstrated its efficacy (Wampold, 2001). This is no more than would be expected by chance, indicating no differential efficacy. Although reports of the superiority of certain approaches over others remain rampant, it is clear that such claims are more myth than fact.

Studies specific to adolescents also have shown a lack of differential efficacy among approaches (Casey & Berman, 1985). Further, any claims of differences in outcomes between treatment models can be attributed to chance (Duncan & Miller, 2000; Wampold, 2001), to problems with outcome measures, methodology, and research design (Casey & Berman,

1985; Kazdin, 2000; Pearsall, 1997; Tramontana, 1980), to the allegiance effect (Luborsky et al., 1999; Wampold, 2001), or to diagnostic categorization (Barrett, Hampe, & Miller, 1978). Due to their relationship with outcomes and implications on future research regarding adolescents and young adults, the *allegiance effect* and *diagnostic categorization* warrant further discussion.

The *allegiance effect* considers the influence of the researcher's allegiance to a particular model with a study. In other words, the more researchers believe in, practice, and support particular models, the greater the likelihood that those models will show favorable results in studies. An example of the allegiance effect can be found in comparison studies involving cognitive-behavioral approaches. Specifically, Lambert and Bergin (1994) found that when the allegiance effect was taken into account for the few EST-related studies demonstrating the efficacy of cognitive-behavioral approaches with disorders of adulthood, the differences completely disappeared.

Although it is a complex issue, there are numerous ways of inferring the allegiance effect (Wampold, 2001). An obvious one would be if a researcher were a proponent of one of the treatments administered in a study. Like biological psychiatrists and pharmaceutical companies interested in validating their viewpoints in order to market their products, mental health professionals are, albeit more indirectly, subject to the influence of entities or organizations with allegiances or ties to particular treatment approaches. These could be in the form of funding sources, third-party payers, political associations, and so on.

Diagnostic categorization is a second area of consideration regarding EST-based research. Of specific concern is the viability of linking treatment modalities with "disorders." Supporters of the EST movement, Chambless and Hollon (1998) have stated, "We do not ask whether a treatment is efficacious: Rather, we ask whether it is efficacious for a specific problem" (p. 9). Within the context of EST research, "problems" are most commonly considered some form of mental disorder. Although it is not mandated, the fourth edition of the *Diagnostic and Statistical Manual for Mental Disorders* (American Psychiatric Association, 1994) is clearly the most frequently used nosology for assigning disorders in research on ESTs (Chambless & Hollon, 1998; DeRubeis & Crits-Christoph, 1998; Kazdin, 2000). This is evidenced by a basic review of literature spanning a 20-year period that found over 2000 books, chapters, and articles proposing specific models of treatment for children, adolescents, and young adults between the ages of 6 and 18 who were assigned disorders such as ADD, ADHD, ODD, conduct disorder, major depression, dysthymia, or associated symptomology (e.g., aggression, anger, low academic grades) (PsychInfo, 1980–2002).

Since its inception, the *DSM* has gone through multiple revisions, expanding in categories from 66 in the first edition to 286 in the fourth. There have been new diagnoses added, others renamed, and considerable changes in the diagnostic criteria for disorders. For adolescents and young adults new psychiatric diagnoses are often identified by an acronym (e.g., ADD/ADHD for attention-deficit/hyperactivity disorder; ODD for oppositional defiant disorder). The pervading idea that diagnosis should precede and then determine a particular mode of treatment is central to EST-based research. Yet, as senior psychotherapy researcher Larry Beutler points out, when it comes to mental health services, "psychiatric diagnoses have proven of little value either to development of individual psychotherapy plans or the differential prediction of psychotherapy outcome" (1989, p. 271).

Although researchers conducting EST-related studies have attempted to monitor for factors that may affect validity and reliability, consider that mental health professionals with expertise in diagnostic procedures are subject to disagreement, inconsistency, and misdiagnosis. Often well-trained clinicians come up with completely different diagnoses for the same individual. The imperfections and shortcomings of diagnostic procedures with adolescents and young adults are well-documented (Evans, 1991; Scotti, Morris, McNeil, & Hawkins, 1996). This is of particular importance as often adolescents are still developing emotionally, cognitively, socially, and physically, as well as transitioning, along with family members, into different stages of life.

It is clear that diagnoses change with the times and tend to reflect political and economic factors and societal tolerances (Beutler & Clarkin, 1990). For example, homosexuality, once considered a mental disease, was "cured" by a vote of the American Psychiatric Association after gay activists protested being identified as sick. Diagnoses are related more to economic, political, market, and social factors than scientific or empirical factors. Due to the aforementioned problems associated with the *DSM*, the issue of diagnosis must be considered an inconsistent variable with adolescents and young adults. Furthermore, evidence supporting an alignment between *any* model and *any* mental health diagnosis must be regarded as questionable.

A final area deserving of attention relates to the generalization of efficacy studies to clinical settings. Kazdin (2000) stated,

There is little or no evidence that these treatments work in clinical settings. That is, an empirically supported treatment, when applied to clinically referred children and families, as administered by clinicians in practice and under conditions where treatment delivery is not so well monitored, has unknown effects. (pp. 85–86)

Even if it were possible to generalize the findings from efficacy to effectiveness settings it is understood that most therapists do not work in sterile, laboratory-based settings. They do not use manualized procedures and protocols. Rigid, structured treatment methods are simply antithetical to the context within which practitioners work with adolescents, young adults, and families experiencing crises and debilitating situations.

Family Therapy Research

As has occurred with the psychological treatments, a plethora of family therapy approaches have been developed (Bailey, 2000; Gurman & Kniskern, 1981, 1991). Representing primarily the second and third waves (although many approaches originally developed for individuals have been expanded to accommodate couples and families), few of these models have been well researched. The evergrowing number of new models continuing to enter an already cluttered scene further complicates this.

Despite a rich, over-50-year history, research in family therapy has faced several undeniable facts. First, the early pioneers of family therapy were extremely charismatic, provocative, and given gurus status. They have promoted (and in some instances still continue to promote) their respective models as superior to others. The selling of theories or "battle of the brands" has been no more apparent than in family therapy.

Next, the research conducted has been inconclusive. On the basis of the most comprehensive meta-analysis of marital and family therapy to date, Shadish, Ragsdale, Glaser, and Montgomery stated, "Despite some superficial evidence apparently favoring some orientations over others, no orientation is yet demonstrably superior to any other. This finding parallels the psychotherapy literature generally" (1995, p. 348). Simply, claims of differential efficacy by proponents of family therapy models are not supported by available empirical data.

Technical Eclecticism and Theoretical Integration

In response to the ineffectiveness and limitations of individual models, the restrictive nature of treatment protocols, and in an effort to offer more diversity and flexibility, some theorists have advocated for technical eclecticism (Beutler & Clarkin, 1990; Lazarus, 1981; Norcross, 1986) and integrative models (Norcross & Goldfried, 1992; Prochaska & DiClemente, 1982; Stricker & Gold, 1993; Wachtel, 1977). For many practitioners these approaches have served as enticing alternatives to individual theoretical approaches and the EST perspective. Their flexibility has made them particularly attractive to practitioners working with adolescents and young adults (Keat, 1996; Prout & Brown, 1999). In fact, there are indications that perhaps more than half of child and adolescent mental health professionals practice approaches that include a "mixture" of techniques in an effort to use "whatever works" (Garfield & Bergin, 1994). Despite the seductive lure of flexibility, there is a limited base of empirical evidence supporting such approaches (Fonagy et al., 2002).

Technical eclecticism is most commonly associated with Arnold Lazarus's (1976, 1981, 1992) *multimodal therapy*. According to Lazarus, the "technical eclectic" " utilizes a systematic approach and uses procedures drawn from different sources without necessarily subscribing to the theories or disciplines that spawned them" (1992, p. 323). By virtue of avoiding alignment with any one theoretical perspective, technical eclecticism stands in stark contrast to ESTs, which adhere to strict theoretical principles.

Whereas technical eclecticism emphasizes technique and intervention, *theoretical integration* involves the combining of differing philosophies in which the goal is a designed framework that will lead to the merging of theoretical perspectives (Goldfried & Newman, 1986; Petrocelli, 2002). Proponents of this movement are not interested in creating a single, unified theory. Instead they seek ways of combining theories in order to generate new hypotheses that are distinct from the individual theories that were integrated in the first place (Arkowitz, 1992).

Supported by those seeking to combine emerging and traditional approaches and methods, technical eclecticism and theoretical integration have offered practitioners increased flexibility in working with adolescents, young adults, and families. At first glance these movements seem to provide an adequate response to ESTs. Under further analysis, however, technical eclecticism lacks a sound theoretical foundation, relying primarily on the success of techniques, a level of abstraction eerily similar to that of ESTs (Wampold, 2001). As noted earlier, models and technique account for little of the variance in outcome. Further, although allowing for creativity and flexibility, theoretical integration, with its lack of theoretical continuity, loses its viability as an option. With over 250 models available, a seemingly endless number of theoretical combinations exists, all of which could be considered intregrative approaches.

The EST movement, family therapy, technical eclecticism, and theoretical integration have each significantly influenced a change-oriented perspective and the field of psychotherapy as a whole. First, although not designed to do so, EST-related studies have indicated that no one model or approach consistently produces more favorable results when compared to others. The same is the case with family therapy approaches. Next, technical eclecticism and theoretical integration have drawn attention to the importance of flexibility in therapy. Because no one approach works all the time, clinicians need alternatives to one-size-fits-all models. In contrast, despite providing more flexibility and an alternative to the highly structured and manualized EST therapies or structured family therapy models, technical eclecticism and theoretical integration have shortcomings related to a technique-only focus and lack of a consistent theoretical base, respectively. This makes research for the latter two models improbable.

It is important to ensure that the debate here is a clear one. The empirical data regarding individual and family therapy approaches, technical eclecticism, and theoretical integration indicate that models produce similar results. However, a lack of differential efficacy does not mean that models are ineffective. Single studies can be found supporting virtually any approach, and clients can and do benefit from specific models.

The issues here are numerous. First, claims of the superiority of models are consistently based on individual studies. Single studies prove very little and can be easily debunked by contrasting studies. Further, as discussed earlier, overall, EST-related psychotherapy studies continue to be plagued with numerous problems, ranging from methodological designs to the allegiance effect. These inconsistencies are well documented and have hampered those attempting to derive conclusions from multiple studies.

Second, the aforementioned theoretical movements emphasize theoretical models or the gurus associated with those models as the change-producing agents. Although it is clear that clients are the primary instigators of change, there is a notable absence of client contributions to change. Because therapists' actions are emphasized, their respective theoretical models and practices come to the forefront. As a result, certain models become privileged over others, thereby contributing to the aforementioned "battle of the brands." In the end, clients are left out of decisions that determine which models will be used. It is the therapist's allegiance to a model—not the client's—that guides treatment. Therefore, therapy is based on the therapists' privileging of models, and clients have little or no voice in determining which approaches provide the best fit for them.

This privileging of models is quite concerning. The EST movement was born out of an attempt to counter the American Psychiatric Association's studies purporting that psychotropic medication was the most effective way to treat mental disorders. Ironically, the very thing that the American Psychological Association and other EST proponents argued against (i.e., privileging medication as superior to psychological treatments) has become a thorn in their side. That is, in the process of attempting to empirically validate models they ultimately created a context where models are privileged. It can be said that psychologists responded to the "myth of the magic pill" by propagating the "myth of the magic method," thereby supporting the notion that EST-based treatments are superior to others. This privileging has left clients out of processes where they have a say in what treatment models, approaches, methods, and techniques are used.

Last, and perhaps most telling, is the focus on developing more methods and frameworks. An emphasis on expanding on the already over 250 models continues, with little consideration of the individual differences between clients (including contextual influences such as culture, spiritual beliefs) and without increasing the participation of clients in processes and practices. As discussed in the next section, it is not therapeutic models and maneuvers that lead to change. The single most significant contributor to change is the client. Though few clinicians would argue this point, most efforts in the area of theory development continue to be void of clients' contributions to change processes.

Movement 2: Research on Common Factors

Forty years of outcome research has demonstrated that although most models effect change, no one approach is significantly and consistently more effective than another (Lambert & Bergin, 1994; Lambert, Shapiro, & Bergin, 1986; Luborksy, Singer, & Luborsky, 1975; Shadish et al., 1995; Smith et al., 1980). Because all models can be beneficial, the "dodo bird effect" comes into play. Saul Rosenzweig referred to the dodo bird's conclusion following the race in *Alice in Wonderland*: "At last the Dodo said, 'Everybody has won and all must have prizes' " (1936, p. 412). Many years prior to the benefit of empirical evidence, Rosenzweig prophetically inferred that various therapeutic models would achieve roughly the same results and clinical effectiveness had more to do with common elements than with differences among theories.

While some researchers have continued with comparative studies to determine what makes one approach more effective than another, others have shifted their attention to what factors or aspects existing among theories contribute to successful outcomes (Frank, 1973; Grencavage & Norcross, 1990; Lambert, 1992). Through a review of these studies, Miller, Duncan, and Hubble (1997) found the following:

> The evidence makes it clear that similarities rather than differences between therapy models account for most of the change that clients experience in treatment. What emerges from examining these similarities is a group of common factors that can be brought together

to form a more unifying language for psychotherapy practice: a language that contrasts sharply with the current emphasis on difference characterizing most professional discussion and activity. (p. 15)

Researchers have learned that when positive change occurs in therapy, there are consistent, non-theory-based commonalities that account for the significant portion of that change. Following Rosenzweig's lead, Jerome Frank (1973; Frank & Frank, 1991) was one of the first to describe components shared by all models of psychotherapy. Through his meta-analysis, researcher Michael Lambert (1992) later identified four specific factors. Lambert originally estimated that the major contributors to outcome, in order of their significance, were *extratherapeutic change (client factors), therapeutic relationship, expectancy (placebo effects),* and *techniques*. Referred to as the "common factors," the four entities have been examined in-depth and gone through some revisions since first being identified. Perhaps the most thorough exploration can be found in Hubble and colleague's (1999) landmark book, *The Heart and Soul of Change: What Works in Therapy*. Let's briefly examine the common factors identified by researchers.

Client Factors

Client factors are what individuals bring to therapy, including their internal strengths, abilities, external resources, and social support systems. They include faith, family relationships, membership in a community or religious sect, or any factors that account for clients contribution to change. These factors account for the most significant portion of improvement that occurs in any form of psychotherapy. Lambert (1992) estimated that client factors account for up to 40% of the variance in outcome. The research is clear that the client is the single most potent contributor to outcome in therapy (Tallman & Bohart, 1999).

Client factors also include external influences such as spontaneous, chance events outside of therapy. These are events that occur during the course of therapy but typically have little or no correlation with the treatment itself. By identifying and amplifying positive, spontaneous changes, therapists can help clients to note that change is constant in their lives. Further, therapists can explore with clients the significance of such changes and work with them to expand and build upon them in the future.

Other essential client factors include resilience and protective factors, having a change focus, and being mindful of clients' contributions to change processes. Resilience and protective factors refer to those qualities and actions on the part of clients that allow them to meet and survive the difficulties and challenges of life. Therapists who are change-focused emphasize pretreatment and between-session change, as well as potentiate change for the future by identifying and amplifying change. Being mindful of clients' contributions to change includes honoring their worldviews and tapping into their worlds outside of therapy. Therapists who are working in these ways are making the most of client factors.

Relationship Factors

The therapeutic relationship is a central factor in successful therapy. Researchers estimate that as much as 30% of the variance in treatment outcome can be attributed to relationships factors (Lambert, 1992). Perhaps the two most significant factors in this realm that affect therapy outcome are the quality of the client's participation and the degree to which clients are motivated, engaged, and join in the therapeutic work (Orlinsky, Grawe, & Parks, 1994; Prochaska, 1995; Prochaska, DiClemente, & Norcross, 1992; Prochaska, Norcross, & DiClemente, 1994).

The therapeutic relationship has been expanded to a broader concept known as the therapeutic "alliance," a more encompassing term that emphasizes collaborative partnership between clients and therapists (Bordin, 1979; Duncan & Miller, 2000). Therapists can promote the therapeutic alliance by accommodating treatment to the client's motivational level, view of the therapeutic relationship, goals and preferred outcomes for therapy, and tasks to accomplish those goals and outcomes.

Clients who are engaged and connected with therapists may benefit most from therapy. In contrast, the strength of the therapeutic bond is not highly correlated with the length of treatment (Horvath & Luborsky, 1993). In other words, the formulation of an instant bond between the therapist and client is commonplace. Most critical here are clients' perceptions of the therapeutic relationship. In fact, client ratings of therapists as empathic, trustworthy, and nonjudgmental are better predictors of positive outcome than therapist ratings, diagnosis, approach, or any other variable (Horvath & Symonds, 1991; Duncan & Miller, 2000; Lambert & Bergin, 1994).

Expectancy and Placebo Factors

Expectancy and placebo factors relate to the portion of improvement derived from clients' knowledge of being helped, the installation of hope, pretreatment expectancy, therapist confidence and enthusiasm, and the credibility of methods and techniques from the perspective of clients (Duncan & Miller, 2000; Duncan & Sparks, 2001). It is the expectation of change and hope that accompanies processes and procedures, not the methods and techniques themselves, that is significant. Lambert (1992; Asay & Lambert, 1999) initially estimated that expectancy and placebo in therapy contributed approximately 15% of the variance in therapeutic outcome. Because Lambert's original estimate was based on a narrow definition (i.e., based primarily on the client's knowledge of being treated and the credibility of the treatment approach), some have speculated that this category of factors may account for as much as 50% of the variance in outcomes (Greenberg, 2002).

Expectancy includes the expectations that clients have upon beginning therapy. Commonly referred to as pretreatment expectancy, this refers to clients' faith and beliefs that therapy can help them with their concerns and problems (Safran, Heimberg, & Juster, 1997; Schneider & Klauer, 2001). Expectancy is also inclusive of both the client and therapist believing in the restorative power of the treatment, including its procedures. Simply expecting therapy to help can serve as a placebo and counteract demoralization, activate hope, and advance improvement (Frank & Frank, 1991; Miller et al., 1997).

Therapists' attitudes in the opening moments of therapy can promote or dampen hope. For example, an attitude of pessimism or an emphasis on psychopathology or the long-term process of change can negatively affect hope. In contrast, an attitude that positive change can occur even in very difficult situations and an emphasis on possibilities and improvement can instill hope. This does not mean downplaying the real-life difficulties that clients face but instead acknowledging such difficulties and simultaneously conveying that there are possibilities for an improved, preferred future.

Model and Technique Factors

Every theoretical model is accompanied by techniques and procedures. For example, behaviorists use methods associated with conditioning, Freudian analysts use analysis of transference, structural family therapists use enactment, solution-focused therapists ask the miracle question, and narrative therapists use externalization. Techniques and procedures include but are not limited to asking particular questions, using specific interventions, assigning tasks, making interpretations, and teaching skills. Most techniques or procedures are designed to get clients to do something different, such as experience emotions, face fears, change patterns of thinking or behavior, and develop new understandings or meanings.

Lambert (1992) suggested that model and technique account for the same contribution to outcome variance as placebo factors—about 15%.

More recently, others have determined that specific ingredients such as techniques contribute even less to therapeutic outcomes (Wampold, 2001). This is in part due to the fact that therapists are much more interested in techniques than clients are. In fact, when asked about what is helpful about therapy, clients rarely mention therapeutic interventions or techniques. Instead, client responses typically fall into the client and relationship factors categories.

It is important to note that the percentages Lambert (1992) initially assigned to the four common factors were based on an interpretation of, not a statistical analysis of, 40 years of data. Nearly a decade later, psychologist Bruce Wampold (2001) completed a scientific evaluation and statistical analysis of the data. The researcher found that Lambert correctly interpreted that the significant portion of variance in psychotherapeutic outcomes is due to general effects. Moreover, Wampold found that specific effects such as technique and model accounted for at most 8% of the variance (only 1% of the overall variance!). This leaves approximately 22% in variance. According to Wampold, this variability is due in part to client differences. He remarked:

> Whatever the source of the unexplained variance, it is clearly not related to specific ingredients. . . . Lest there be any ambiguity about the profound contrast between general and specific effects, it must be noted that the 1% of the variability in outcomes due to specific ingredients is likely a gross upper bound. Clearly, the preponderance of the benefits of psychotherapy are due to factors incidental to the particular theoretical approach administered and dwarf the effects due to theoretically derived techniques. (pp. 207–209)

Wampold's (2001) findings confirm that non-theory-based elements, contributing 70–92% (or more) of the variance, are by far the most significant contributors to therapeutic outcome. Therefore, although research pairing treatment models with disorders has provided little justification for approaches theoretically different from one another, research around the question "What works in therapy?" has provided significant direction for the fields of psychology and psychotherapy. Empirical evidence has indicated that successful outcomes have more to do with general effects than specific ingredients.

A handful of theorists have taken note of and indirectly referred to the general effects within their proposed approaches with adolescents, young adults, and families (Berg & Kelly, 2000; Johnson & Lee, 2000; Keim, 2000). These theorists have not addressed the overall relevance of the general effects and have instead emphasized one, or perhaps two, particular factors, most notably the therapeutic relationship and alliance. Others have attempted to directly articulate how most or all non-theory-based effects are replicated within models with adolescents, young adults, and families (Selekman, 2002; Sells, 1998). Although paying homage to the literature on common factors, study of the latter approaches reveals significant shortcomings. These will be discussed next.

BEYOND THE GENERAL EFFECTS:
WEAVING NEW THREADS

What we have learned from outcome research has contributed to processes and practices that are more collaborative, client-informed, outcome-driven, and change-oriented. Yet growth must be accompanied by a willingness to continually reexamine what has been learned and how that translates into practice. That said, approaches that have laid claim to integrating the literature on the common factors with adolescents, young adults, and families warrant further investigation (Selekman, 2002; Sells, 1998). Specific to approaches that purport adherence to the common factors, the areas of investigation are as follows:

1. In viewing the common factors as independent ingredients in isolation from one another, the impact and significance of their collective interplay may be minimized.
2. Client orientations (i.e., influences and attribution of context; client theories) have been virtually ignored.
3. Despite research that has identified the role of therapist variables as significant to treatment outcomes, there is a distinct absence of discussion of such in the literature.

Maximizing Change: From Independent
to Interrelated

Approaches based on the common factors tend to emphasize each of the factors as separate ingredients. Although three of the four factors (with the exception of model and technique) fall into the category of general effects, each is understood as making an independent contribution to outcome. This distinction can be helpful for the purposes of understanding research outcomes. By outlining the various factors that play a role in outcomes, therapists and students can better understand areas that ought to be emphasized in therapy. In contrast, when discussion turns to their application in clinical practice, the distinctions made between each factor can actually be misleading. This is in part because the common factors cannot be understood in isolation or void of context. In this sense, context relates to individual differences and the various influences including but not limited to culture, ethnicity, gender, genetics, family history, spirituality/religion, and so on.

By viewing the common factors as independent ingredients, the effect of the overall interplay of the factors may be extremely diluted or even lost. For example, many theories emphasize the therapeutic relationship yet pay little attention to client factors such as internal strengths and external resources. Others focus more on client factors yet largely ignore the role of hope and expectancy. Arguably, some factors may make more of a contribution to outcome; however, research can only offer a general range in terms of the contributions of common factors. How important a determinant the factors are in outcome is contingent on clients and is influenced by context. Conceptualizing the common factors as distinct, independent entities, (and thereby lending more attention to one or another) minimizes the relative effectiveness of their interrelatedness. Moreover, this presents a paradox. That is, when common factors are viewed as independent entities, there is an increase in the risk that they will ultimately be seen as "things" that can be excavated through methods and techniques.

A change-oriented perspective is based on the premise that although independent contributions may be made by various factors, the chance of successful outcomes increases when therapists use processes that maximize the general effects as a whole. Throughout this book multiple ways of promoting the interplay of the general effects by learning from adolescents, young adults, and others involved in therapy what is needed to help facilitate positive change are explored.

Client Orientations

Despite the plethora of treatment models available, many therapists pay little attention to the importance of young people and others' orientations regarding the influences on the concerns and problems that brought them to therapy. Instead, explanations tend to reflect therapists' ideas about causality. It is therapists' explanatory theories that point to whether a problem is related to thinking, reinforcement contingencies, relational interactions, or some other phenomenon, influence, or aspect. Once again, this represents therapy that is theory-driven.

We are continually at risk of allowing our theories to determine what is necessary for change to occur. Whether this involves progressing through stages, processing events from the past, completing homework assignments, or some other theory-driven process, this privileges therapists' theories over clients' orientations. It also contributes to theories' taking on lives of their own and becoming "real" in our eyes. This phenomenon has been referred to as *theory countertransference* (Hubble & O'Hanlon, 1992).

In its strictest, technical meaning, countertranference refers to an emotional, largely unconscious process, taking place in the therapist and triggered in relationship with the client, that intrudes into the treatment. A similar process of projection can take place in the theoretical milieu when therapists unconsciously intrude on clients with their theoretical biases and unrecognized assumptions. It's important that therapists are aware of how their theoretical constructs influence the content, processes, and directions in therapy (Bertolino & O'Hanlon, 2002). Theory countertransference can blind therapists from learning about clients' perspectives on the contexts within which their concerns, complaints, and possibilities for positive change are situated.

The research on common factors has demonstrated unequivocally that clients' contributions to change far outweigh any specific effects (i.e., techniques, methods, models). This underscores the importance of consulting with clients, not theories. It also provides an antidote to theory countertransference. When young people and others involved are invited into conversations where their ideas and preferences are encouraged, therapists learn about the influences of context and how to work within the parameters of those belief systems. In addition, the more therapists work within clients' worldviews, the more open clients are likely to be with ideas, processes, and practices that honor their views yet offer slightly different perspectives. These subtle differences can assist in facilitating positive change.

Interestingly, even though some theorists have referred to the importance of common factors in outcomes, their treatment remains model-driven (Selekman, 2002; Sells, 1998). A change-oriented perspective emphasizes the contributions of adolescents, young adults, and others in therapy. One of the ways this is done is by attending to clients' orientations regarding influences on both problems and possible solutions and ideas about how positive change might occur. Client orientations include the influences of context and theories of change.

The Influence of Therapist Variables

The particular treatment models that therapists practice do not positively affect outcomes. Strict adherence to manualized protocols does not positively affect outcomes. Therapists as persons, however, do account for a large proportion of the variance. Wampold stated, "A preponderance of the evidence indicates that there are large therapist effects (in the range of 6–9% of the variance in outcomes accounted for by therapists) and that these effects greatly exceed treatment effects" (2001, p. 200). It is clear that therapist effects contribute more to the variance in outcomes than treatment effects.

Numerous variables and influences (e.g., age, gender, ethnicity, style, personality, values, expectations) contribute to therapists' practicing differently (Beutler, Machado, & Neufeld, 1994). Just as with client variables (previously discussed with regard to context), few theories take into account the influence of therapist variables in the application of treatment protocols, procedures, and methods. Moreover, as researchers in EST-related studies have learned, different therapists providing the same treatments, even if based on manualized protocols, can produce different outcome effects (Luborsky, McLellen, Diguer, Woody, & Seligman, 1997; Shapiro, Firth-Cozens, & Stiles, 1989). This suggests that the effect of therapist variables ought to be given significant attention when the general effects in psychotherapy outcomes is researched.

A change-oriented perspective recognizes that therapist variables do influence treatment. They can enhance or inhibit positive change and client growth. To address this, therapists are asked to explore their beliefs about adolescents, young adults, and families, change processes, and other areas. This is explored further in the next chapter. A continual examination and reexamination of personal and professional philosophies and how they influence treatment provides an isomorphic process whereby therapist training and supervision parallel therapy itself (Liddle, 1988; White & Russell, 1997).

As a second way of attending to the influence of therapist variables, instead of using theoretical constructs as guides in treatment, a change-oriented perspective shifts attention back to clients' experiences and ratings of the therapeutic relationship and alliance. In doing this, clients are invited to share their perceptions of therapy processes and how therapists are working with them. The intention is to ensure that therapists gain feedback regarding what is working and what is not, and that clients' experiences guide treatment.

Most approaches for working with adolescents, young adults, and families do not take into consideration the collective contribution of the general effects, the issue of context, or therapist variables. There is clearly a need for a new direction. A change-oriented approach fulfills this need by weaving together the aforementioned threads with the findings regarding the question, "What works in therapy?" Through collaborative, client-informed, outcome-oriented processes and practices, the fibers that form a new perspective with young people and families are thereby woven and strengthened.

A NEW DIRECTION: THE
JOURNEY BEGINS...

The next chapter explores how a change-oriented perspective offers a sound, flexible, and respectful alternative for working with adolescents, young adults, and families. The discussion that follows in the coming chapters does not represent an endpoint but part of an ongoing journey to find the most respectful and effective ways of helping young people and their families to achieve the changes they desire. The change-oriented philosophy presented takes a next step in the evolution of psychotherapy by building on research findings and client feedback. To this end, numerous clear, practical ideas and ways of working with adolescents, young adults, and families are discussed.

Chapter 1

A Change Orientation with Adolescents, Young Adults, and Families

WELCOME TO THE WONDERFUL WORLD OF POSSIBILITIES AND CHANGE! This chapter delves into the foundations of a change-oriented approach with adolescents, young adults, and families. It begins with an exploration into what you believe about young people, families, and the possibilities of change. This is followed by a discussion of ideas associated with a change-oriented perspective.

A REALITY CHECK: PREPARING FOR A PHILOSOPHICAL LEAP

As mentioned earlier, there seems to be a virtually endless stream of theoretical models and associated explanations as to *why* adolescents and young adults struggle and experience difficulty growing up. Corresponding with each model's explanations for the causes of problems are prescriptions for resolving them. For example, cognitive therapists see people's problems as related to thinking. Family systems therapists tend to see problems as indicators of relational and hierarchical dysfunction. And solution-focused therapists believe clients have untapped reservoirs of abilities that they don't even know about.

This way of thinking holds that explanations and, ultimately, models and techniques drive therapy—leaving the contributions of clients and other non-model-specific effects as relatively insignificant to change processes. Because most clinical training focuses on teaching models it's easy to begin to see them as representative of truths and realities.

Although models do not represent reality, to challenge one's theoretical viewpoint is to challenge one's view of reality. Perhaps, then, the most difficult "leap" for many clinicians is to shift from thinking in terms of models as truths to exploring processes that are more reliant on clients as the engineers of change.

THE HEART OF THE MATTER:
A PHILOSOPHICAL SHIFT = A
CHANGE ORIENTATION

The introduction offered ample evidence that indicates the need for a new direction in therapy with adolescents, young adults, and families. However, research does not speak to the heart of the matter—practitioners' core beliefs. Regardless of the professional literature, you believe what you believe for a variety of different reasons, all of which are your own, and all of which potentially effect therapy.

The importance of therapist variables also was raised in the preceding chapter. Although there are many variables worthy of discussion, perhaps the one that permeates therapy the most is therapists' beliefs. There are many contextual influences that contribute to how we view the world and our beliefs about the nature of people and their problems. The same can be said for our beliefs about change processes and the possibilities for solutions. Just as clients develop theories through contextual influences, therapists construct their worlds based on culture, family history, social relationships, genetics and biology, religion/spirituality, gender, sexual orientation, nutrition, politics, economics, and so on (Bertolino, 1999; Bertolino & O'Hanlon, 2002; Bertolino & Schultheis, 2002). All of these influences are filtered through personal and professional experiences, some of which were, or will be in the future, more meaningful than others.

Contextual influences shape our personal and professional views and, ultimately, how we work with young people as they show up in our theories, therapeutic processes, and practices. Beliefs are represented in theories and can vary significantly, yet they affect therapeutic processes nonetheless. The impact of our theories on therapy is undeniable. Therefore it is essential that we remain open to personal investigations of our beliefs.

There are many ways that "impossibility" can arise, most notably in our theories. A belief that improvement or positive change is impossible frequently shows up in the ways we describe or talk about adolescents, young adults, and family members ("He doesn't want to change," "She's resistant," "They're unmotivated," "Those are pervasive familial patterns," or "Once you have ADD, you have it forever," etc.). These descriptions can infiltrate therapy in very negative ways. Such beliefs can inhibit positive change and dampen hope and the expectation of positive change. Moreover, these beliefs can be a threat to longevity in the field as they can significantly contribute to the burnout of individuals and "staff infections" (Bertolino, 1999; Bertolino & Thompson, 1999). The latter occurs when negativity permeates individuals and spreads to other staff members. The result of staff infections can be devastating and include fear, loss of hope, less effective services, malaise, and a host of other negative effects.

The remedy is a change orientation—a belief that positive change and successful outcomes are possible with adolescents, young adults, and families. Such a perspective can circumvent therapy by freeing us from predetermining theoretical restraints that suggest impossibility. A change orientation can facilitate creativity and spontaneity. It also helps to distinguish each of us from one another through our "fingerprints" in therapy. Fingerprints represent the subtle nuances and idiosyncrasies that are evident in our "styles" of therapy. For example, some therapists are good storytellers. Some use humor well. Still others have a calmness about them that is attractive to clients. These variables are, in part, what clients respond to and in all likelihood account for some percentage of the unexplained variance in psychotherapy outcomes (Wampold, 2001).

A shift to a change orientation requires personal exploration and commitment. It involves going beyond a scientific, rational mode of thinking and searching within yourself. Your mission, should you choose to accept it, is one of opening yourself up to exploring what you believe about adolescents, young adults, and families. In my teaching and practice, supervisees and students are routinely asked questions to aid with this exploration:

1.   What do you believe about working with adolescents, young adults, and families (and people in general)?
2.   How did you come to believe what you believe and know what you know?
3.   What have been the most significant influences or determining factors on your beliefs?
4.   How have your beliefs affected your work with young people and their families?
5.   Do you believe that change is possible even in the most "difficult" adolescents/young adults/families/situations? (If you answered "yes," proceed to question #6. If you answered "no," proceed to question #7.)
6.   How do you believe that change occurs with young people and their families? What does change involve? What do you do to promote change? (Skip to question #8.)

7. How do you work with young people and their families with this belief? (Skip to question #9)
8. Would you be in this field if you didn't believe that young people and their families could change? (If you answered this question, end here)
9. Given that you do not believe that change is possible even with the most "difficult" adolescents/young adults/families/situations, how have you managed to remain working with such persons?

Take some time to think about these questions. You may also want to record your responses in some way. This would offer you the opportunity to compare your current responses with later ones once you have finished this book. It is important that we ask ourselves these and other questions that challenge us to review our theoretical conceptualizations about adolescents, young adults, and families. The practices and processes we use to effect change directly reflect our underlying beliefs and assumptions.

Theoretical assumptions reflect therapists' beliefs in models and do not require empirical support. A change orientation is not based on random assumptions. Instead, general effects, incidental aspects, and common factors based on empirical evidence and, more importantly, client feedback, inform a change-oriented perspective and provide a foundation for therapy. All pathways emphasize collaboration, competency, respectfulness, and effectiveness (Bertolino & O'Hanlon, 2002). Clients are the most influential contributors to outcome and therefore should be the compasses that guide treatment (Bohart & Tallman, 1999). Any allegiances formed must be with adolescents, young adults, and others involved with therapy, not with models.

CHANGE-ORIENTED IDEAS WITH ADOLESCENTS, YOUNG ADULTS, AND FAMILIES

A change-oriented perspective is inclusive and client-informed, promoting the interplay of the common, change-effecting factors. In upcoming chapters a brief overview of the common factors provided in the introduction is expanded on. Here, some of the core ideas that relate to a change-oriented approach with adolescents, young adults, and families are identified and amplified. Derived from the literature on both general and specific therapeutic effects as well as client feedback and clinical practice, these ideas include *clients as agents of change; honoring the therapeutic relationship and alliance; client orientations as guides to change; a change orientation; expectancy, hope, and placebo; directions, goals, and outcomes;* and *means and methods.*

Clients as Agents of Change

Adolescents, young adults, and others associated with their therapy are the single most important contributors to therapeutic outcome. Therapists can be seen as assisting with change, but it is young people who are the agents of change. It is the ability that these people possess as self-healers that makes them the heroes of therapy. It has, in fact, been said that all change is self-change (Prochaska et al., 1994). Change-oriented therapy embodies processes that help to identify and build on internal strengths and external resources of adolescents and young adults and to strengthen their ability to "mature out of" developmental phases or spontaneously change, manage the trials and tribulations of life, overcome problems, and find viable solutions.

Strengths and Resources

It is common for adolescents and young adults to be viewed as and subsequently treated as irrevocably maimed, damaged, incapable, or lacking ability in some way. When problems occur, mental health professionals, educators, and others who interact with them often assume that young people do not have the coping, anger management, or others skills necessary to deal with life. Moreover, parents or caregivers may be unnecessarily blamed for parenting skills or for their sons' and daughters' "conditions." This perception not only significantly downplays the contributions of adolescents, young adults, and family members to the processes of change but also is disrespectful of such persons.

Young people have abilities, strengths, and resources that can be helpful in solving problems and resolving conflicts. This is not to suggest that they have all the competencies they will ever need or that they have untapped reservoirs with answers to every problem in life. Instead, young people are seen as both in the process of learning *and* as having competencies—internal and external resources that have been helpful in the past, in similar or different contexts in relation to presenting concerns, and that can be utilized in the present and future. Internal competencies include strengths, abilities, resilience, and coping skills. External resources relate to the role of family, friends, communities (religious or otherwise), and other potential contributors to the lives of young people (Bertolino, 1999; Bertolino & Thompson, 1999; Bertolino & O'Hanlon, 2002).

Strengths can go unnoticed and underutilized when therapists, who have been trained to discover problems or pathology and "underlying conflicts," continue to search for and find inabilities, liabilities, and deficiencies. "Pathologies" are often the result of unhelpful views on the part of therapists or other professionals involved. Subsequently, these views can become situated in language and magnified, thereby becoming "problem areas."

Spontaneous Change

Change is constant. Therapists orient toward identifying and amplifying the ongoing contributions of young people and others in the service of change. Being change-oriented means taking care to notice moments of change in or outside of therapy and incorporating those changes into therapy. The significance of change is dependent on the attribution of meaning by clients and others. What is important is recognizing that because change can happen in multiple ways in the lives of young people and their families, there will be numerous opportunities to tap into what occurs spontaneously or in a less deliberate fashion.

Development, Maturation, and Transition

Adolescents, young people, and families will experience ups and downs, transitions, and movement through different phases of life both as individuals and as part of larger systems. Learning how clients attribute meaning to those movements is essential. It's important to honor the experiences of clients and invite them into conversations where they can explore the relevance of developmental, maturational, and transitional processes and changes in their lives. The idea is not for therapists to impose beliefs on clients but to normalize their experiences and offer alternative possibilities that may promote change in the direction of their preferred goals and futures.

Honoring the Therapeutic Relationship
and Alliance

A common misperception is that therapeutic relationships are *formed* and then remain in a constant, set state. Although we cannot completely escape our everyday verbal references to relationships in the noun form (i.e., as "things"), it is essential that we attend to relationships differently. Relationships grow and evolve, ebb and flow. They are not static. Young people and those involved are sensitive to seemingly endless influences and, in particular, changes in the processes and practices carried out in therapy.

Interestingly, the strength of the therapeutic bond is not highly correlated with the length of treatment (Horvath & Luborsky, 1993). There can be an instant bond between a young person and his or her therapist. This notion runs counter to traditional teachings that suggest that adolescents, in particular, tend not to trust adults and that therefore rapport will take many sessions to build. The amount of time it takes for young people to feel comfortable in relationships varies and is highly contingent on their experiences and perceptions. Said differently, it is not whether therapists believe they are connecting with young people, but whether young people experience connection with their therapists.

Client ratings of therapists as empathic, trustworthy, and nonjudgmental are better predictors of positive outcome than therapist ratings, diagnosis, approach, or any other variable (Duncan & Miller, 2000, Horvath & Symonds, 1991; Lambert & Bergin, 1994). Client ratings of the relationship are the *most* consistent predictor of improvement (Duncan & Miller, 2000; Gurman, 1977; Lafferty, Beutler, & Crago, 1989). Those who are engaged and connected with their therapists are likely to benefit most from therapy. Therapists who are tuned into the importance of clients' relational needs and are monitoring relationships are better able to ensure that they feel heard, understood, and connected.

Empathy, Acknowledgement, and Validation

Central to the therapeutic relationship and a change-oriented approach with adolescents and young adults is that they feel heard and understood. Therapists listen and attend, acknowledging and validating whatever is experienced. This includes young people's feelings, sense of self, bodily sensations, sensory experience, and automatic thoughts. It is important that therapists acknowledge and validate all internal experience. This can be done in a variety of ways. Empathy, genuineness, and unconditional positive regard are essential (Rogers, 1951, 1961). It is also important to tune into ways young people talk about their lives, situations, and concerns—the ways they use language. Client satisfaction ratings are significantly related to similarity in the client-therapist linguistic style (Patton & Meara, 1982). Therefore, special attention is paid to accommodating and matching adolescents' and young adults' use of language. Other ways include the use of verbal and nonverbal behaviors, questions, constructing clear outcomes, and processes that encourage and facilitate positive change.

Personal Agency and Accountability

Although all of what adolescents and young adults feel experientially is okay, their views are not always helpful and the actions they undertake are not always okay. That is, some of the ways that they view the world are helpful and direct them toward goals, but others do not and contribute to "stuckness." While it's important to acknowledge young people's views, we do not have to agree with them. Therefore, therapy may involve deconstructing clients' views such that they are able to save face and simultaneously begin to see and experience themselves or their situations differently. Likewise, some of the actions, interactions, and behaviors that young people undertake are positive, legal, and propel them toward goals—others are illegal or cause danger to self or others. In all cases, therapists must take appropriate action to ensure the safety of the client and others.

Client-Informed: Alliance and Collaboration

As previously discussed, the therapeutic alliance is an expansion of the relationship and a more encompassing term used to refer to the collaborative partnership between clients and therapists. Orlinsky and colleagues (1994) concluded that the quality of the client's participation in therapy is the most important determinant of outcome. The degree to which young people and others are included in processes (e.g., how to meet, when to meet, etc.), directions of therapy, establishment of goals, and methods to achieve those goals is paramount. Negative outcome is often traced to clients' being excluded from therapeutic processes. As Duncan, Hubble, and Miller stated, "Impossibility, we decided, is at least partly a function of leaving clients out of the process, of not listening or of dismissing the importance of their perspective" (1997a, p. 30).

Adolescents and young adults are routinely left out of therapeutic processes. They are used to having clinicians work *on* them as opposed to *with* them. The latter reflects a commitment on the part of the therapist to invite youth to be part of conversations and processes. Regardless of whether or not they are accepted, invitations should nonetheless be open. This allows young people to move in and out of therapeutic processes in ways that are right for them. Efforts to form collaborative partnerships begin prior to the start of "formal" therapy. Adolescents, young adults, family members, and others involved are consulted with about when and where sessions should be held, who ought to attend sessions, and so on (Bertolino & O'Hanlon, 2002). As therapy proceeds, so do collaborative efforts.

It is often assumed that adolescents and young adults lack a sense of direction. The idea is that others are much more capable of making decisions for them. Therapy can become one-dimensional when anyone and everyone but the young person seems to know best. From a change-oriented perspective the voices of the young are encouraged and valued. They are seen as capable of choosing directions that fit with them. The following story from Rosen (1982) about psychiatrist Milton Erickson illustrates this idea:

> When Erickson was a young man a horse wandered into his yard. Although the horse had no identifying marks he offered to return it to its owners. To accomplish this, he mounted the horse, led it to the road, and let the horse decide which way it wanted to go. He intervened only when the horse left the road to graze or wander into a field. When the horse finally arrived at the yard of a neighbor several miles down the road, the neighbor asked the young Erickson, "How did you know that horse came from here and was our horse?" Erickson replied, "I didn't know—but the horse knew. All I did was keep him on the road." (pp. 46–47)

Collaboration in this sense means showing young people the road and letting them choose the direction. This is a cornerstone of therapy that is client-informed. A collaborative stance is also extended to those outside helpers (family members, social service workers, parole officers, juvenile officers, teachers, etc.) who may be involved in the therapy.

Many therapeutic models require that therapists take charge and accept responsibility for making change occur. From a change-oriented perspective, therapists are seen as *facilitators* of change. Clinicians use language, questions, and other processes to promote change. Ideas and questions are not imposed on young people and others. They are "offered" in a nonauthoritarian way as possibilities for consideration. In this way young people and others involved with therapy have the space to agree or disagree, modify, or correct what has been offered.

Being collaborative does not mean "Never be directive." As with any population, working with adolescents and young adults can require that practitioners become more or less directive depending on client preferences and context. From a change-oriented perspective, one can be directive by challenging views and behaviors and promoting accountability while simultaneously conveying respect. Numerous respectful and creative ways of facilitating change while promoting accountability are offered in upcoming chapters.

Client Orientations as Guides to Change

Each model or theory of therapy offers an explanation as to why adolescents and young adults have problems and how to intervene to solve those problems. Depending on the perspective, problems can be seen as being influenced by biological, cognitive, developmental, relational, or other contextual properties. With adolescents and young adults there is no shortage of explanatory theories. Ironically, there exists no solid evidence to support the idea that clinicians must explain the roots of dysfunction, explore past events, or focus on pathology to help clients change (Beutler, 1989; Held, 1991, 1995; Prochaska & DiClemente, 1982, 1984, 1986).

Although therapists' theories rarely jumpstart positive change, clients' orientations are instrumental. Client orientations include *influences of context*—what they attribute their concerns and problems to as well as what are considered resources—and *theories of change*—their ideas about how positive change will come about. Although young people and others involved won't necessarily have well-formed theories about the nature of problems, they typically have ideas regarding influences that can be identified through careful attention to language. As change-oriented therapists we *invite, learn, honor,* and *match* client orientations.

Inviting involves creating a context where adolescents, young adults, and family members feel understood, thereby creating space where their ideas, stories, and narratives can be shared. *Learning* relates to an openness and commitment on the part of therapists to understand, as much as possible, how young people and others associated with therapy view their situations. This includes learning about the influences of context, preferences about who should be involved with therapy, and so on. *Honoring* clients' orientations speaks to the importance of acknowledgement and validation. It's important that the perceptions, ideas, and beliefs of young people, parents, caregivers, and others are respected and validated. This does not mean that therapists must agree with such perspectives. Acknowledgement and validation simply let people know that we don't blame them or see them as crazy, maimed, bizarre, or having bad intentions. *Matching* involves therapists' using processes and practices that are respectful of and consistent with clients' ideas about their concerns and problems, possibilities for attaining solutions, and the means and methods for achieving those hoped-for changes.

Through these processes we can gain a better understanding of how young people and others involved have constructed their worlds. We can then help them to achieve the change they desire within the orientations or worldviews they have established. When their orientations seem to contribute to stuckness, we collaborate with young people and others in finding valid, alternative perspectives that open up possibilities for positive change.

Influences of Context

Concerns, problems, possibilities, and solutions do not exist in a vacuum. They are situated in and influenced by context. Context has two connotations. First, it refers to the healing environment and relationship and the meanings attributed to it by participants (Frank & Frank, 1991). Next, as mentioned previously, it refers to individual differences and variables that may influence problems, possibilities, and solutions, including but not limited to culture, family history and background, social relationships, genetics and biology, religion/spirituality, gender, sexual orientation, nutrition, and economics (Bertolino, 1999; Bertolino & O'Hanlon, 2002; Bertolino & Schultheis, 2002).

Because it is very difficult to identify any one aspect of context as being the true *cause* of a problem, it's more helpful to view contextual propensities as *influences*. Thus, any one problem can have multiple influences. What is most important is the emphasis clients place on aspects of context. Young people, caregivers, and others involved in therapy continue to demonstrate that they are motivated predominantly by what they believe influences their problems. Clients may not enter therapy with clear-cut theories of causation, but they do often have ideas about the nature of or influences on their concerns. Oftentimes these ideas are embedded in their language and can be cultivated through careful listening. More powerful than therapist explanations are clients' perceptions and attributions regarding the influences of context.

Theories of Change

As an adjunct to contextual influences, another aspect of clients' orientations relates to their ideas about how positive change might occur with their situations or lives. Several theorists have discussed this idea in terms of learning clients' *theories of change* (Duncan & Miller, 2000; Duncan & Sparks, 2001). Clients' theories of change represent their ideas, attitudes, and speculations regarding how they situate themselves in relation to problems, what might bring about change, at what rate and when change might occur, who might be involved, and what factors, including contextual influences, might be involved in facilitating change. Duncan and Miller discussed the importance of attending to clients' theories:

> Honoring the client's theory occurs when a given therapeutic procedure fits or complements the client's preexisting beliefs about his or her problems and the change process. We, therefore, simply listen and then amplify stories, experiences, and interpretations that clients offer about their problems, as well as their thoughts feelings, and ideas about how those problems might be best addressed. As the client's theory evolves, we implement the client's identified solutions or seek an approach that both fits the client's theory and provides possibilities for change. (p. 84)

Client theories are filtered through contextual influences and help us to better understand their worldviews and how to help them. Recall that young people and others involved won't necessarily enter therapy with clear-cut ideas, but will give indications of how they view themselves and their situations by the words they use. Through careful listening, questioning, and direct inquiries, we invite clients into conversations where details can be learned about how they expect change to occur. We have conversations with adolescents, young adults, and others about how they feel their problems developed, how they have tried to resolve them and to what degree those efforts have or haven't worked, what they've considered but haven't tried, and what they might consider in the future to attain the change they desire. Moreover, the processes and practices that therapists offer are client-informed and match clients' ideas and facilitate positive change. Learning clients' orientations and theories is essential because their ideas are a much more accurate guide than therapists' theories to finding pathways with possibilities for positive change.

A Change Orientation

While traditional models propose theories of dysfunction and disorder—why people are stuck—a change-oriented approach orients toward how change is *already* occurring in the lives of young people and their families. Erickson was one of the first practitioners to work in this way. He focused less on explaining *why* his patients were having problems and more on how he could help them to change in positive ways. Miller and colleagues (1997) echoed Erickson's nontraditional, change-oriented approach to problems, reporting that a growing body of literature suggests that:

> Therapeutic time is spent more productively when the therapist and client focus on and enhance the factors responsible for change-in-general rather than on identifying and then changing the factors a theory suggests are responsible for causing problems-in-particular.... Indoctrinating clients into a particular model of problem causation might actually ... [undermine] the very factors responsible for the occurrence of change by drawing clients' attention to whatever a particular theory suggests is causing their suffering. (p. 127)

An explanatory-only focus on the part of clinicians working with adolescents and young adults can be counterproductive as it may unnecessarily stigmatize and blame them for problems. Further, as demonstrated previously, there is little evidence suggesting that theoretical explanations lead to change. If this were the case, there would be no need for therapy. Therapists could just explain away the troubles of adolescents and young people. An emphasis on explanations is only indicated when a young person, parent, or other (not including the therapist) involved in therapy believes that such a focus is necessary for positive change to occur (Bertolino & O'Hanlon, 2002). In such cases, therapists honor such perspectives and work with clients to determine valid explanations. The significant difference here is clients are seeking explanations as opposed to therapists imposing the idea that explanations must be found.

Clients' problems will fluctuate in frequency, intensity, duration, and so on. Change is constant; problems are not static. There will be better days, worse days, symptom-free, and symptom-laden times. By orienting toward change, therapists can enlist change-effecting propensities such as client competencies and support systems.

Future Change

A change-oriented approach with adolescents and young adults emphasizes present and future change (Miller et al., 1997). A focus on the present and future does not dismiss the possible significance of past events. As with an explanatory focus, if an adolescent, parent, or other is oriented toward the past, the respectful path is to follow him or her and remain client-informed. Alternatively, clinicians do not hold the assumption that clients must explore the past and go through cathartic experiences to resolve conflicts.

Therapists must contend with theoretical maps and constructions that can greatly alter the course of treatment (Efran & Lukens, 1985). Therapists who maintain the view that future change is possible can convey this belief through the use language and interaction. This, in turn, can engender hope, promote adolescents', young adults', and others' expectancy for change, and facilitate future change. Conversely, therapists who are guided by pathology or unhelpful theoretical assumptions that close down possibilities for change can extinguish hope and create a context where positive change seems impossible.

Change Is Predictable

Regardless of the model employed, the average length of time that clients attend therapy is six to ten sessions (Garfield, 1989; Koss & Butcher, 1986; Levitt, 1966; Miller, 1994). Further, Miller and colleagues wrote that "all large-scale meta-analytic studies of client change indicate that the most frequent improvement occurs early in treatment" (1997, p. 194). Most major positive impact in therapy happens during the first few weeks and six to eight sessions (Fennell & Teasdale, 1987; Howard, Kopta, Krause, & Orlinsky, 1986; Howard, Lueger, Maling, & Martinovich, 1993; Ilardi & Craighead, 1994; Smith et al., 1980). Further, studies have demonstrated that 60–65% of clients experience significant symptomatic relief in the first one to seven sessions, 70–75% after six months, and 80–85% at one year (Brown, Dreis, & Nace, 1999; Howard et al., 1986; Howard, Moras, Brill, Martinovich, & Lutz, 1996; Lambert, Okiishi, Finch, & Johnson, 1998; Smith et al., 1980; Steenbarger, 1992; Talmon, 1990; Talmon, Hoyt, & Rosenbaum, 1990).

Whether in individual or family therapy, adolescents and young adults can benefit from treatment that extends beyond eight sessions. However, as treatment progresses, there is a course of diminishing returns with more and more effort required to obtain just noticeable differences in client improvement (Howard et al., 1986). Even though the amount of change decreases over time, as long as progress is being made, therapy can remain beneficial. Further, if clients are "early responders" and experience meaningful change in the first handful of sessions, the probability of positive outcome significantly increases (Garfield, 1994; Lambert, 2002). In contrast, when clients show little or no improvement or experience a worsening of symptoms early on in treatment, they are at significant risk for negative outcome (Lebow, 1997).

In many mental health settings, regardless of the theoretical model employed by the therapist, the majority of clients attend just a single session of therapy (Talmon, 1990). Though people end therapy after one session for a variety of reasons, often the reason is that they got what they wanted in a single session. This research suggests that therapists ought to attend to each session as if it were the only one by focusing on what clients want as opposed to consulting their respective theories to determine what needs to happen during initial sessions.

The issue of treatment length with adolescents in particular has been debated at length. From a change-oriented perspective this is a non-issue. First, the evidence shows that on average clients only attend a handful of sessions regardless of the therapist's orientation. Therefore, it is essential that therapists work to maximize the effectiveness of each interaction and session. That said, some clients will need one, three, or eleven sessions, and others will need thirty sessions. It is not the number of sessions that is most important, but collaborating with adolescents, young adults, and others involved to determine where they want to go, when things are better, and when goals and preferred outcomes have been achieved. This, by nature, makes for therapy that is generally briefer and client-informed.

Next, as mentioned earlier, adolescents and young adults go through both individual and familial developmental transitions. A change-oriented approach accommodates these transitions by incorporating a "revolving door" philosophy. This allows for entry, termination, and reentry, depending on the needs of young people and their families. It is not contingent on a set number of sessions. Instead, therapists and clients collaborate to determine when therapy is no longer necessary. Therapy can restart if the same or a different concern arises. This flexibility allows families to seek help whenever they feel it is necessary—through the ups and downs of raising adolescents and young adults. This is in contrast to the view that people must remain in therapy for years or that therapy is a one-time affair, where problems are fixed in one fell swoop and life becomes problem-free.

Expectancy, Hope, and Placebo

There are many general effects that contribute to positive change and successful outcome. None may be as amorphous, yet essential, as expectancy, hope, and placebo. Estimates indicate that this combination of elements contributes 15%–50% (Greenberg, 2002; Lambert, 1992) of the variance in outcome. Although empirical studies may suggest a wide variance, what is clear is the importance of the presence and promotion of these aspects with adolescents, young adults, and families. Hope, in particular, can play a key role for young people and families surviving from one day to the next.

Pretreatment Expectancy

People would not bother with therapy if they didn't believe it could be beneficial in some way. This is commonly referred to as pretreatment expectancy (Safran, Heinberg, & Juster, 1997; Schneider & Klauer, 2001). The expectation and hope for positive change, however minimal, that accompanies therapy is an important factor for young people and their families—one that counteracts demoralization. Pretreatment expectancy is also very important for therapists. Going into therapy, those who hold the belief that change is possible, even in the most difficult of situations, maintain hope, and expect, anticipate, and continuously monitor for positive change. This is evidenced by their use of processes and practices that are collaborative, respectful, honor young people's theories of change, and ultimately build on, create, or rehabilitate hope.

Involuntary or Mandated

Most adolescents and many young adults do not initiate therapy and are often sent against their wishes. There are at least two crucial issues here. First, in terms of successful outcomes, clients who have been mandated to engage in therapy do just as well as those who attend voluntarily as long as they feel connected with and understood by their therapists (Tohn & Oshlag, 1996). That is, clients' ratings of their therapists are excellent indicators of outcome (Horvath & Symonds, 1991). Therefore, how therapists respond during initial interactions with mandated youth can make a significant difference in whether or not they remain in therapy. A strong therapeutic relationship and alliance can also promote hope and increase the expectancy that positive change will occur in the future.

Second, the mere appearance of mandated youth or caregivers at sessions is quite telling. Not every young person mandated or advised to attend therapy actually follows through. The same can be said for parents and caregivers. Whether viewed by referring parties as part of the problem and in need of therapy or as responsible for ensuring that young persons attend therapy, not all adults follow through.

When adolescents, young adults, caregivers, or others involved respond with statements such as, "I didn't have a choice, I had to come," "They would have locked me up," or "They threatened to take her away," it's important that practitioners do not fall into the abyss of "impossibility-land" (Bertolino & O'Hanlon, 1999). This is a place where young people are viewed by clinicians as resistant, unmotivated, incapable of change, and perhaps worst of all, as having bad intentions ("She needs her daughter to be sick," "He doesn't want to change," etc.). When therapists begin to view clients in these ways, creativity, spontaneity, expectancy, and hope can diminish for all involved. Impossibility-land not only closes down avenues of positive change for young people but also provides a direct path to therapist burnout.

From a change-oriented perspective expectancy and hope offer the remedy to impossibility. We do not hold that adolescents, young adults, and others involved want to be "sick" or that they have bad intentions. It is believed that people want better for themselves and others. When things are going poorly, most people, at some level, would like their lives to improve at least minimally. This is not about looking at the world through rose-colored glasses. It is recognizing that if people have choices, most will want things to be better rather than worse. Therefore, when young people, caregivers, and others show up for sessions despite not wanting to be in therapy, they are directly making some effort to improve their lives. Therapists identify these efforts and amplify them by talking with young people and others in sessions. This is explored further in the next chapter.

At first glance it may seem that a different protocol is necessary with young people sent to therapy involuntarily. The philosophy behind a change-orientation is simply that positive change is possible. Therefore, with all situations, not just with youth attending against their wishes, we recognize that philosophy or theory-informed pessimism or negativity (when it is not with the intent of matching and joining with clients) on the part of therapists can dampen hope and perhaps even contribute to higher dropout rates and treatment failures.

Technique and Placebo

An issue of debate among mental health professionals relates to the role of techniques in facilitating change. As we have learned, methods and techniques contribute little to the variance in outcomes. Nevertheless, all therapeutic processes involve techniques or rituals (Frank & Frank, 1991). What is important here is whether the processes and practices used by therapists contribute to the expectancy for change and increase hope, and whether clients *and* practitioners believe in the treatments and the rationales behind them.

Instead of maintaining allegiances with favorite techniques, therapists can determine the viability of their methods by checking with clients. In other words, although most clients will not know whether a "technique" is being used, how they respond to therapists' use of questions, for example, can make a difference. Further, clients' beliefs about particular focuses (i.e., emphasizing thoughts, behaviors, interactions) in therapy weigh in heavily. When clients believe that therapists are working with them in ways that are consistent with their views of concerns and problems and ways of resolving those concerns and problems, hope increases. On the contrary, a mismatch (e.g., the therapist focusing on cognitions and insight when the client sees the problem as relational) can dampen hope and the expectancy for positive change.

An increase in hope can produce a placebo effect. That is, a mere increase in expectancy and hope for clients can contribute to positive change. In many cases it will not be the technique or method that leads to a specific change, but rather the client's belief in the technique or method. It is also noteworthy that clients' confidence in therapists and their processes and practices can make a difference in therapy. Clients who are confident that they are "in good hands" and trust their therapists are likely to experience an increase in expectancy and hope as well as an increase in placebo effects that may accompany methods and techniques.

Opening Moments...

Throughout therapy it is important for therapists to build on the expectation of change and promote hope. Perhaps most important are early interactions with young people. Adolescents, young adults, and others involved in therapy form opinions quickly. The ways that therapists respond during initial interactions can significantly affect future interactions and therapeutic processes. Initial sessions and interactions offer numerous opportunities to promote the expectancy for change and hope. These include but are not limited to:

- Attending to conversational and relational preferences
- Attending to client differences
- Acknowledging and validating the perspectives (i.e., influences of context, orientations, and theories of change) of young people and others involved
- Conversations regarding the severity of concerns or problems
- Viewing change as inevitable and positive change as possible
- Conversations regarding who should attend sessions, where to meet, the length of therapy, etc.
- Conversations regarding diagnosis
- Collaborating around goals and ways of achieving those goals

Directions, Goals, and Outcomes

Therapy that is theory-driven directs practitioners to theory-specific goals (e.g., changing distorted thinking, developing social skills). As a result, adolescents and young adults are often left out of processes, as it is assumed that others know "what is best." Because a change-oriented approach is client-informed, it is reliant upon what young people and others involved would like to have different in their lives. This includes their preferences in terms of directions, goals, and outcomes.

Although this will be explored in depth in Chapter 3, here it is necessary to distinguish between directions, goals, and outcomes. *Directions* relate to a general sense of where young people and others involved would like their lives or situations to be headed in the future. *Goals* represent what such persons want to see change from session to session. *Outcomes* are young people's and others' perceptions of the impact of services on the major areas of their lives (individually, interpersonally, socially, etc.).

The Importance of Direction,
not Terminology

Many adolescents, young adults, and family members have difficulty thinking in terms of "goals." The terminology is unimportant. Whether you speak of "achieving goals," "developing meaning," "discovering purpose," or use some other syntax, what is crucial is learning from those involved what they would like to see change as a result of coming to therapy.

Practitioners who do not have a sense of what others' concerns are, what they want to have change, and what will constitute successful therapy are at risk for therapeutic ambiguity. This can contribute to therapy that is chaotic, confusing, and without any sense of structure. Consequently, both clients and therapists can experience frustration, anger, or other feelings or thoughts that may lead to a loss of hope and thoughts of giving up. This can translate into an increase in session no-shows and client dropout. Moreover, therapists are at risk of referring to young people and others as resistant, unmotivated, or incapable of change.

The Benefits of Collaboration

As with change-oriented processes in general, the benefits of collaborating with young people and others involved about directions and goals are numerous. When clients are invited into conversations where their voices are encouraged and valued, client factors, the therapeutic relationship and alliance, and expectancy and placebo all become more important in terms of their respective contributions to outcomes. This further exemplifies the relevance of the interrelatedness of the general effects.

Means and Methods

It is clear that general effects account for the majority of the variance in outcomes (Hubble, Duncan, & Miller, 1999; Lambert, 1992; Wampold, 2001). This does not imply that specific ingredients, namely means and methods, are irrelevant in facilitating positive change. Instead the indication is that means and methods ought to emerge out of interactions with clients, match their orientations, and maximize the potential contribution of general effects. In the preface of the most recent edition of his classic text *Persuasion & Healing: A Comparative Study of Psychotherapy*, Jerome Frank (Frank & Frank, 1991) stated:

> My position is not that technique is irrelevant to outcome. Rather, I maintain that, as developed in the text, the success of all techniques

depends on the patient's sense of alliance with an actual or sym-
bolic healer. This position implies that ideally therapists should
select for each patient the therapy that accords, or can be brought
to accord, with the patient's personal characteristics and view of
the problem. (p. xv)

Frank's statement illustrates the importance of the therapeutic relationship and alliance and client factors, both of which are significant general effects. This translates into therapy that is collaborative and client-
informed as opposed to model-driven.

Theories, Means, and Methods as
Possibilities, Not Realities

We have learned that although there is no differential efficacy between
models this does not mean that models are unhelpful. It merely calls
attention to the allegiances that therapists often have with their models.
The privileging of models reflects therapy that is theory-driven. This
means that many clients have little to no choice in which models and
methods are used in therapy. They are merely beneficiaries of the models that therapists have been trained in and or believe in. It therefore
leaves the most significant contributors to outcome—clients—as either
minimally involved in or completely out of therapeutic processes.

Therapy that is change-oriented is based on clinicians' engaging
young people and others involved in an exploration of their orientations and ideas about the influences on concerns and problems and
how positive change might occur. This makes for therapy that is client-
informed. Although clients' orientations will drive therapy, therapists
who have diverse backgrounds in terms of their knowledge of theories
can draw on such knowledge to match clients' ideas about problems,
possibilities, and potential solutions. By having knowledge of theories,
therapists can engage in conversations with clients where a multitude
of possibilities can be generated and explored. Therapists can encourage dialogues that may open up space for new client perspectives to
emerge. Thus, knowledge of theories is beneficial as it allows therapists
to view situations involving adolescents, young adults, and families
from varying perspectives without having to align with any one model
or viewpoint.

Knowledge of theories brings along with it a wider repertoire of
means and methods that may be helpful in therapy. Theories do not
represent reality. They offer alternative ways of viewing concerns and
problems that may contribute to new possibilities for problem resolution. Unlike therapy that is model-driven, change-oriented therapists

offer new ideas, in the form of means, models, and methods, into conversations while adolescents, young adults, and others involved determine the validity of such ideas. Means, methods, and techniques are never imposed; they are introduced into conversations so that clients can accept, reject, modify, or alter them in ways that make most sense to them and open possibilities for positive change.

Specific Ingredients as Rituals

All therapists use rituals. Rituals include processes and practices that are most easily identified through specific ingredients such as methods and techniques. In the best tradition, rituals are procedures practitioners use to promote hope and facilitate change and what has become known as iatrogenic healing (Rossi & Ryan, 1983). In the worst tradition, rituals reflect clinicians' dogmatic beliefs and can inhibit positive change and perhaps contribute to therapists-induced injury or iatrogenic injury. Bertolino and O'Hanlon (2002) wrote:

> Iatrogenic injury refers to methods, techniques, assessment procedures, explanations, or interventions that harm, discourage, invalidate, show disrespect, or close down the possibilities for change.... In contrast, iatrogenic healing refers to those methods, techniques, assessment procedures, explanations, or interventions that encourage, are respectful, and open up the possibilities for change. (p. 61)

Rituals can effect change, but are not necessarily casual agents of change. Wampold remarked that treatment procedures "are beneficial to the client because of the meaning attributed to those procedures rather than because of their specific psychological effects" (2001, p. 27). The importance of rituals is in mobilizing general effects including client, placebo, and relationship factors, thereby opening up space for future change.

Client Orientations and Individual Differences

Our aim is to match or fit means and methods with young people and others' orientations as to how change might come about. Means and methods should be respectful and inclusive of the individual differences that contribute to the uniqueness of people. Wampold stated, "Because specific ingredients of most treatments, particularly ESTs, are designed and implemented without consideration of race, ethnicity, or culture, these treatments are recommended for a disorder, problem, or complaint blind to the client's cultural values" (2001, pp. 221–222). Change-oriented therapists are as much students as practitioners. As Anna Leonowens says in the Rodgers and Hammerstein musical *The King and I*, "By your students you'll be taught." As practitioners we will have some general knowledge of different cultures, religions, and so on; however, we want to take care to not use generalizations as guides.

Generalizations and biases contribute to oppression and clients being marginalized. It is essential that we remember the importance of learning from young people and others what we need to know about cultural, ethnic, religious, and other influences in order to help them. This can convey respect, tap into the general effects, and provide information that can help in the matching of means and methods with young people's and others' concerns so that positive change can be promoted.

Motivation

Motivation is a major issue for many clinicians working with adolescents, young adults, and families. Although there are many divergent views on this topic, this is not an "either/or" (i.e., either they are motivated or they aren't motivated) proposition. From a change-oriented perspective, motivation exists on a continuum. That is, for young people and family members motivation ranges from very low to high depending on the issues. Often what appears as a lack of motivation or as resistance on the part of young people is due to working on goals or outcomes that have little interest to them. Duncan, Miller, and Hubble (1997b) stated:

> There is no such thing as an unmotivated client. Clients may not, as we have found all too often, share ours, but they certainly hold strong motivations of their own. An unproductive and futile therapy can come about by mistaking or overlooking what the client wants to accomplish, misapprehending the client's readiness for change, or pursuing a personal motivation. (p. 11)

Adolescents and young adults are typically motivated toward desired experiences or goals (e.g., money, freedom) and away from unpleasant or unwanted experiences (e.g., boredom, restrictions) (Bertolino, 1999). The same can be said for parents, caregivers, and others who may be involved in therapy. Therefore, crucial to the effectiveness of means and methods is how well these efforts match the degree of motivation exhibited by young people, family members, and others involved.

Matching levels of motivation is another aspect of client orientations. It relates to learning where young people and others situate themselves in terms of their concerns (e.g., involved, not involved, their problems, other people's problems) and what they feel needs to happen for their lives or situations to improve (e.g., nothing, new perspectives, new actions, change in interactions). By better matching means and methods with clients' levels of motivation and how they perceive their situations, we increase the chance of successful outcomes.

Informed by the research on common factors and general effects, the ideas offered in this chapter provide the foundation of a change-oriented perspective with adolescents, young adults, and families. They emphasize change, collaboration, competency, possibility, respectfulness, and the importance of accountability and effectiveness on the part of clinicians. Although these ideas provide an underlying philosophy, the true engineers of therapy are adolescents and young adults. Clients are what make therapy work.

The next chapter explores how these ideas translate into practice. But before proceeding with an in-depth exploration of how to put these ideas to work, I'd like to offer an acronym for this new philosophy with adolescents and young adults:

H.O.P.E.
H – Humanism: Connect with adolescents and young adults through respect and genuineness.
O – Optimism: Be on the lookout for positive change; it is always possible.
P – Possibilities: Search for possibilities and use creativity to facilitate positive change.
E – Expectancy: Expect positive change.

Keep in mind this simple yet essential word as you continue your journey through the pages of this book and, more importantly, your work with adolescents, young adults, and families.

Chapter 2

Creating a Culture of Respect: Collaboration as a Key to Connection and Change

MANY THERAPISTS HAVE TRADITIONALLY VIEWED ESTABLISHING THE therapeutic relationship with young people as akin to giving patients anesthesia before performing surgery: First the gas is given, then the operation follows. Therapists working with adolescents and young adults often consider the therapeutic relationship as something that is *done* just prior to intervention. It is as if establishing the therapeutic relationship is a precursor to the *real* therapy. This prevailing idea is both unhelpful and misleading.

This chapter explores how the therapeutic relationship *is* treatment and offers numerous ways that practitioners can promote positive change by honoring clients' perceptions of the processes and practices. Before delving into these ideas, however, the chapter puts into context the importance of the therapeutic relationship from the perspective of both clinicians and clients. This is followed by a brief discussion about the importance of putting words to work and ensuring that philosophy translates into practice.

A TALE OF TWO PERSPECTIVES: HONORING THE VOICES OF CLIENTS

When successful outcomes have been achieved during the course of therapy, one rather innocent question can elicit varied responses from treatment providers and clients: "What was helpful?" This single inquiry often evokes answers from practitioners that are both similar to and quite divergent from those of clients. For practitioners, two responses are most frequent. The first relates to the therapeutic relationship. Clinicians consistently identify the importance of unconditional positive regard, empathy, and good listening and attending skills, in general. Clients also recognize the importance of the relationship. In fact, the majority of client responses relate directly to dynamics or elements of the therapeutic relationship. Given the parallel, before discussing the second most common response from practitioners, let's explore this further.

From the beginning of most graduate programs students are taught the importance of the therapeutic relationship. Much time is spent on learning and practicing listening and attending skills. Instructors monitor and evaluate the progress of students and provide feedback. By the time they have completed their introductory or foundations classes, there is little doubt in students' minds that the therapist-client connection is essential to the success of treatment.

Once out of school or training, most clinicians continue to value the therapeutic relationship. Furthermore, when practitioners identify the therapeutic relationship as one of the most important contributors to outcome, they are correct. As noted in the introduction, along with client factors, the therapeutic relationship and alliance is among the most significant contributors to outcome. Moreover, in terms of single variables, clients' ratings of the therapeutic relationship are the best predictor of outcome (Horvath & Symonds, 1991; Lambert & Bergin, 1994; Duncan & Miller, 2000). From the perspectives of both clients and therapists, there is little debate over the importance the therapeutic relationship. Still, we have learned much more about it in recent years. Some of these findings stand in stark contrast to traditional teachings and the anesthesia metaphor offered previously. These will be explored shortly.

The second response from practitioners to "What was helpful?" corresponds with models and techniques. That is, clinicians often equate a significant portion of outcome to the effectiveness of their interventions and methods. Once again, at the university level, the same kind of emphasis that is put on the therapeutic relationship is frequently placed on theories and models. In addition to learning attending and listening skills, students quickly learn about theories or, as they sometimes say, "What to do in therapy." Depending on the program, students may be taught primarily individual theories (e.g., Adlerian, cognitive, behavioral, gestalt) or systemic family therapy approaches (e.g., structural, strategic, Mental Research Institute [MRI], conjoint) or a smattering of both. Not all "major" theories are taught in all programs. What theories and models students are exposed to depends on the department, the program, and its faculty. It is not uncommon for the faculty of some programs to hold specific models in high esteem and require that students learn them.

This pattern is duplicated in the plethora of seminars and workshops offered internationally. In these trainings, mental health professionals and students are taught techniques, methods, and models to help them improve their therapeutic effectiveness. For example, a recent sampling of some titles of workshops for working with adolescents, young adults, and families includes the following: "The Impossible Teen: 10 Effective Strategies for Working With Out of Control Adolescents," "The Angry Adolescent: Seven Therapeutic Solutions," "The Explosive Teenager: Proven Methods for Therapeutic Change," and "From Boys Into Men: A New Cognitive-Behavioral Approach for Adolescents Transitioning Into Adulthood." Despite empirical evidence that model and technique factors account for *very little* of the variance in outcomes, it continues to be the area that receives the *most* attention in clinical training.

Although clinicians and clients agree on the importance of the therapeutic relationship, there is significant divergence regarding model and technique factors. Therapists routinely attribute positive change to these factors; clients do not. Clients rarely report that a method, model, technique, or maneuver was a main catalyst in positive change. This is supported by empirical data that continue to demonstrate that model and technique factors account for very little of the variance in therapeutic outcomes (Lambert, 1992; Wampold, 2001). Despite the empirical evidence *including* the voices of clients, clinicians routinely credit their techniques as the catalysts of change—leaving clients contributions out of the picture. What's more, practitioners *continue* to seek the latest, greatest methods as opposed to learning more from clients about what works for them.

As illustrated in upcoming chapters, methods, models, and techniques can assist in facilitating change. But these models and techniques should be born out of the therapeutic relationship and alliance and incorporate general effects such as client factors and expectancy and hope. Care must be taken to find ways of promoting change that are client-informed, respectful, and effective.

STARTING OFF ON THE RIGHT FOOT: STRENGTHENING THE THERAPEUTIC RELATIONSHIP AND ALLIANCE THROUGH COLLABORATION

When does therapy truly begin? Of course, it depends on one's theory. Many would say it begins when an individual, couple, or family attends a first therapy session. Others would argue that therapy starts with any initial contact with a practice, program, agency, or clinician (e.g., a phone call, referral to a provider). Let's remove the confusion by recalling a principle of physics—change is constant. From the moment that therapy becomes an option for adolescents, young adults, and families (voluntarily, mandated, or otherwise), multiple opportunities to increase the chances for positive change are apparent. Many of these occur *prior* to meeting with clients face-to-face and strengthen the therapeutic relationship and alliance.

Recall that the therapeutic alliance is an expansion of the relationship and includes involving clients in virtually all processes. Given that the quality of the client's participation is considered an excellent predictor of outcome (Orlinsky et al., 1994), it is important to include young people and others involved in therapy whenever possible in order to let them know that their preferences are valued and respected and to learn more about their orientations (ideas and perspectives) so that therapy can be accommodated to better meet their needs. This is particularly important with adolescents and young adults who feel marginalized and voiceless. By including young people whenever possible, we increase the chances of getting things off to a good start and achieving successful outcomes.

The following *collaboration keys* (Bertolino & O'Hanlon, 2002) can be used to begin thinking about how collaboration can enhance the therapeutic relationship with young people both prior to the first therapy session and in initial interactions and meetings.

Collaboration Key #1: The Interview

Most adolescents and young adults do not seek therapy on their own initiative; more often it is a parent, teacher, juvenile/probation officer or other "authority" who believes that therapy is necessary. Regardless of whether adolescents are attending on their own volition or against their wishes, it is very important that we attempt to reach out to them whenever possible, inviting them to share their voices.

Including young people in the process of finding a therapist can be helpful. For example, therapist Lynn Loar (2001) has recommended that families be given a list of qualified therapists whom the adolescents can then contact and interview. This allows them to weed out the therapists they don't feel comfortable with and schedule appointments with the ones they think provide the "best fit." This process provides an early opportunity for therapists to join with young people by answering questions, describing what sessions are like, and dispelling any misconceptions or myths. Additionally, young people who are involved in therapist selection are likely to be more invested in the success of therapy. If you are contacted by a young person who wants to ask you questions about therapy or methods, remember that your willingness to openly answer questions is essential to the therapeutic relationship. You don't want to be labeled as a resistant therapist!

This process can also be used with young people sent to therapy against their wishes. The idea is akin to what has been referred to as the "illusion of alternatives" (see Cade & O'Hanlon, 1993; O'Hanlon, 1987; Rossi, 1980). Adolescents or young adults may not be given a choice about what will happen (in this case, to attend therapy); however, they are given a choice about how it will happen (choosing a therapist). Even if a therapist has already been chosen by someone other than the adolescent still can be offered the opportunity to "check out" or interview the therapist prior to the initial in-person session. This involves the young person contacting the therapist and asking a few questions about the process of therapy. Whether or not they accept these invitations to become involved in interviewing and choosing therapists depends on young people themselves. What is important is the effort to reach out and encourage involvement from the start.

Some clinicians take exception with the use of the term "interviewing." They view it as antithetical to collaborative therapy in that it implies an asymmetrical relationship. Interviewing in this context does not refer to the therapist changing his or her posture. In fact, the therapist remains open, flexible, and genuine as in in-person sessions. Interviewing here refers to encouraging the adolescent or young person to take the lead and become involved in the some of the decisions that are made early on (e.g., who to see, when to schedule the first appointment). Here is an example of how this might look:

Adolescent: [Dials number of therapist on list.]
Therapist: Hello, this is Bob Bertolino.
Adolescent: Yeah, I'm supposed to call people and talk to them. I have to see a therapist.
Therapist: Thanks for calling. So, someone told you to call?
Adolescent: Yeah, my mom. I don't have a choice.
Therapist: You mean you don't have a choice about seeing a therapist?
Adolescent: Nope.
Therapist: That must have taken a lot on your part to call. I admire that. What ideas do you have about how I can help you with this?
Adolescent: I guess... well, what do you do when you meet with people?
Therapist: That's a great question. There are many things, but the main thing is I want each person to know that I respect him or her. I also want to take the time to make sure that I understand where each person is coming from. After that, if people choose to continue

working with me, then I find out what they want and how we can get those things to happen.

Adolescent: Would you take their side?

Therapist: You mean your parents?

Adolescent: Yeah.

Therapist: Everyone is entitled to his or her opinion. Because your parents are your parents and they care about you and are responsible for you, they are going to have opinions about what is best for you. I'll support them. I'll also support you because you're entitled to your opinion. You don't have to agree with what your parents want for you, you just have to accept that that's how they see it. Do you know what I mean?

Adolescent: Yeah. That's cool. Well, what if I don't like therapy? Will you tell them I don't have to come any more?

Therapist: If you were to choose to see me and you found that you didn't like it I would certainly want to know. Knowing what's going on with people helps me to learn what is working and what is not. It can help me to make adjustments so people feel better about coming to therapy. So if you felt it wasn't working out, I'd want to talk about it. As far as you not having to come back, I wouldn't claim to know what's best for you and your family. I can only say that I would want things to work out for all of you. So if you didn't like therapy I would support you the same way that I would support your parents. I would help you and your family to arrive at a decision that makes sense for all of you.

Adolescent: Okay ... do I have to tell you everything?

Therapist: You only have to tell me what you feel comfortable with. So that's for you to decide.

Adolescent: Okay, I'll give it a try.

Therapist: You mean you want to set an appointment?

Adolescent: Yeah.

There are many possible scenarios aside from the one just offered. For example, in our emergency shelter, which is a voluntary program for 10–18 year olds, youth are encouraged to ask questions about the program, the structure, rules, staff, and other areas they may be curious about (Bertolino & Thompson, 1999). They can do this by calling the shelter prior to setting up an intake meeting or in the intake meeting itself. Staff members are patient to answer questions and help youth to feel comfortable. They recognize the importance of initial interactions, whether on the phone or face-to-face. The way that staff members respond during initial interactions can promote or dampen hope.

The importance of offering adolescents and young adults opportunities to become involved early on in decisions regarding therapy is paramount. For parents and caregivers, there are opportunities to involve adolescents in interviewing therapists. For therapists, there are opportunities to increase the involvement of youth and promote hope and the expectancy of change that accompanies the start of treatment or therapy.

Collaboration Key #2: Determining Who Should Attend Sessions

Mental health services reflect a trend that began with the advent of psychotherapy, nearly 100 years earlier. Models continue to be the driving force behind decisions regarding whether adolescents and young adults should be seen for individual or family therapy. As discussed in the introduction, those adhering to models that are consistent with the psychological paradigm or first wave see the root cause of problems as existing within the mind or psyche of individuals. It is believed that people are essentially held captive by internal cognitive processes or are shaped or conditioned by external factors. Therefore, the target of treatment is the young person. Although family therapy may be considered, within the psychological paradigm focus remains on helping individuals to change internal processes and therefore improve interpersonal relationships.

In contrast, the systemic-relational paradigm, which represents the second wave, holds that problems are interpersonal in nature and originate from dysfunctional patterns of interaction. The target of therapy is relationships, and all or as many family members as possible are involved in treatment.

Although many first- and second-wave theorists argue otherwise, there are no "right" answers regarding who should be seen in therapy. As noted earlier, one of the factors that can inhibit positive change is when therapists' rules or preferences regarding therapy run counter to or do not match those of clients (Miller et al., 1997). Thus, decisions about who will attend therapy should be client-driven. One way of learning clients' orientations toward their concerns and problems is by asking the people making the appointments to bring to therapy whoever they think will be helpful in resolving the concern. People initiating contact can also choose to consult with others (e.g., family members) to decide how to proceed. This way, before formal therapy has even started, clients' ideas about how to begin and how positive change might occur are acknowledged and respected. Following is an example of how a therapist might talk with a parent setting an appointment for therapy:

Parent: My son is the main one getting into trouble. Should I just bring him to the appointment or should I bring the whole family? I've never done this before.

Therapist: That's a good question. Since I can never know you or your family the way you do, I'd like to ask, do you or anyone else in your family have a preference about who should come to the first session?

Parent: I know my son needs to go—he's what started all of this. But I know he'll only go if I make him because he already told me, "I don't need a shrink!"

Therapist: Okay. There are different ways to approach this. One is to invite the people who you think can help with the concerns that you or your family are having. Another possibility is to ask each person involved if he or she would like to come. You could also just make a decision yourself as to who should come in. We can always make adjustments later by having more or fewer people come in.

Parent: Okay, then I think I want everyone—both of my kids and my husband to come in. But I have another question. Can therapy still work even if everyone doesn't come? I mean, I don't know if my husband will come in. He doesn't think there's a problem.

Therapist: Sure. There are going to be times when certain family members might not be able to attend. Some might not be able to make it because of work or a scheduling conflict and others just flat-out won't want to. It's your call as to whether or not you make someone come. Even if we begin the first session with certain people present, we can always make changes in subsequent sessions. We may find that it's more helpful to have certain people present and not others. There aren't any right or wrong ways of going about this, so whatever you decide is okay. Therapy can work without every family member being present. I'm confident that we can move toward the change you want with those who come in.

Parent: That sounds good. I think we should start with just my son and me. That makes the most sense to me. Let's set an appointment.

Therapist: Okay.

Parents, caregivers, and those who are typically the ones making decisions about therapy often have ideas about who ought to attend sessions. Youth also have ideas (most often not to attend therapy!). As a result, sometimes "family" therapy involves just a couple of family members or "couples" therapy with just one member of a couple. Positive change can occur whether the therapist is working with an individual, one member of a couple, three members of a five-person family, or some other "nontraditional" configuration.

In working with adolescents and young adults, officials from outside entities such as family and juvenile court systems, social service agencies, and schools may mandate or recommend that certain family members go to therapy. For example, some parents and caregivers are sent to parenting classes. Adolescents and young adults are often referred to therapy by law enforcement or court officials. This brings to light at least two areas worthy of further discussion.

First, many outside helpers who refer young people and family members to therapy are doing so with goals and outcomes in mind. Recommendations regarding who should attend therapy and particular forms of intervention (family therapy, parenting classes, anger management groups, etc.) often represent what referring persons are most familiar with, have been told is most effective, or have the most faith in. In virtually every case, those who made the referral are seeking resolution to the problem that led them to become involved in the first place. In other words, the method of intervention is less important to referrers than the overall goals and outcomes are.

When clinicians understand what goals and outcomes referrers are seeking, opportunities to have conversations with such persons to discuss the means and methods for achieving those results often arise. In my experience, many court officials, school representatives, and so on will negotiate and perhaps even allow clinicians to decide who attends sessions and how to achieve change *as long as* goals and outcomes are reached. Therefore, therapists who have ideas about issues (such as who should attend sessions) that diverge from those recommended or ordered by referring bodies are encouraged to open up conversations with such persons.

Second, many parents, caregivers, and youth may feel that they don't have choice about attending therapy. In Chapter 1 it was noted that not everyone who is mandated follows through on therapy. Therefore, a decision to follow through with a referral ought to be acknowledged. This can facilitate connections between therapists and clients and neutralize what some would refer to as resistance.

It is important that people aren't blamed but are held accountable for their behaviors and actions. Many clients, upon recognizing that therapists want them to be accountable (e.g., know where their kids are, maintain consistency with rules and consequences for violating rules) but do not think they are "bad," "inadequate," or "crazy" parents, will open themselves up to conversations about how therapy might be useful. The following case example illustrates this idea.

Tricia and Diane: R.E.S.P.E.C.T.

Tricia, a 14-year-old, was referred to me by the local family court. The referring juvenile officer had mandated that the girl attend therapy because she had assaulted her school principle and had been truant for 57 days. When I didn't hear from the family within a week of receiving the referral, I telephoned the teenager's legal guardian, her mother. As soon as I introduced myself, Diane began to shout over the phone.

"I know why you're calling and this is total bull. She was referred because she's pregnant and you're a man and couldn't possibly know anything about that!" she exclaimed.

I responded, "It sounds like you've got a lot going on. Is this a good time to set up an appointment or would like me to call back later today?"

"What difference would it make? We have to do this so let's just get it over with," she replied.

We scheduled an appointment for a week later. Based on our conversation, I really believed that the family would not show up for their scheduled session.

The following week, as I was meeting with another client, I heard someone yelling outside my door, in the vicinity of the waiting room. It dissipated rather quickly, so I continued with my session. After the session, the receptionist came into my office. Pointing toward the waiting room, she said, "That's your next appointment and she's not happy."

I went into the waiting room and introduced myself to Diane and Tricia. As soon as we sat down to talk, Diane raised her voice and began talking in a lecturing tone.

"Like I told you on the phone, the only reason we are here is because she's pregnant and you can't possibly understand that, being a man. There's nothing you can do about it so this a waste of time."

When she finished, I replied, "I really didn't know she was pregnant until you told me on the phone." I picked up the paper referral. "It says here that the referral to therapy was made because Tricia assaulted a school official and hasn't been attending school regularly," I read.

"That's a complete crock!" she bellowed. "They can go to hell and so can you. And I've got an ear infection and it's slick outside. If I slip I'm going to sue the court, you, and every other jerk in this charade. You're just another fool in the mix."

While Diane's feelings were okay, some of her actions were not. I realized that I couldn't let her continue her put-downs and outbursts. So I acknowledged her and shifted the conversation by requesting permission to speak to her daughter, which she granted. I then asked Diane to go to the waiting room. As she exited I could hear her muttering profanities. I spoke with Tricia for about 10 minutes. She said very little yet seemed to agree with much of what her mother had revealed. When I asked her what her thoughts were about attending therapy she shrugged her shoulders as if to say, "I don't know."

After meeting with Tricia, I invited her mother back in to my office. Upon entering, she again raised her voice. "I'm really sick of this crap! You're as big a fool as all those people at the court. You're at the end of a long list of stupid people," she spouted.

After her statement, I addressed her: "It seems that you've got a lot going on, and based on your reactions you've had a lot of people involved, most of which you don't want involved. It's perfectly okay for you to be angry with me or anyone else that's involved. However, it's not okay for you to put me or anyone else down and take verbal jabs. I have a sense that you're going through a lot and I can certainly understand the intense feelings. It's the name-calling and threats that I won't tolerate. Now, I'd like to take a moment to speak about this dilemma. Because your daughter was referred here I am going to have to respond to the court. There are essentially two options that I know of. The first is for you and your daughter to come to therapy here. Although I haven't heard about everything that's going on, I'm confident that we can get things going in a direction that the both of you prefer. The second option is for you to decide not to come."

Diane immediately interrupted: "If we don't come in you'll call her juvenile officer and tell her how bad we are—that I'm a bad mom and she's bad—you'll say that we're noncompliant."

I followed, "I can understand that you might see it that way. You're partially right. If you decide not to come back then I will call Tricia's juvenile officer and tell her that you made the decision to not return. However, I will not tell her that you are a bad mom or that Tricia is bad. I'm not judging who you are in any way. I can only report your actions to her juvenile officer—you came back or you didn't." What happens after that is between you and the juvenile officer."

I continued, "I know you don't feel well. I'm sorry you've got an ear infection and I appreciate that you took the time to come here. Many people don't keep their appointments. So, thank you. Now, I don't want you to make a decision right now. What I'd like to ask is that you go home and get some rest. You can call me tomorrow and let me know what you've decided."

The entire session lasted just 20 minutes. About a half-hour after the mother and daughter left, the receptionist buzzed me. "You know that lady who was here a while ago?" she asked. "Well, she's on the phone." My stomach sank and my shoulders drooped. I wondered to myself, "Is she calling to yell at me again? Does she have more to say?"

I picked up the receiver. "Hello, this is Bob."

On the other end, Diane spoke, this time very softly, "I'm very sorry. I shouldn't have talked to you the way I did. I'm very ashamed. And I did it in front of my daughter. My husband left a few weeks ago and it's been a constant struggle. Tricia's been in trouble and her brother is having problems too. I just don't know what to do and I feel like the weight of the world is on my shoulders. If it's not too much to ask I'd like to bring Tricia in and her brother, too."

I never experienced another outburst, put-down, or verbal lashing from Diane. The family kept their appointments and completed therapy. After 7 months, Tricia was released from probation and the brother's behavior had improved. Most notably, Diane was feeling more supported and had, in her words, "turned one of life's many corners—for the better."

Many parents, caregivers, and young people enter therapy feeling blamed, inadequate, or a host of other things. Often these feelings are the result of interactions with other mental health professionals, educators, court officials, or people in positions of influence. The anecdote is simple. It's respect. Being respectful does not mean giving clients permission for actions that are hurtful to themselves or others. It means taking care to acknowledge and validate people's feelings and experiences while simultaneously promoting accountability.

Finally, there may be times when practitioners believe that expanding sessions to include one or more new people may be helpful. In such cases, therapists should offer such ideas, not impose them. Bertolino and O'Hanlon (2002) stated:

> The difference here is that a collaborative therapist would not hold or present the idea that this must occur or that this is the only way that positive change will take place. Instead, the therapist might suggest that bringing in another voice might offer a new perspective or lead to the generation of some new ideas. Ultimately, clients decide whether such ideas are acceptable to them and whether they are within their personal theories about how change will come about. (p. 32)

By inviting clients into conversations where their preferences are honored, therapists continue to strengthen the therapeutic relationship and alliance and learn about clients' orientations. This information helps us to understand how clients believe change might occur and increases the likelihood of positive outcome. Because clients' preferences about who should attend can change over time, it's a good idea to continue to consult with them throughout the course of therapy.

Collaboration Key #3: Determining the Format of Sessions

Most therapeutic models carry with them traditions regarding who should attend sessions and how clients should be seen. Specifically, they define whether clients ought to be seen individually or as families. Ironically, with adolescents, research indicates that when the two variants are compared, individual therapy is as effective as family therapy (Kazdin, 2000; Szapocznik, Kurtines, Foote, Perez-Vidal, & Hervis, 1986). Yet many training programs still indoctrinate students in preferred practices, lending respect to models, not necessarily to clients. Change-oriented therapists refer to theories as possibilities, not as realities. Clients' ideas and preferences are what drive therapy.

Adolescents, young adults, family members, and others involved often have ideas about how to meet for therapy. When multiple people attend therapy there may be some members who want to be seen together and others who do not want to spend any time individually with therapists. Further, with adolescents in particular, parents and caregivers often have identified them as the problem and want or expect that they be seen separately. This can also change from session to session.

When multiple people are present it is important to honor each person's perspective and work together to create an agreement. This means that some negotiating between clients and therapists may need to occur. Therefore, therapists must be aware of theory countertransference and how it can interfere or conflict with clients' orientations and preferences.

It is often helpful to talk with clients about their preferences for meeting in initial sessions. When asked how they would like to meet, clients commonly respond in one of two ways. The first is to identify the persons they feel are most responsible for problems, hinting that these people should be given significant attention, either in individual meetings or as part of family sessions. The second is to say, "What do you think we should do?" or "What do you usually do?" Following are two illustrations of talking with family members about how to meet.

Therapist: There aren't any right or wrong ways about how to meet in sessions. Some people prefer to keep everyone together. Others are more in favor of having each person spend some individual time with the therapist. Some like a combination of both. And that may change from session to session. Does anyone here have a preference about how we should start?

Parent: This is new for us. So whatever you think is best.

Therapist: Okay that's fine. Would anyone else like to share his or her thoughts about it? [no response from the other family members.]

Therapist: Okay. Would it be okay with each of you if we continued meeting just like we are now? [Head nods around the room indicate "yes."]

Therapist: What about if we split up on occasion and I met with some or all of you separately from time to time—would that be okay with each of you? [Head nods around the room indicate "yes."]

Therapist: Great. If you continue to meet with me we can make changes from session to session. All you need to do is voice your opinion.

Therapist: There aren't any right or wrong ways about how to meet in sessions. Some people prefer to keep everyone together. Others are more in favor of having each person spend some individual time with the therapist. Some like a combination of both. And that may change from session to session. Does anyone here have a preference about how we should start?

Parent: Well, we tried therapy before and it didn't work. It think it's because we argued so much and talked over each other so we really couldn't get anywhere. So my vote is that we do something else.

Therapist: Do you have any ideas about what might be a good way start?

Parent: I think we should try meeting like this, but if we start arguing maybe we should talk with you separately. That might be a good idea anyway—to talk to us separately once in a while.

Therapist: That makes sense. Who else agrees or has another idea? [Two of the family members agree, and one does not give a verbal response.]

Therapist: Okay, so two of you agree. Sean, you didn't say anything, but I saw your shoulders drop. What do you think?

Sean: I don't care. This is stupid. I don't have anything to say anyway.

Therapist: That's okay. I just wanted to be sure that if you had an opinion you were able to share it. Will it be okay with you if you and I spend a few minutes together once in a while?

Sean: I guess.

Parents and caregivers often want more direct responses from therapists. When therapists are invited to share their ideas there is no reason to be bashful. Therapists do have ideas and when they match clients' spoken or unspoken preferences the likelihood of achieving successful outcomes increases. As with other processes, therapists offer ideas into conversations, noting clients' responses to those possibilities. Therapists take care to not impose ideas or present them as correct ways (Bertolino & O'Hanlon, 2002). Here is an example of how to do this:

Parent: I'd really like to know what you think we should do. I mean, you see families every day and know what works. What do you think?

Therapist: Yes, I do work with families on a daily basis. And I'd like to share with you one of the things I've learned from this. What fits and ultimately works for one family may not necessarily fit and work for another family. I've got some ideas that may or may not be right for you. But all of you will the judges of whether or not one or more of them fit for you. Before I offer them into the mix, I want to be sure that you feel comfortable letting me know if the way we're meeting, or anything else about therapy for that matter, isn't working and that a change is in order. Okay? [Head nods around the room indicate "yes."]

Sometimes circumstances necessitate that therapists take more directive approaches. One is when families request therapists' opinions and ideas. Another is when there are multiple clients and it is too difficult to clearly delineate what each person is concerned about and wants to see change. At times, it may be helpful to separate clients to give each person time to voice their concerns and expectations for therapy. Certainly there are benefits and drawbacks to keeping people together and separating them. What is most important is eliciting clients' ideas about the processes being used.

A third circumstance that can require therapists to be more directive is when clients prefer ways of meeting that might contribute to harm (Bertolino & O'Hanlon, 2002). Volatility, hostility, or other mitigating circumstances between clients may necessitate individual rather than joint sessions. For example, if an adolescent begins to use verbally abusive statements with a parent and the therapist's immediate efforts do not curb such behavior, it may be necessary to split the two up by dismissing the adolescent or having the parent leave the room. The behavior may be indicative of what happens at home, but that does not make it acceptable. In such cases clients can be brought back together when there is an agreement to treat others more respectfully. Client safety and well-being are always the primary considerations.

Collaboration Key #4: The Timing and Length of Sessions

Most practitioners who work with adolescents, young adults, and families are sensitive to the time restrictions facing this population. School and employment schedules, childcare issues, and other commitments and responsibilities must be contend with. While adults generally have more flexibility in their schedules (e.g., they can see therapists before or after work, schedule sessions over lunch breaks, take time off), young people don't always have as many options. Further, when several people attend sessions, multiple schedules come into play.

When therapists meet with families in outpatient/outclient settings or in their homes, sessions often need to be scheduled within very restrictive time frames (e.g., after school, on days off from after-school jobs, between sports schedules). This can pose a challenge for clients and therapists. Residential treatment programs often afford more flexibility. In addition, some adolescents may be more comfortable in sessions if they are seen at specific times during the day. For example, some youth respond better in early morning sessions while others do better with late afternoon meetings. Therapist and program flexibility in timing can make a difference in establishing a context where the needs of youth are better met.

Akin to the timing of sessions is the length of sessions. There are many influences that determine the length of interactions, meetings, and sessions with young people and families. Although these could be discussed at length, a common thread is that external influences are driven primarily by economics and therapist theories. Therapists face multiple restrictions (e.g., having to see a minimum of 25–30 clients per week, keeping therapy sessions to 50 minutes, providing intensive home-based services 20 hours a week for 6 weeks) that are rooted in economics and affect how therapy services are carried out. In addition, therapists' preconceived theoretical constructs about "correct" ways of conducting therapy sessions can largely influence the timing and length of sessions. Whether such restrictions are based on economics or therapist theories, what often goes unrecognized is the impact that exists beyond service delivery—the effect it has on clients.

The lives of young people and families rarely fit neatly inside of the cookie-cutter molds within which many mental health services are delivered. Although many clients adapt well and come to appreciate 50 minute hours, others may need longer sessions or perhaps multiple meetings each week. For example, families who travel great distances to see therapists or are seen in remote home settings that require therapists to travel long distances may need flexibility in terms of the length of sessions. Likewise, clients who are exploring intense, painful issues may need longer sessions. Conversely, young adolescents with short attention spans may at times need briefer sessions. In short, therapists who have fewer guidelines regarding the length of meetings can extend further options to clients to better accommodate their needs.

Perhaps most crucial is the consideration of individual differences. What may be deemed as standard or commonplace in terms of therapy time frames isn't always respectful of clients who have their own ideas about how change may come about. Culture, ethnicity, family background, spiritual/religious beliefs, and other influences can shape how people expect to interact around their concerns and problems. Sensitivity to these differences can increase the expectancy and hope that often accompanies the start of therapy. Even when it is not possible to change the time of or length of meetings due to organizational, funding, or other requirements, acknowledgement of such parameters can let clients know that practitioners are sensitive to their needs and open to accommodating them whenever possible. Here is one way that a therapist might speak of this:

> One of my hopes is that you'll share with me any thoughts you might have about the timing and scheduling of our meetings, the length of our meetings, how often we meet, or any other ideas you may have about our sessions. Because there are many ways to approach therapy, that information can help me to better understand your needs and expectations. Although I can't make promises that I'll be able to accommodate every request, I want you to know that I'm committed to doing whatever I can to ensure that this is a positive experience for you and that we make progress toward the changes you want in your life/situation.

Collaboration Key #5: Determining the Location and Setting of Sessions

The actual location or setting of sessions with adolescents, young adults, and families is an often unrecognized yet significant contributor to the strength of the therapeutic relationship and alliance. Session settings can also reflect client orientations and contextual influences such as culture, ethnicity, family background, and so on. In other words, like with all people, the life experiences and backgrounds of young people make them feel more comfortable in some settings than in others.

There are at least two ways to consider the relevance of location for sessions or meetings. The first relates to initial meetings. Most programs are designed to provide services in one of two contexts: the office or the home. In such cases clients typically don't get a choice. They are seen in whatever context is designated by the particular program. Other situations may allow more flexibility. Some programs offer the option of sessions' being held in homes or in an office. If this is the case, clients should be the ones to determine where sessions are held.

When it comes to where sessions are held, there are many arguments supporting both sides. Some argue that unless families are seen in their homes, therapists do not get a "real" picture of what things are "truly" like. They may believe that families who don't want to be seen in their homes are probably "hiding things." Others claim that families, particularly those with adolescents and young adults who have been in trouble with the law, should be held responsible for arranging transportation, making it to meetings on time, and so on. These arguments certainly make sense from *therapists'* perspectives.

We have a much better chance of facilitating strong therapeutic relationships and alliances with clients when we work to accommodate their ideas about where to meet. Options can always be eliminated later, if necessary. We prefer to give people choices whenever possible, thereby increasing the chances of keeping them in therapy. If families don't make it to initial first sessions or drop out early, we may never know if therapy would have been helpful. Conversely, when we attempt to meet families' needs we increase the likelihood of them continuing in therapy. This in no way lowers the standards for accountability. Young people and family members are accountable for their choices and actions (e.g., not showing up or being late for office-based sessions, not being present when therapists arrive for in-home sessions).

A third option is to meet in a location other than the home or office. Many adolescents, young adults, and family members feel more comfortable in such contexts. For example, I have met with youth in restaurants, cars, on buses, street corners, basketball courts, indoors, and outdoors. "Therapy" can occur at any place and any time. The following case example illustrates this concept.

Brian: "He Hates to Sit and Talk"

Brian, a 15-year-old, was placed in an emergency shelter where I worked as a therapist. Prior to my meeting with Brian, his mother informed me, "Therapy won't work with Brian. We've already tried it." When asked to elaborate, the mother would only say, "He hates to sit and talk. And even if he does sit down with you, he won't say anything more than 'yes' or 'no' to your questions."

Before my first meeting with Brian for therapy, I asked him if he preferred to talk inside the house, in an office, outside in the yard, or on a walk around the neighborhood. With a surprised look, Brian responded, "Can we really go outside and talk?"

"Sure," I responded.

Brian and I ended up talking outside on the stairs of the emergency shelter. During that time, Brian, perhaps for the first time, expressed himself and talked about what he had been experiencing. In future meetings we shot baskets, walked down to the local waterfront, and even talked inside in an office.

Due to logistics, space restrictions, or other limitations, some clinicians will not be able to meet with young people outside of their specified settings. Bertolino and O'Hanlon stated, "Although it may not always be possible to change the meeting place, consulting with clients about their comfort level with regard to different contexts can let them know that you are sensitive to their needs" (2002, p. 34). The idea is to include young people and others in therapy processes and accommodate, whenever possible, their ideas about what makes most sense to them.

Collaboration Key #6: Determining
the Frequency of Sessions

The frequency of meetings is contingent upon clients' and therapists' availability, mandates from referral sources, organizational or program philosophies and guidelines, and so on. Once again, this is an area where many clients have opinions about the frequency of sessions and time between them. With adolescents and young adults, involvement in the scheduling of sessions can be another way of including them in therapy processes.

Asking young people, family members, and others involved for their ideas about how they would like to proceed is helpful during initial sessions. Do not assume that clients will want to return for future sessions; instead invite them into conversations where they determine what is best. This can include deciding not to return to therapy, scheduling future sessions, or referral to other mental health professionals and services.

If clients decide to return for future sessions, they can be asked when they would like to return for another appointment. Although many opt for weekly visits, quite interestingly, responses can vary to this inquiry. For some, every-other-week visits will suffice; others may want to be seen more frequently. Although clients' and therapists' availability affects scheduling, the involvement of young people and others in decisions is what is essential. Here is an illustration of how such a conversation might look:

Therapist: If it's okay with you, I'd like to hear your ideas about what you think should happen next. There are many possibilities. We could set another appointment. You could decide you'd rather not come back....

Parent: I think we should set another appointment.

Therapist: Okay. Does anyone else want to add anything?

Adolescent: Do I have to come back?

Parent: Yes, you do.

Therapist: [to the adolescent] I appreciate your being able to speak your mind. Knowing that your mom thinks it's a good idea to set another appointment, what might make the next session a little better for you?

Adolescent: All she does is talk. Why do I have to be here?

Therapist: If we took some time for just you and me to meet would that be okay with you?

Adolescent: I guess.

Therapist: [to the parent] Are you okay with that?

Parent: Sure. I think that's a good idea.

As therapy progresses changes may occur in the frequency of sessions. For example, if positive change has occurred and goals are being reached sessions could be dropped to once a month. Sessions with adolescents experiencing school problems could be suspended over the summer and resume again in the fall. Flexibility on the part of practitioners can allow young people and families to be seen in ways that fit with them and their lifestyles, thereby increasing the chances of successful outcomes.

Collaboration Key #7: The Revolving Door

Perhaps one of the most overlooked issues of working with adolescents, young adults, and families is that of providing services when they are needed. Families often must jump through many hoops in order to receive services. These include getting authorization from insurance companies and third-party payers, finding local providers, squandering time on waiting lists, securing transportation, and so on. Not surprisingly, once services are in place, many families are reluctant to end therapy, even when their situations have improved, fearing that they will not be able to retain services should they experience future problems.

Many organizations and agencies that provide services to youth and families are set up in ways that make accessing mental health services difficult. Complicating issues include a scarcity of mental health practitioners and time restrictions regarding the length and intensity of services (e.g., limited number, length, or frequency of sessions). Such problems often in a mismatch between organizational designs and client needs.

One the solution is a revolving door in service provision. Programming must offer easy access to people who are in immediate need and allow people to move in and out of therapy as necessary. This is consistent with what many young people and families need as they move through life and its trials and tribulations. An increasing number of people seek therapy to straighten out a few things and then move on. They may return later if necessary, but they're not in it for the long haul. The following case example illustrates this.

CORY: "I'M GETTING A COMPLEX"
Fourteen-year-old Cory was referred to therapy after shooting another teenager with a BB gun. Although Cory had not been mandated to attend therapy, a family court official that he do so had strongly suggested. In response, his mother brought him to see me. As I had in each session, at the end of the fourth session I asked Cory and his mother how they would like to proceed. Because Cory had been doing well, his mother suggested that we meet

again in two weeks. We all agreed and an appointment was set for two weeks later.

Cory and his mother had been very consistent about showing up for sessions, so I was surprised when, two weeks later, they did not make their scheduled appointment. I attempted to telephone the family but my calls were not returned. I then sent a series of three letters to the family, but again no one responded. After a few weeks passed without any contact from the family, I closed the case file.

About six months later, I received a telephone call from Cory's mother. She asked if she could bring him back to therapy. I agreed. At the appointment, I began by asking both Cory and his mother about the incident with the BB gun, the concern that brought them to therapy previously. Both Cory and his mother reported that he had been doing well and had not been in trouble of any kind. I was very curious about why they had chosen to return. The suspense was quickly abated when Cory's mother stated that Cory recently had met his biological father for the first time. For Cory, this meeting had stirred up feelings of anger about his father's lack of interest in him in the past.

For the next few weeks, Cory and his mother consistently attended their scheduled sessions. Following the third session, a fourth was scheduled for three weeks later. Then, just as with the first series of sessions, Cory and his mother did not show up for their next scheduled appointment. Once again, I attempted to contact them through telephone calls and letters, and, once again, I received no response.

Nearly a year later, I was taken by surprise when Cory's mother contacted me, seemingly out of the blue. She told me that Cory had been struggling with his grades and seemed uninterested in school. There was no mention of previous sessions or concerns. She simply asked to bring Cory back to therapy. I again agreed.

This time I was determined to find out what had led to Cory and his mother's dropping out of therapy on the previous two occasions. Early in the session I asked, "I have to tell you that I'm a bit confused here. This is the third round of sessions that we've had. After the first two, you disappeared. And I'm still wondering if I did something wrong or just what happened."

To this the mother replied, "Oh, no. You've been great. That's why we keep coming back. What happens is we come for a few sessions until we can handle things better. Then we come back if we need to."

"Okay," I replied. "But I would greatly appreciate it if you could do me a favor. The next time you feel like things are where you think you can handle them, will you let me know so that I don't get a complex?"

The mother laughed and replied, "Sure. I'll be sure to remember this time."

Over the course of two months I met with Cory and his mother for six sessions. We focused primarily on school-related concerns, although we did delve into a few other areas that came up from session to session. Then, what *seemed unthinkable happened again: The family did not show up for a scheduled seventh session.*

As time passed, I periodically wondered about Cory and how he had been doing. I was also puzzled by the pattern that had occurred with therapy with them. Nearly a year later I was again surprised, although less so than before, when Cory's mother called for an appointment. He was now 17 years old. This time Cory did most of the talking, seemingly taking the reigns of therapy. He explained that his girlfriend had broken up with him and that he was "bummed out" because he had to decide what to do after graduation. We talked about the issues and I again asked Cory and his mother to please let me know when they felt that they had a better handle on things. I went on to meet with Cory for three sessions, with his mother sitting in on occasion. Following the third session, his mother said, "We're doing well. Thanks again and we'll see you down the road if we need to."

Cory and his mother's approach to therapy were similar to the general practitioner model. That is, people go to see their general practitioners (medical doctors) when they have a concern. These concerns are dealt with and they go about their lives. They expect to see their doctors in the future as needed, and in accordance, their doctors expect to see them again. Families, particularly those with adolescents and young adults, experience different concerns and problems at different times (Carter & McGoldrick, 1989). We aren't in the business of trying to help clients to live problem-free lives. We want them to know that we value our relationships with them and will do what we can to provide the services they need as they encounter the challenges of life.

As noted earlier, although some clients need ongoing, long-term therapy, research indicates that clients only attend a handful of sessions regardless of therapists' orientations, and that most significant change in therapy typically occurs in the first several sessions.

It is also noteworthy that a sizeable number of studies have shown that the provision of psychotherapy is not only cost effective but actually results in significant reductions in medical expenditures—especially among people with a history of overutilization (Chiles et al., 1999). In one study, for example, Guthrie and colleagues (1999) found that brief psychological consultation resulted in significant reductions in inpatient stays, consultations with primary care physicians, nursing visits, use of *all* medications, and care provided by relatives.

Thus, economics is only one of the benefits of offering services to people prior to a full-blown crisis. Offering services when clients first need them is also respectful to them, as it accommodates their ways of changing. Finally, this represents a proactive posture, with an orientation toward *prevention*.

The revolving door is another philosophical cornerstone of a change-oriented perspective. It reflects a position where clients and our relationships with them are valued. This means that once we become involved in therapy with adolescents, young adults, and family members, we are forever part of their lives. This is important for young people as they often seek connection and stability in their lives. Simply knowing that their therapists have not abandoned them after they have transitioned out of services can make a significant difference for young people.

This idea runs counter to the philosophy promoted by many organizations, agencies, programs, and individuals who hold that when treatment ends, the therapist-client relationship also ceases. I once had a graduate student who on two occasions received written warnings after he had taken phone calls from youth who had been in the residential facility at which he worked. He was told that once youth left, the facility and staff members were to have no contact with them, as contact might "keep them from moving on" or "hurt them therapeutically." The student was extremely upset because he had not violated any "boundaries" or done anything covert—he had merely talked with teenagers who occasionally called. All these young people wanted was a few minutes of his time, and he gave it to them.

From a change-oriented perspective, we remain a part of clients' lives and, in turn, they are forever a part of ours. This does not mean that we continue being their therapists until the end of time. Instead, we communicate to young people that if they need to contact us after therapy has ended they can do so. We let them know that if they need to talk or are considering coming back, we will help them in whatever ways we can. Sometimes this means talking on the phone, starting up therapy again, or referring them to another agency or therapist. Although we convey that clients are welcome to return to therapy in the future, we don't guarantee our personal availability. What is essential is the connection that is so vital to young people. This philosophy was discussed in one of my previous publications (Bertolino & Thompson, 1999) in relation to youth in residential facilities:

> Many youth, for one reason or another, find themselves shuffling in and out of a multitude of placements over the course of months or years. We refer to this as the "shelter shuffle".... Many crises arise in residential placement as a direct result of youth doing the shelter shuffle, and rehearsing and enacting internal narratives of rejection, instability, and anger.... [Many youth] will have little sense of being grounded or having any permanent, or at least stable "roots".... To counter this we continue to value the relationships that are created, to listen, to acknowledge, and to

validate.... Once we come in contact with a youth, that relationship continues indefinitely—each story continues to evolve.
Our impact extends beyond the walls within which we
work.... Supporting and strengthening youth and their families
and being available to help is ongoing. Although we view residential treatment as a transitioning point for youth, we must always remember that their struggles to survive are an everyday issue.... [Therefore] whenever we have youth contact us after placement, we consider it a gift. (pp. 167–168)

I once heard a quote that has stuck with me for years: "Children
and youth do not fall through the cracks. They fall through people's
fingers." This poignantly stresses the importance of having a philosophy
that is client-informed as opposed to theory-driven. Every day, in each
interaction, relationships with young people and families do make a
difference.

Collaboration Key #8: Pretreatment Change

Because change is constant and people's problems are in a state of flux,
there are opportunities to help identify subtle differences prior to first
sessions or meetings. This concept has been referred to as "presession"
or "pretreatment change" (Weiner-Davis, de Shazer, & Gingerich, 1987).
The idea was originally created as a way of helping clients to notice when
their situations or lives had gone better in relation to their concerns
or problems. To inquire about pretreatment change, practitioners ask
during initial therapy sessions: "Many times, people notice in between
the time they make the appointment for therapy and the first session
that things already seem different. What have you noticed about your
situation?" (Weiner-Davis et al., 1987, p. 360). It has been estimated that
15–60% of clients experience some form of positive pretreatment change
(Lawson, 1994; McKeel & Weiner-Davis, 1995; Weiner-Davis et al., 1987).

Merely inviting clients into conversations about pretreatment change
can be beneficial. Particularly in families with adolescents or young
adults, one or more persons individuals may see their situations as unchangeable. They feel that "it's always been this way and it will never
change." Problems seem constant, with little or no differences in intensity. These clients remain focused on how their situations and lives stay
the same as opposed to how they are continually changing. By inviting
clients to notice variations you help them begin to question their own
orientations and theories to problems.

A focus on pretreatment change need not wait until first sessions.
During initial phone contacts when appointments are set, therapists

can invite parents, caregivers, young people, and others to notice any differences. Further, emphasis should be on change in general, not just positive change. In fact, therapists who emphasize just one direction may miss opportunities to learn about variations in problems. To introduce this idea, during initial contacts therapists might ask:

> Now that we've got a time set and we know where we'll be meeting, I was wondering if I might ask for your consideration in a matter. I'd like to invite you, in between now and our first meeting together, to notice any differences or variations with the situations, concerns, or problems that led you to make this appointment. You might notice changes with the intensity of problems—when things are a little better or worse, with how long they last, what brings them to an end, who's around when they occur or don't occur, and so on. I'll leave that up to you. I'd just like to invite you to consider noticing any differences and then telling me about them when we meet. If you'd like you can ask others to do the same thing. If you or others want to write down these differences that's fine too, or you can just remember them. Just do what makes the most sense to you.

Inviting clients to notice differences helps them to make a small shift away from focusing on how things seem to remain the same. If such individuals then notice any differences, however subtle, they may begin to alter their orientations to problems, casting doubt on their own theories and beginning to view their situations and problems differently. Therapists can then follow up on the question in first sessions. Information gained can help clinicians to learn the who, what, when, where, and how's of problems—that is, the influence of problems over young people and families and the influence of young people and families over problems. In turn, when clients report a reduction in or elimination of problems therapists can explore how those changes came about, what they mean, and how those changes can continue into the future.

Even those who do not accept the invitation to notice differences may experience a momentary shift in attention, which can contribute to a change in orientation. Frank and Frank (1991) noted that providing new learning experiences is an important element of the rituals and procedures used by therapists. This is a major facet of a change orientation: helping young people and others to temporarily step out of the spaces that are obstructing their views—to step out of their perspectives and view their situations differently. If they are able to do this, opportunities exist to make changes in their orientations.

That said, when clients notice differences they seem to carry more weight and lead to more change than when therapists or other "professionals" suggest them. Therefore, therapists work to create contexts for new experiences and learnings. Therapists then invite clients into such situations where they can see the world differently. This is the strength of self-discovery.

Collaboration Key #9: Process-Informed

Therapy that is client-informed and change-oriented is highly contingent on efforts to encourage client voices, whether it's in the form of ideas, perspectives, preferences, observations, evaluations, or other perceptions. Therapists should collaborate with clients around processes that will help them to learn what is working, what is not, what they need more or less of, what adjustments would be helpful, and so on. Therefore, beginning with initial interactions, we must talk with young people and others involved about what therapy will entail and introduce them to therapeutic processes that are intended to magnify their voices. Interestingly, studies have demonstrated that explaining therapy processes and rationale to clients prior to formal therapy decreases dropout rates (Garfield, 1994).

As noted earlier, client ratings of the therapeutic relationship are a better predictor of positive outcome than therapist ratings (Duncan & Miller, 2000; Horvath & Symonds, 1991; Lambert & Bergin, 1994) Research conducted over the last several decades has found that a combination of the *client's* rating of the therapeutic alliance and the experience of meaningful change in the initial stages of treatment is a highly reliable predictor of eventual treatment outcome (Duncan & Miller, 2000). One study of 2000 therapists and thousands of clients indicated that therapeutic relationships in which no improvement occurred by the third visit did not on average result in improvement *over the entire course of treatment* (Brown, Dreis, & Nace, 1999). The researchers of that study note that variables such as diagnosis, severity, and type of therapy (including medication) were "not . . . as important [in predicting outcome] as knowing whether or not the treatment being provided is actually working" (p. 404).

Therapist perceptions of the therapeutic relationship are sometimes incongruent with client perceptions. Therapists may believe that they have strong connections with clients when clients are experiencing something quite different. Because clients, without prompting, infrequently speak about their experiences of therapy with their therapists (i.e., their perceptions of how things are going), such disparity in perspectives can contribute to unsuccessful outcomes and higher dropout rates.

Given this concern and the potential for therapists to use practices that are based on their interpretations of the strength of the therapeutic relationship and alliance, it is important to build in processes for monitoring clients' experiences. This involves talking with clients early on about ways of "checking in" with them. The following example is a way of introducing clients to this idea:

> I'd like to share with you a little about how we like to work at our agency/clinic/practice. We are dedicated to helping the people we work with to achieve the results they want in therapy. From the start I'll be talking with you about your experience with therapy. I'll check in with you to find out what's been helpful to you, what's not, what's working, and what's not. There are several ways that I can learn from you how you think things are going. For example, I might suggest a brief pencil-and-paper questionnaire. Or I might just ask you a few questions. Your ongoing feedback will let me know if any changes are necessary. Is this okay with you?

Being process-oriented means inviting clients' views and using them as the compasses that guide therapy. This makes for therapy that is client-informed. The next chapter provides some specific examples of questions that can help you learn how young people and others involved are perceiving the therapeutic relationship and alliance.

Collaboration Key #10: Outcome-Informed

At an increasing rate, mental health professionals are being required to demonstrate that their practices and approaches produce results. This movement ought to be welcomed. In order for psychotherapy to be seen as a viable option among many, we must continue to implement ways of monitoring the degree to which our therapeutic efforts affect change. This translates to being outcome-informed.

As with being process-informed, we want to introduce clients to ways of monitoring outcomes—including progress and change—that will be involved throughout the course of therapy. Outcomes refer to the benefit subjectively derived by clients from the services provided. This includes the idiosyncratic meaning the client attaches to the benefit of services. Outcomes also encompass clients' perspectives regarding the impact of the services on major areas of their lives (personal distress, close interpersonal relationships, and larger social roles). By monitoring outcomes, therapists are able to learn from clients whether and to what degree services provided are beneficial. This helps therapists to understand which services are helpful and which ought to be challenged.

Questions or pencil-and-paper questionnaires can be used to monitor outcomes. One way of introducing the importance of monitoring outcomes follows:

> In addition to talking with you about your experience in therapy, I'll also be curious to learn whether or not the work we've done together has been of benefit to you. To do this I'd like to periodically ask you a few questions or have you do a brief pencil-and-paper questionnaire to let me know if and how what we've been doing in therapy has been effective. This way I'll be able to learn from you if therapy has helped with the concerns you came in with, if anything needs to change in terms of the services we've provided, or whether a referral to another service would help you to get what you want.

Upcoming chapters offer ways of monitoring outcomes with young people and others. In being both process- and outcome-oriented, therapists help to create a context where clients are the engineers of change.

When therapists collaborate with clients around the aforementioned collaboration keys, general effects such as client and relational factors, expectancy, and hope are enhanced. Collaboration keys also represent the building blocks upon which future change-oriented processes and practices can be built.

Chapter 3

There's No Place Like Home: Strengthening the Therapeutic Relationship and Alliance

ALL PHASES OF THERAPY PRESENT NUMEROUS OPPORTUNITIES TO INVITE adolescents, young adults, family members, and others involved into conversations where their preferences can be heard, acknowledged, and incorporated into therapy. Many of these opportunities occur either prior to in-person contact or early in initial sessions or meetings. By collaborating with young people and others we begin to create a culture of respect where therapy is change-oriented, client-driven, and outcome-informed. This chapter explores in depth further ways of tapping into the general effects and facilitating change during initial interactions and sessions.

MAKING CONTACT: EVERY MOMENT COUNTS

The idea that therapy takes place in an office, between a therapist and client, for a specific number of sessions, and with a standardized length of time for each session is an extremely limited perspective. It implies that change occurs within certain parameters. With adolescents and young adults, it is imperative that we extend our thinking beyond preconceived, traditional ideas about what constitutes "therapy." Because opportunities to promote positive change exist at every turn, this involves recognizing the importance of making the most out of each and every interaction.

Even brief, seemingly insignificant interactions can contribute to meaningful change. In fact, young people often report that informal interactions meant more to them than standard, formal therapy sessions required in their respective programs. The young people's perceptions of their relational interactions with mental health professionals are of utmost importance. Without inquiring, we cannot know which interactions are most significant to young people. We can, however, remember that each contact represents an opportunity to connect and, ultimately, contribute to positive change with young people.

Although the length of time it takes for adolescents and young adults to feel heard and understood varies, we must bear in mind that there is little correlation between the strength of the therapeutic alliance and the length of therapy. Therefore, it is often possible to achieve immediate therapeutic bonds with young people.

BE YOURSELF: SELF-DISCLOSURE
IN CONTEXT

People who strive to put on their "therapist hats" in their professional lives and take them off in their personal lives may underestimate the importance of being themselves regardless of the context. Although therapy itself necessitates a different relationship with people, a therapist's core identity ought to be consistent across contexts. This is even more important when working with young people, who know when therapists are behaving in "fake" or unauthentic ways.

We must also remember that therapy is a two-way relationship. If adolescents or young adults have divulged a lot about themselves and do not feel they know anything about their therapists, a sense of disconnection can occur. Most, if not all, young people need to know that the people they are sitting with from day to day are real human beings. They will close down conversations quickly if they feel that they are being analyzed, manipulated, or coerced. Therapists who are unwilling to use self-disclosure to any degree are likely to be at an extreme disadvantage in working with young people. Although it's up to therapists to find their personal levels of comfort in terms of what is offered into therapeutic conversations, we must remain aware of the significant benefits of therapist self-disclosure.

We know that the strength of the therapeutic relationship and alliance is largely based on client ratings. When adolescents and young adults are asked what made a difference for them in therapy, they routinely provide feedback that points to their therapists and the therapeutic relationship ("My therapist listened to me," "The social worker I saw was funny," etc.). This feedback often includes comments about how therapist self-disclosure made a difference for them. Furthermore, self-disclosure can help therapists to acknowledge young people's social realities, normalize their everyday experiences, offer hope, new perspectives, and possibilities, and evoke previous solutions and successes.

The connections formed with young people are essential to the success of therapy. They contribute to a foundation of genuineness, trust, and care. Young people are particularly sensitive to situations and people that lack genuineness. It is therefore essential that therapists are themselves and bear in mind that positive change has more to do with general effects (relational factors, hope, expectancy, client contributions, etc.) than their models or techniques.

THE WORLD AS WE KNOW IT:
STORIES AS LIFE

Many therapeutic approaches offer clever ways of engaging clients in dialogue during initial meetings. Because change-oriented therapy is client-driven, not theory-driven, emphasis is on creating opportunities for young people and others to begin sessions in ways that make them feel most comfortable. From the opening moments of therapeutic encounters, clients are encouraged to speak about topics with which they feel comfortable and are not required to engage in discussions that make them uncomfortable. Permission *to* and *not to have to* is extended to all participants in therapy (Bertolino & O'Hanlon, 2002; O'Hanlon & Bertolino, 2000). This is crucial with young people, as they often enter therapy with the understanding that they must divulge things they would rather keep to themselves.

We want to give young people and others enough "space" to share their stories. That is, we work toward creating a context where clients know that they have plenty of room to speak about what is most important to them. Stories are people's explanations, interpretations, perceptions, and evaluations rolled into their views of themselves, their lives, others, and the world. They are how people make sense of the world. We take care to acknowledge multiple perspectives, recognizing that all views are valid, with no one story being a more accurate representation of the "truth" or "reality" than another.

For many young people and others involved, being able to tell their stories freely is the most important part of therapy. In fact, for many clients the most important part of the therapeutic process is the opportunity to tell their stories and be heard (Lawson, McElheran, & Slive, 1997). There is no substitute for listening and attending to people. When therapists apply their own agendas without allowing clients to relate their experiences and stories, it is therapists' theories that become valued. In such instances, a "one model fits all" approach takes precedence, leaving out the uniqueness of clients and their circumstances. I addressed this issue in a previous publication (Bertolino, 1999):

> When a therapist attends mainly to his or her theory, and attempts to fit the client into its confines, the person may go unheard. If we did this in our everyday conversations, people would walk out on us or stop talking. After all, when you talk with others, do you ordinarily start to intervene with problem- or solution-loaded questions right from the start? Probably not. Do you let the person say what he or she needs to say? Probably. The idea here is that . . . [clients] and others ought to have space for their stories to be told and heard. (p. 37)

It is usually best to start therapy from a position that allows young people and others involved to share their stories without theoretical interruptions from the therapist. Although we want to tune in closely to how clients use language and the ways in which they describe their lives and situations, it is important not to immediately delve into a search for problems or solutions. The value of inviting young people and others involved to speak about that with which they feel comfortable cannot be measured, as it allows clients to choose where to begin and brings forth their personal expertise.

HOW DO YOU SEE IT? TUNING INTO CLIENT ORIENTATIONS

By inviting adolescents, young adults, and others involved to share their stories and experiences freely, we create a context where their voices are honored. Although young people often limit or edit their words, they are more likely to understand that what they have to say is important and will be respected. This, in turn, allows clients to teach therapists about their perceptions and experiences.

As discussed earlier, client orientations include individual differences and variables that may influence problems, possibilities, and solutions. These differences are affected by numerous factors including culture, family history and background, social relationships, genetics and biology, religion/spirituality, gender, sexual orientation, nutrition, and economics (Bertolino, 1999; Bertolino & O'Hanlon, 2002; Bertolino & Schultheis, 2002). Client orientations relate to how young people and others involved understand and perceive their difficulties and what they believe influences those difficulties. By listening closely to the words clients use when telling their stories, we can begin to understand whether problems are influenced more by family, social relationships, culture, and so on. Of course, client orientations do not represent physical reality; they merely indicate how clients are viewing their social realities and situations and to what they attribute their concerns. We don't have to agree with their perspectives. We do, however, want to learn about and honor clients' orientations and work within them to facilitate positive change.

This approach is similar to the model practiced by medical physicians. Physicians seldom search for illness in areas that are not of concern to patients—if a patient complains about a sore throat, the doctor doesn't ask about the big toe on the patient's left foot. Nonetheless, therapists continue to be trained to ask questions about the past and to uncover pathology, regardless of clients' concerns. This is indictative of therapy that is theory-driven.

Client orientations also influence their ideas about how change will occur—that is, what young people and others involved believe may help to resolve their concerns and problems, what they have done to try to solve them, and how those attempts have faired. By understanding client orientations we can learn how such influences affect possibilities and solutions—hence, positive change.

If young people and others involved are not invited into collaborative relationships where their stories are heard, if they are cut off during conversations, or if attempts to intervene are made too quickly, therapists risk not learning about their perceptions and experiences regarding problems, possibilities, and solutions. This can negatively influence the therapeutic relationship and alliance and attempts to facilitate positive change. For example, clients can become disheartened when therapists suggest remedies that do not match their views of their situations or ones that have already been tried and have failed. Therapists credibility can suffer when attempts at problem solving or solution building are misguided or premature. This can be avoided if clients are given the space to share their stories and if therapists give more attention to learning and honoring clients' orientations to change. In Chapter 5, various ways of learning and matching client orientations will be explored at length.

THE THERAPEUTIC ALLIANCE:
LEARNING AND ACCOMMODATING
CONVERSATIONAL AND
RELATIONAL PREFERENCES

Therapy involves a series of choices. What do we attend to or not attend to? What do we focus on or not focus on? What questions do we ask? Throughout the twists and turns of therapy sessions clinicians must make decisions. A change-oriented approach emphasizes the voices of adolescents, young adults, and others involved in determining nearly every aspect of therapy. One of the key ways of facilitating collaboration is by monitoring the therapeutic relationship and alliance by learning clients' conversational and relational preferences. In fact, the client's rating of the alliance in the *second* session is the best predictor of success (Kopp, Akhtarullah, Niazi, Duncan, & Sparks, 2001).

Clients' preferences about the therapeutic relationship are reflected in conversation. That is, young people and others involved have expectations and opinions about the types of conversations they prefer and the positions therapists ought to take (e.g., be more/less directive, more/less active, more/less laid back). The following case example illustrates this idea.

MICHELLE: "I NEED BOTH"

Michelle, an 18-year-old, came to see me because she had been experiencing problems with substance abuse. During our initial session she stated that she had recently seen a social worker at a local community mental health center. When I asked what her experience in therapy had been like, she stated, "The social worker I saw was very nice. She listened really well." I then asked Michelle how she knew the social worker had been listening to her. She responded, "She would say 'uh-huh' and nod her head." I followed, "Is that what you feel you need from a therapist?" To this the 18-year-old replied, "That's not all I need. I didn't go back after a few sessions because I didn't think we were getting anywhere. I need someone to help me come up with some answers." After hearing this, I said, "Let me see if I follow you. Are you saying that what you need is someone who listens really well and also works with you to come up with answers?" "That's right. I need both," she replied. I had a good idea about what I could do to let Michelle know that I was listening well, but I knew I needed to spend time learning more from her about how she thought I might help her in coming up with answers. Through the remainder of the therapy I continued to check in with her to ensure that she was getting what she needed, to determine if any changes or modifications were necessary, and to check that the ways in which we were approaching her situation were right for her.

Even though we have our own preferences and biases, we want to be sure that we are working in ways that clients deem are helpful and effective.

There are various junctures at which therapists can learn more from clients about their conversational preferences and their perceptions of the processes that have already taken place. Following are some questions to consider asking at different times during interactions and sessions.

In initial sessions:
- What is most important for us to talk about?
- What is most important for me to know about you and your situation/concern?
- What do you want to be sure that we discuss during our time together?
- What ideas do you have about how therapy or coming to see me might be helpful?
- In what ways do you see me as being helpful to you in reaching your goals/achieving the change you desire?
- What do you feel/think you need from me right now?
- How can I be helpful to you right now?
- What do you see as my role in helping you with your concern?
- What, in your estimation, do therapists who are helpful do with their clients?

Checking in as sessions progress:
- Have you felt heard and understood?
- Do you feel/think we're talking about what you want to talk about?
- Have we been working on what you want to work on?
- How has the session been for you so far?
- Are we moving in a direction that seems right for you?
- What has the conversation we've been having been like for you?
- What has been helpful or unhelpful?
- Are there other things that you feel/think we should be discussing instead?
- Is there anything I should have asked that I have not asked?
- On a scale from 1 to 10, with 10 being completed satisfied, how satisfied are you with how things are going so far?
- Are there any changes we should make at this point?
- At this point, how has what I've been doing been for you?
- Is there anything I should be doing differently?
- To what degree has what we've been doing met your expectations for therapy so far?

At the end of sessions:
- How was the session/meeting for you?
- What was helpful or unhelpful?
- Did we talk about what you wanted to talk about?
- Did we work on what you wanted to work on?
- How was the pace of our conversation/session/meeting?
- Was there anything missing from our session?
- Is there anything I should have asked that I did not ask?
- Is the way we approached your concern/situation fitting with the way you expect change to occur?
- Are there any changes you would recommend if we were to meet again?
- Did you feel heard and understood?
- Is there anything you would need me to do differently if we were to meet again?
- How would you explain your experience in therapy today to others who may be curious?

This is an example of how a therapist might talk with family members about their experiences in a therapy session:

Therapist: If you don't mind, I'd like to take a moment to talk with you a little about how you think the session went today. This will help me to learn from you how things went and if any changes ought to be made should we meet again. Is that okay with the both of you? [Head nods indicate "yes" from each client.]

Therapist: Great. Can each of you tell me how you think the session went?

Parent: [looking to her son] Why don't you go first?

Adolescent: I don't know.

Therapist: Was there anything that you liked or didn't like?

Adolescent: I don't know. It was okay.

Therapist: What about it was okay?

Adolescent: You didn't take my mom's side.

Therapist: Okay. Did you feel that I understood your point of view?

Adolescent: Yeah. You knew where I was coming from.

Therapist: Is there anything in particular that I did that let you know I was understanding where you were coming from?

Adolescent: You just listened and didn't say she was right and I was wrong.

Therapist: I see. That's helpful to you to know that I'm not going to choose sides—even though I am going to hold each person responsible for his or her actions.

Adolescent: Yeah.

Therapist: Was there anything else you found helpful or unhelpful?

Adolescent: Not really.

Therapist: Okay. If we end up meeting together again and something comes up I hope you'll let me know.

Adolescent: I will.

Therapist: [turning to the parent] How was the session for you?

Parent: I think it was fine, but I don't think we really figured anything out. You know, what to do about it.

Therapist: Can you say more about that?

Parent: Well, we talked about a lot of things but didn't really figure out what to do to make things better.

Therapist: What do you think would need to happen, if we were to meet again, to help us figure out how to make things better?

Parent: I think if we talked more in the next session about some ideas— if we problem-solved more.

Therapist: So it would be helpful in the next session to spend more time problem solving and coming up with specific ideas to help with your concern. Is that right?

Parent: Yes.

Therapist: Okay. Great. Thank you for the feedback. We can do that in our next session. Was there anything else you'd like me know about today's session?

Parent: I think that's it.

Therapist: [looking toward both clients] I'll check in with you in each session to see how things are going, but if anything comes up at any point for either of you, I hope you'll please let me know. I'm very committed to making sure that your experience in therapy here is a good one.

Some argue that clients, particularly young people, are not honest when asked the aforementioned types of questions or when alliance measures are used—that they simply tell the therapist what he or she wants to hear. That is always a possibility. However, when clients are not invited into conversations where their feedback is respected, they usually do not voluntarily speak up. Further, when clients are not being approached in ways that they deem as respectful and helpful they may respond by dropping out of therapy prematurely.

If clients indicate that they need something different from conversations and relational postures, it is up to us to make adjustments. Sometimes young people or others involved do not have much feedback to offer about the processes taking place. That is to be expected. When this occurs, therapists simply move on, leaving the invitation to offer feedback an open one that clients may choose to accept at any point. What is important is simply inviting clients to share their views.

For those interested in going beyond questions to measure clients' ratings of the therapeutic relationship and alliance, numerous instruments are available (Horvath & Greenberg, 1994). These pencil-and-paper questionnaires often take little time for clients to complete and are reliable, valid, and applicable across a wide variety of settings.

LANGUAGE AND THE THERAPEUTIC RELATIONSHIP AND ALLIANCE

From the start of therapy it is important that therapists tune into the ways that young people and others talk about their situations. Our aim is to create a context where young people and others involved feel heard and understood and are therefore comfortable in sharing their experiences and stories. This includes ensuring that clients have permission to express their emotions and internal experience. A change-oriented approach with adolescents and young adults emphasizes the importance of attending and listening and encouraging emotional expression. This does not mean that the expression of emotion is necessary for change to occur—only that clients ought to have the space to experience what they may. Carl Rogers's (1951, 1961) seminal ideas of unconditional positive regard, empathy, trustworthiness, and genuineness come to the forefront when we emphasize attending and listening. Research has identified these and corresponding relational elements as being important factors for positive outcome. In practice, these ideas translate into acknowledging, validating, and matching the ways in which adolescents, young adults, and others use language.

Acknowledgement means attending to what young people and others have communicated both verbally and nonverbally (Bertolino & O'Hanlon, 2002). This involves letting people know that their experience, points of view, and actions have been heard and noted. A basic way of acknowledging is to say "Uh, huh" or "I see." Another way is to reflect back, without interpretation, what clients have said. For example, a therapist might say, "You're sad" or "I heard you say that you're angry." This can also be done by attending to and acknowledging nonverbal behaviors. For example, a therapist might say, "You shuttered as you spoke" or "I can see the tears."

Validation means that we give permission to young people and others to experience whatever it is that they are experiencing and let them know that those experiences are valid (Bertolino & O'Hanlon, 2002).

People are not bad, crazy, sick, or weird for being who they are and experiencing what they do. Validation also lets young people and others know that others have experienced the same or similar things. To validate we add words such as "It's/that's okay" or "It's/that's all right" to acknowledgement and reflection. For instance, a therapist using acknowledgement and validation might say, "It's okay to be angry," or "It's all right if you're mad," or "I heard you say that you're sad, and you can just let that be there."

As discussed previously, acknowledgment and validation are often lost when focus turns to "intervention." It is assumed that therapists are either acknowledging and validating *or* intervening. First, acknowledging and validating *is* intervention. For some young people and others involved, simply feeling understood, perhaps for the first time, is enough to facilitate positive change. It is therefore important that we continue to attend to young people and others' internal experience throughout the therapeutic process. However, although we acknowledge and validate all internal experience, we do not validate and give permission for all actions and behaviors, as some may be harmful. Second, therapists acknowledge, validate, *and* simultaneously search for possibilities for change. It is not a matter of doing one or the other. Therapists who are change-oriented carefully listen and attend to their clients, collaborating with them to promote change through respectful processes and practice.

At the core of respectful processes and practices and promoting change are the ways in which practitioners use language. It has been said that language is a virus. In a positive way, this means that language can promote hope and expectancy that accompanies therapy. At a basic level, there are specific ways of acknowledging and validating young people and others while subtly working the language that they use to move from impossibilities to possibilities (Bertolino, 1999; Bertolino & O'Hanlon, 2002; Bertolino & Thompson, 1999; O'Hanlon & Beadle, 1994, 1999; O'Hanlon & Bertolino, 2002). These methods offer ways of using language as a vehicle for creating change and reflect what Jerome Frank (Frank & Frank, 1991) identified as therapeutic rituals. All approaches make use of rituals—methods and procedures—to facilitate change processes and promote hope. Although rituals are not necessarily causal agents of change, they can mobilize placebo factors and enhance the therapeutic relationship, highlight client competency, promote change, and orient treatment toward future possibilities. Following are several ways of acknowledging and validating the experiences of young people and others involved while simultaneously opening up possibilities for change and strengthening the therapeutic relationship and alliance.

Dissolving Impossibility Talk:
Acknowledgement and Possibility

My first job in the field was as a residential counselor at an emergency shelter for runaway and homeless youth. The program operated a 24-hour-a-day, 365-day-a-year crisis hotline. In the emergency shelter, youth and families sought immediate assistance for a variety of concerns. In this environment, the importance of establishing a connection with callers in crisis and working toward problem resolution quickly was clear. If this did not happen, callers might hang up or people that had walked in might leave, possibly resulting in harm to themselves or others.

The dilemma with crisis calls, in particular, was finding a way of acknowledging what youth and family members were experiencing while using directive questions to gain valuable information. Achieving a balance between acknowledgement and straightforward questions about the callers, their situations, what they needed, and what they wanted to change was crucial: Directive questions without acknowledgement might lead to callers' feeling invalidated; acknowledgement without directive questions might not facilitate movement toward desired change. Combining acknowledgement with direction helped to open up possibilities and provided the internal validation that clients were seeking, which helped to alleviate crisis.

Through traditional training we learn the importance of acknowledging and validating the internal experience of clients; however, if we only reflect back their experiences and views many will continue to use words to paint themselves into corners. In other words, youth, family members, and others will use words and phrases in describing their views of themselves and their situations that close down possibilities for change. It can be very difficult for therapists to find possibilities within problem-laden descriptions. One of the ways to introduce possibilities is to add a twist to the idea of pure reflection. Following are three ways of doing this.

1. *Use the past tense.* Reflect back clients' responses or problem reports in the past tense.

    Adolescent: I'm very angry.
    Therapist: So you've been very angry.

    Parent: He'll never do any better.
    Therapist: He hasn't done better.

    Young adult: Things aren't going well.
    Therapist: Things haven't been going well.

When a young person, family member, or other gives a present tense statement of a problem, acknowledge and reflect back the problem using the past tense. By doing this, the possibility of a different present or future is introduced. This is a very subtle linguistic shift that involves both acknowledgement and validation with the simultaneous introduction of possibility into the conversation.

If we only acknowledge and validate, some clients will move on, most will not. They will continue to describe situations of impossibility. Further, if we simply stress that adolescents, young adults, family members, or others should move on, they may experience that as invalidation. The hybrid of acknowledgement and validation through reflection and an emphasis on possibilities through subtle but effective changes in language provide therapists with a way of introducing possibilities into otherwise closed-down statements and conversations.

2.   *Translate "all or nothing" statements into "partial" statements.* When young people, family members, or others use words such as *everything, everybody, nobody, always,* and *never,* try to introduce qualifiers into their language. These qualifiers can be related to time (e.g., recently, in the last while, in the past month or so, most of the time, much of the time), intensity (e.g., a lot, a bit less, somewhat more), or partiality (e.g., some, most, many). We do not seek to minimize or invalidate clients' experiences. Instead, we want to gently introduce the idea of possibilities.

Young adult: I'm always down.
Therapist: You've been down a lot.

Adolescent: Nothing ever goes right in my life.
Therapist: Much of the time things haven't gone right in your life.

Parent: He's become nothing but trouble.
Therapist: In the last while he's been nothing but trouble.

By using qualifiers to help clients go from global to partial, we can introduce possibility into impossibility-laced statements. This can create little openings where change is possible.

3.   *Translate "truth" statements into "perceptual" statements.* When young people, family members, or others make statements about truth or reality, rephrase them as subjective realities.

Young adult: Things will never change.
Therapist: Your sense is that things will never change.

Parent: I'm a terrible parent.
Therapist: You've gotten the idea that you've been a terrible parent.

Adolescent: I can't make good decisions.
Therapist: It seems to you that you haven't made good decisions.

Clients' statements do not represent the way things are, but rather their perceptions of events, situations, or themselves. By reflecting back their statements as such, possibility can be introduced.

Notice that it's possible to combine different methods of changing language. "You've been down a lot of the time" uses both past tense and a partial statement. "It seems to you that you haven't made good decisions" uses past tense and a perceptual statement. The more therapists practice such changes in language, the more comfortable and consistent they become in identifying and attending to words, phrases, and statements that suggest impossibility.

It is important to recognize that therapists must be sure to capture the essence of the clients' experience when introducing possibilities. We do not want to echo the voices of society that suggest to clients that they must "move on" or "get over it." Many parents, adolescents, and young adults have heard enough of such talk, which they generally translate into invalidation and blame. If clients feel like their experiences are being minimized or if they feel pushed to move on they often respond with statements such as "Not most of the time! All the time!" If a client reacts in such a manner, the therapist is not getting it right. He or she must then move to validate further so that the client feels heard and understood. This can be done even while keeping an eye on possibilities. For example, a therapist might respond to the previous client statement by saying: "Okay. Your sense is that things have been bad all the time." In this way we continue to acknowledge and validate while simultaneously interjecting the idea of possibility into a statement that implies impossibility. We are not coercing clients but rather inviting them into different perspectives. We want to let young people and others know that we have heard and understood their suffering, concerns, felt experience, and points of view without closing down the possibilities for change. Even though things have been difficult, painful, or overwhelming, positive change is possible.

Future Talk: Acknowledgement and a Vision for the Future

Research suggests that given the choice, most clients prefer focusing more on the present and future than on the past. Yet the language some young adults and others use to describe themselves and their situations seems to hold them prisoners of the present or past, with little or no sense of a future without problems, pain, or suffering. Again, acknowledgement is the building block we use to offer small changes in language that open up possibilities for future change.

This idea is akin to the moving walkways in airports that take people to their destinations with little or no effort additional effort. We can use language in a similar way to move clients along in the direction of possibilities without them actually having to take steps toward those goals and preferred outcomes. Following are three ways of doing this.

1. *Assume future solutions through future talk.* Use expressions such as *yet* and *so far* to acknowledge the possibility that young people, family members, or others involved can find solutions. These words presuppose that even though things feel stuck or unchangeable in the present, they will change sometime in the future. This simple shift in language can help to create a "light at the end of the tunnel."

   Young adult: Things will never go right for me.
   Therapist: So far things haven't gone right for you.

   Adolescent: I'm always in some kind of trouble.
   Therapist: You haven't found a way to stay out of trouble yet.

   Parent: As a parent, my life is going downhill.
   Therapist: Your life as a parent hasn't gone in the direction you'd like yet.

   Although we are only making small changes in language, in actuality, we are introducing the possibility that change may occur in the future. This seemingly simple shift gently challenges closed-down views and can open doorways to further, more significant changes.

2. *Turn problem statements into goals.* Take young people, family members', or others' problem statements and change them into a statement about a direction or preferred future.

   Parent: His behavior will never improve.
   Therapist: So you'd like to see his behavior change in the future?

   Young adult: I'm worthless.
   Therapist: So one of the things that we could do is to help you to find some self-worth?

   Adolescent: I'm always in trouble.
   Therapist: So one of the things we could focus on here is to find a way to change your relationship with trouble?

This particular way of changing language serves several purposes. First, as with all of the methods outlined to this point, it offers a way of acknowledging clients. Second, it helps to clarify the importance of clients' statements in the eyes of clients (Bertolino & O'Hanlon, 2002). In the course of attending and listening to the stories of young people, family members, and others, it can become difficult for therapists to discern what is most concerning for them. Therapists must routinely make decisions regarding which words, phrases, comments, and remarks should be given more or less attention. Turning problem statements into goals helps therapists understand whose statements are most important. This is an example of how this might look with an adolescent with multiple concerns:

Adolescent: I don't have any friends. I'm not doing very well in school. Everything is going downhill.

Therapist: It sounds as if you've got a lot going on. And if I'm hearing you right, some of the things that we could focus on here are developing friendships, doing better in school, and just getting things going in a better direction for you.

Adolescent: Kind of . . . I mean, I do want friends but I really want to get my grades up first. That's the most important thing. Then I think I'll feel better about the way my life is going.

By utilizing a collaborative posture and recasting the problem statement into a statement about a preferred future or goal, young people, family members, others, and therapists can begin to gain some clarity about what clients want different in their lives. In this way, therapists can set aside their ideas about what should or should not be focused on and let clients to indicate their preferences.

3.   *Presuppose changes and progress.* Assume changes and progress toward goals by using words such as *when* and *will*.

Adolescent: All I do is get into trouble.

Therapist: So when you've put trouble behind you, you'll feel as though things are heading in a better direction.

Young adult: No one wants to hang out with me.

Therapist: So when you get the sense that you have found people who might be interested in hanging out with you, we'll know that we've made some progress.

Parent: I'm always getting angry and then saying things I shouldn't say.

Therapist: So when you are able to experience anger without saying things that you might later regret, you'll feel better about things.

The psychiatrist Milton Erickson used presupposition in his hypnotic work with patients to link specific movements on the part of his patients with the suggestion of internal, automatic changes. For example, he might say, "When your hand begins to lift, I wonder what changes you'll make within yourself?" We can use the same general concept to presuppose future changes and progress toward goals and preferred futures. To do this, use the word *when* in restating what the client said, followed with either *how* or *what* combined with *will* to form a question for the client:

Young adult: No one wants to hang out with me.

Therapist: So when you get the sense that you have found people who might be interested in hanging out with you, what will be different for you?

It can also be helpful to add the use of conjecture, wonderment, or speculation (Andersen, 1991; Hoffman, 1990; Penn & Sheinberg, 1991). The use of conjecture allows therapists to respond either with statements or questions. In other words, questions can be framed as speculation or as inquiries about how future changes will make a difference for young people and others (Bertolino & O'Hanlon, 2002). To use conjecture, simply add "I wonder" or "I'm curious."

Parent: I'm always getting angry and then I say things I shouldn't say.

Therapist: So when you are able to experience anger without saying things that you might later regret, I wonder what will be different in your life.

Here's how to combine conjecture with the use of a question:

Adolescent: All I do is get into trouble.

Therapist: So when you've put trouble behind you, I'm curious as to how your life will be different?

For young people, family members, and others experiencing hopelessness, pain, fear, and other intense feelings, such emotional reactions are often intensified by a lack of a vision for the future. Clients have little sense that the pain or suffering they are experiencing in the present will somehow be alleviated or dissipate altogether. It is clear that people who have a sense that their pain will end and that things will improve in the future are much more able to cope with the day-to-day struggles of everyday life. Presuppositional language offers a small but significant pathway with possibilities for future change—without minimizing the problems and suffering that young people or others are currently experiencing, thereby building on the general effects of hope and expectancy.

Beginning with our initial interactions with young people and others and throughout therapy we are inviting clients to tell their stories. Such invitations let clients know that we are interested in their experiences and views, want to form collaborative relationships, and learn their theories of change (Bertolino & O'Hanlon, 2002). We facilitate this process through attending and listening, acknowledging and validating. We also are listening for words, phrases, and statements that reflect views or stories that suggest impossibility and may inhibit change. When we hear suggestions of impossibility, we work to make subtle changes to create openings for possible future changes. Let's explore several more methods that can be helpful in attending to young people and others' experiences without imposing our theories.

Giving Permission

All people have internal experiences such as feelings, sensations, involuntary thoughts, and images. Although we have choices in controlling actions, internal experience is another matter. For many adolescents, young adults, and caregivers the notion that certain feelings are unacceptable or not okay can contribute to invalidation and the intensification of problems. We want to let young people and others involved know that whatever they are experiencing internally is okay, acceptable, and that they can move on. There are two kinds of permission:

1. *Permission to:* "You can."
2. *Permission not to have to:* "You don't have to."

Some young people, parents, caregivers, and others feel stuck, thinking that they are bad or terrible for having some experience or thought, or that they shouldn't think or experience it. In these instances, clients need to be given permission to think or experience whatever is going on with them internally. Perhaps the best way of doing this is to normalize, which provides validation and permission. This can let clients know that they're not bad, crazy, or weird—that others have felt similarly. It's important to note that giving permission for internal experience does not mean giving permission for action. What people experience internally is different than the actions they undertake. Here are some ways to give permission to:

Young adult: I know I shouldn't think about quitting school. I just can't help it. I must be a bad person.

Therapist: It's okay to think about quitting school and that doesn't make you a bad person.

Parent: I can feel the anxiety building...
Therapist: You can go with it and just let it be there. I'm right here. Just let it flow through until it passes.

Other people feel that they are being dominated by internal experiences or that they should be having some internal experience that they are not. They might need permission not to have the experience. Here are some ways of giving permission not to have to:

Adolescent: People keep telling me that I need to remember the abuse, but that's the problem!
Therapist: You don't have to remember the abuse if it's not right for you.

Parent: In the support group I attend for parents who've lost their spouses, everyone keeps saying that I need to express my anger because that's a stage of grieving. But I've never felt anger. Is something wrong with me?
Therapist: Each person goes through grief in his or her own way. Some people will experience anger and some won't. It's okay if you don't go through someone else's stages and take your own path to healing.

Although either type of permission can be given independently, it can be useful to give both types at the same time.

Young adult: Should I be angry or not? I don't know.
Therapist: You can be angry and you don't have to be angry.

Parent: That was a really bad situation. I can't believe I'm not more upset about it.
Therapist: It's okay to feel upset about it and you don't have to feel upset about it.

If we only give one type of permission, some clients may feel pressured to experience only one part of the equation or may find the other side emerging in a more compelling or disturbing way (O'Hanlon & Bertolino, 2002). For example, if we only say, "It's okay to remember," the client might say, "But I don't want to remember!" We can counter this bounce-back response by giving permission to and not to have to.

As stated earlier, be careful regarding which actions you extend permission to. For example, therapist could say, "It's okay to feel like hurting yourself and you don't have to feel like hurting yourself," but should not say, "It's okay to cut yourself and you don't have to cut yourself." Never give permission for harmful, destructive behavior.

Inclusion

Some young people and others involved in therapy feel as if they are in binds and experiencing opposite or contradictory experiences that seem to present conflict. In these cases, should include any parts, objections, feelings, aspects of self, or client concerns that might have been left out or seen as barriers to the therapy or goals and preferred outcomes. We use what the client has brought to therapy and include anything that may have been left out, devalued, or seen as irreconcilable. To do this we use *and* to link client experiences. Here are some ways of doing this:

Adolescent: I need to tell you something but I just can't.
Therapist: It's okay to feel like you can't tell me and maybe there is a way you can tell me.

Young adult: I hate my life. Nothing will ever change for the better.
Therapist: You can hate your life and things can still change for the better.

Parent: My husband makes me so angry. I can't be around him.
Therapist: You can be angry with your husband and find a way to be around him.

If young people or others are feeling stuck, it's often because they are leaving out some part of their experience or don't feel as if they have room for it. The use of inclusion allows therapists to pull together ideas and feelings that seem to be in opposition and may be hindering the change process. This can free clients up to experience all aspects of a situation and move on.

Utilization

Outcome research suggests that whatever clients bring to therapy with regard to their internal strengths and abilities and external resources ought to be utilized in the service of change. One way of doing this is by using what young people and others bring to therapy—no matter how small, strange, or negative the behavior or idea seems—to open up the possibilities for change. This is in direct contrast with more traditional approaches that often view such things as symptoms or liabilities. Following are some ways of utilizing client behaviors and ideas as vehicles for change.

Parent: He wastes his time playing those stupid computer games.
Therapist: So you've learned to play computer games? How did you do that?

Young adult: My family is extremely conservative.
Therapist: So you've had some experience dealing with people who
   tend to be more conservative.

Adolescent: I'm terrible at sports.
Therapist: Now that you've ruled out sports, how can it be helpful to
   you to know that your efforts may be better utilized on other things?

Utilization allows therapists to take behaviors and ideas that are typically seen as deficits, inabilities, or symptoms and turn them into assets.
This can be a helpful way of getting young people, parents, and caregivers moving, if they aren't already doing so, in the direction of the
change they are seeking.

Although the promotion of connections with young people and others involved occurs throughout therapy, a context for change is created
early on. To facilitate positive change and strengthen the therapeutic relationship and alliance, we create space in which clients are encouraged
to share their stories. We do not attempt to lead young people, parents, caregivers, or others into *our* ways of thinking. Instead, through
acknowledgement and validation and by using language in subtle ways
to create small openings for change, we introduce possibilities into otherwise closed-down situations.

Chapter 4

From Here to Where? Establishing Direction Through Collaboration

REGARDLESS OF THE MODEL EMPLOYED, IT'S IMPORTANT THAT SOME direction is established in therapy. A lack of direction can lead to confusion and frustration. Therapists working with adolescents, young adults, and families often must deal with multiple people with different concerns. Therefore, clarity on the part of all parties involved is essential to the achievement of successful outcomes. This chapter explores ways of working collaboratively with young people, caregivers, family members, and outside helpers in determining complaints, concerns, and directions in therapy and focuses on how collaborative processes and practices in the area of assessment can facilitate positive change.

WORKING WITH STANDARDS: COLLABORATION AND FORMAL ASSESSMENT

Many practitioners working with adolescents, young adults, and families are required to use formalized assessment procedures as part of their intakes or initial sessions. These assessment procedures generally involve specific protocols, forms, or instruments that are used with all clients. Because clients' perceptions of the therapeutic relationship and alliance are essential to the success of therapy, it is important that practitioners explore using formal or standardized assessment methods in ways that are respectful and useful in the eyes of clients. This can be

achieved by letting each young person, family member, or other participant go through the same or similar procedures. It can also be helpful
to talk with clients about the purpose of the assessment. The following
(Bertolino, 1999) are two ways of doing this.

> If it's okay with you, I'd like to ask you some questions that we
> ask of all people who come to see us. The information you give
> will help us to understand what you're concerned about and how
> that's affected you, what you'd like to see change, what's worked
> and hasn't worked for you in trying to manage your concerns, and
> how we can be of help to you. And as we proceed, if you feel like
> or think we've missed something please be sure to let us know.
> We want to make sure that we fully understand your needs. How
> does that sound?

> There are some questions that I'd like to ask you that we ask of
> everyone who comes here. The questions will help me to under-
> stand what's happening with you or in your life that's of concern.
> Once we get finished with those questions, we'll move on to some
> others that will tell me more about what you do well and what
> has worked or might work for you in the future regarding your
> concerns. How does that sound?

Most formal assessment procedures utilized with young people and
families are designed to discover problems. Emphasis is on identifying deficits and pathologies that are "uncovered" through various techniques and methods. However, formal assessment processes need not be
pathology- or problem-focused, which often alienates clients. Instead,
formal assessment offers numerous ways of maximizing the general
effects by:

• Strengthening the therapeutic relationship and alliance;
• Building on or creating hope for the future;
• Creating space for clients to tell their stories;
• Identifying and matching clients' ways of using language;
• Helping therapists learn about clients' concerns and complaints;
• Eliciting and evoking clients' strengths, abilities, and resources;
• Revealing clients' orientations to change.

From this perspective, assessment provides a way of facilitating
change from the initial interaction. Furthermore, rather than focusing primarily on pathology and problems, attention is given to clients'

concerns *as well as* client factors such as internal strengths and community resources. Vaughn, Cox Young, Webster, and Thomas (1996) stated:

> We believe that an exclusive focus on pathology, deficits, and risk factors without evaluation and documentation of strengths, resources, and mitigating factors can put both the client and institution at risk for unnecessary hospitalizations, increased length of stay, and ineffective treatment. We therefore gather assessment data concerning the problem, but we maintain a balance between history, strengths, exceptions, and the *client's* goals. (p. 107)

Attending to both concerns and problems *and* strengths and resources allows us to gain valuable information from young people and others. Focusing only on pathology and problems often makes clients feel further invalidated and blamed. This is of particular concern for many young people, parents, and caregivers. In addition, "problems" can become reified in the eyes of clients and therapists. That is, the more clients talk about their problems and the more therapists emphasize what's wrong through questions, the more both parties become subject to the idea that things are actually worse than they first imagined!

The concerns and problems that adolescents, young adults, and others face tend to ebb and flow, vacillating on a continuum between things working and not working. In therapy we want to learn about both ends of the continuum and consider the gray area in between. We can then learn about both the influences problems have had over people and the influence people have had over problems. Formal assessments should be viewed as yet another means of bringing possibilities to light as opposed to an instrument or procedure that reinforces a sense of impossibility.

In tapping into the general effects, we must acknowledge what people experience internally, being careful not to minimize their pain and suffering, and simultaneously search for openings with possibilities. Even when the information obtained during assessment seems very problematic, we want search for *exceptions*—when things are different with regard to the problem (de Shazer, 1988, 1991; O'Hanlon & Weiner-Davis, 1989). Exception-oriented questions ask for information about times when the concern or problem is less dominating, occurs less frequently, or is completely absent. We also inquire about what the person did differently in such instances. This helps to identify internal strengths and external resources and serve as a way of intervening in the present while providing building blocks for future change.

Following are some examples of the many general questions that practitioners can use at the start of assessment to search for exceptions and begin to understand the influence that young people, family members, and others have over concerns and problems.

- It seems that when the concern that brought you in is happening, things are pretty difficult. When does the concern seem a little less noticeable to you?
- Tell me about a time recently when things went a little bit better for you with regard to the concern that brought you in.
- How did that happen?
- What did you do differently?
- What's different about those times?
- What's different about the times when you're able to get more of an upper hand with the problem?
- What people, places, or things were helpful to you?
- How will you know when things are better?
- What will be different in your life?

We're searching for small differences as opposed to extremes. We do not ask, "When don't you have the problem?" That's too big a leap for most clients and can prove invalidating for caregivers, in particular, who may get the sense that practitioners are trying to gloss over problems. It's important that we let clients know that we understand their pain and suffering and not give short shrift to their concerns. We therefore use questions that elicit small differences. This can be enough to get things moving in the direction of positive change.

The multifaceted lives of most adolescents and young adults allow for many areas of exploration: family/social relationships, education, hobbies/interests, employment, and previous treatment experiences, among others. In each of these areas therapists can gather information about concerns and about strengths (resilience, coping skills, etc.), abilities, and resources as well as exceptions and differences. The following questions that can assist therapists in each of these areas.

Individual qualities:
- What qualities do you possess that you seem to be able to tap into in times of trouble?
- What is it about you that seems to come to the forefront when you're facing difficult situations/problems?
- What is it about you that you keep going despite all that you've faced?
- Who are you that you've been able to face the challenges that life has presented to you?
- What would others say are the qualities that you have that keep you going?

- What have the qualities that you possess allowed you to do that you might not have otherwise done?
- Given the type of person that you are, what do you do on a regular basis to manage the challenges that you face?
- How have you managed, in the midst of all that's happened, to keep going? How have you done that?
- Tell me about a time when you were able to deal with something that could have stopped you from moving forward in life. What did you do?

Family/social relationships:
- Who are you closest to in your life/family/etc.?
- What do you appreciate most about your relationship with your parent/caretaker/family member/spouse/friend/colleague?
- What would he/she/they say are your best qualities as a son/ daughter/family member/spouse/friend/husband/wife, father/ mother/colleague?
- How is that helpful for you to know that?
- What does it feel like to know that?
- Which relationships have been more challenging/difficult for you?
- How have you dealt with those challenges/difficulties?
- Whom can you go to for help?
- Who has made a positive difference in your life?
- How so?
- What difference has that made for you?
- When are others most helpful to you?

Education:
- How did you manage to make it to/through a specific grade, middle school, high school, trade school, junior college, a four-year university, two years of college?
- What qualities do you possess that made that happen?
- What did you like best about school?
- What did you find most challenging/difficult about school?
- How did you manage any difficulties that you encountered while in school (e.g., completing assignments, tests, getting to school on time, moving from one grade to another, teacher/classmate relationships, sports)?
- In what ways did school prepare you for future challenges?

Hobbies/interests:
- What do you do for fun?
- What hobbies or interests do you have or have you had in the past?
- What kinds of activities are you drawn to?

- What kinds of activities would you rather not be involved in?
- What would you rather do instead?

Employment:
- How did you come to work at your current place of employment?
- How did you get yourself into a position to get the job?
- What do you think your employer saw in you that might have contributed to your being hired?
- What have you found to be most challenging or difficult about your job?
- How have you met or worked toward meeting those challenges/difficulties?
- What keeps you there?
- What skills or qualities do you think your employer sees in you?
- What qualities do you think you possess that are assets on the job?
- (if self-employed) How did you have the wherewithal to start your own business?
- (if unemployed) What kind of employment would you like to see yourself involved in the future?
- What would be a first step for you in making that happen?

Previous treatment experiences:
- What did you find helpful about previous therapy (individual, couples, family, group, etc.)?
- What did the therapist do that was helpful?
- How did that make a difference for you?
- What wasn't so helpful?
- (if currently or previously on psychotropic medication) How is/was the medication helpful to you?
- What, if anything, did/does the medication allow you to do that you wouldn't have otherwise been able to do?
- What qualities do you possess such that you were/are able to work with the medication to improve things for yourself?

Formal assessment offers practitioners an opportunity to learn from young people and others involved what is worked in the past (to any degree) and what might work in the future. We then help them to apply or replicate what's worked in the past in the present and the future. It is also important to find out what hasn't worked. For example, if a young person has been in therapy before but did not find it helpful, we want to know what was unhelpful so that we do not replicate that aspect of therapy in our work with the client.

ONGOING ASSESSMENT:
DETERMINING DIRECTIONS
FOR CHANGE

The process of learning from young people and others what they would like to have change and monitoring for change is referred to as *ongoing assessment*. The following questions can be used as a starting point to help therapists understand what concerns and directions young people and others involved in therapy are interested in.

- Where would you like to begin?
- What is most concerning you at this point?
- What is most important for me to know about you/your situation?
- What would you like to focus our attention on during our time together?
- What did you (hope/wish/think) would be different as a result of coming to treatment?
- What would have to be minimally different in your life to consider our work together a success?
- What would you like to have change be different in your life?
- What would you like to be different in your life?
- What goals do you have for yourself?
- How will you know when things are better?
- How will you know when the problem is no longer a problem?
- What will indicate to you that therapy has been successful?
- How will you know when you no longer need to come to therapy?
- What will be happening that will indicate to you that you can manage things on your own?

First and foremost, these types of questions are very important in that they offer space for young people and others to continue to share their stories and experiences. It is essential that clients know it is safe to talk about subjects they feel comfortable with and that they do not have to speak about subjects that make them uncomfortable. We invite clients to respond to questions in whatever ways feel right for them.

Second, such questions assist practitioners in learning valuable information from young people and others involved. This information can be helpful in learning about clients' orientations to their concerns and problems as well as about potential possibilities for change and solutions. For example, young people and others sometimes answer these types of questions by describing what they *don't* want. This represents their concerns and problems. Through careful listening, therapists can learn what influences those problems, when they occur, and so on. This will be discussed further in the following chapter.

Third, the aforementioned questions provide a pathway to learning what young people and others *do* want. What they do want represents what they would like to see change and their preferred directions and goals. Note that some young clients do not align with terms such as "goals." It is important to remember that it is not the term that is most relevant, but rather gaining some sense of direction and clarity about how people want their lives to be in the future. A lack of clarity can translate into numerous difficulties for both clients and therapists. It is therefore imperative that practitioners collaborate with clients to determine what specifically they are concerned about and want to have different in their lives and when they are ready to transition out of therapy.

To help young people and others to gain clarity about what they want different in their lives, we emphasize the role of a future vision. This idea was explored in depth by Viennese psychiatrist Viktor Frankl (see 1963, 1969), an existentialist who created Logotherapy. Frankl spoke of the importance of clients' having a vision for the future and how that vision could affect their actions in the present as well as their views of the past. Frankl seemed to know about the importance of an imagined future that is different from the past—a future in which things work out. That is what many young clients lack: a well-articulated, good connection to a future with possibilities.

Our mission is to help clients create a sense of a future where things are different and possible. Some young people have a sense of that possibility-filled future, and we can help them to rehabilitate it and begin moving powerfully toward it. Others have no sense of it and may need to begin to imagine that it is possible to have a future that is different from the past or better than the past.

Waters and Lawrence stated, "One of the great deficits of most therapy is the lack of a proactive vision of what people need to move towards instead of a sense of what they need to move away from" (1993, p. 9). Consistent with outcome research, we work with young people and others to create visions of what they want different in their lives and then work with them to take steps to achieve those outcomes. We also learn what difference it will make for clients when they've achieved the change they desire.

Goals represent clients' visions of the future—when their lives are more manageable and the concerns, complaints, or problems that brought them to therapy are less intrusive or absent altogether. Often clients' goals are simply the opposite of their problem descriptions.

However, as with concerns and problems, their descriptions of goals can be vague, providing little clarity to practitioners. For example, clients often make statements such as "I want to be happy," "I just want some peace," "I have anxiety," "I don't want to be depressed," or "I don't want him to be so impulsive." These vague, nondescriptive statements do not clearly depict what clients want. As a result, therapists' belief systems, biases, and theoretical opinions may become activated and projected onto young people and others. Therapists may assume that they know what clients mean and react accordingly. This can lead to misguided attempts to help clients.

For example, imagine that a parent mentions that she believes her teenage son is "acting out." Such a phrase can mean different things to different people. If we do not take time to find out what the parent means by the phrase "acting out," we are at risk of responding to our own subjective frame of reference. This may not be consistent with the parent's perspective. If therapists base their attempts to promote positive change on vague descriptions, attempts at finding solutions and possibilities may be futile, as the interventions offered may not fit with clients' views of concerns and ideas about how to resolve them (Bertolino & O'Hanlon, 2002). Thus, we must collaborate with adolescents, young adults, family members, and others to establish clear descriptions of their concerns, directions, and, ultimately, goals for therapy. Following are two ways of collaborating with young people and others to clarify concerns and complaints as well as directions and goals: *action-talk* and *videotalk*.

Putting Words Into Action: Gaining Clarity Through Action-Talk

To move from vague, nondescriptive accounts of young people and others' concerns and preferences, we use *action-talk* (Bertolino, 1999; Bertolino & O'Hanlon, 2002; O'Hanlon & Bertolino, 2002). Practitioners can use action-talk in numerous ways; here, it involves determining how clients *do* their problems and, subsequently, what they will be *doing* when positive change has occurred or goals have been met. When therapists hear vague, non-sensory-based words, phrases, and statements, they should ask clients to describe their concerns in behavioral, action-based language. In this way therapists can get clear views of what clients are doing when their problems are interfering with their lives. For example, if a client says, "I'm having relationship problems," we first ask her to describe how she *does* her relationship problems. We learn through action-talk that this means that she yells at her partner when he's late, calls him a "liar," and then refuses to talk with him for at least a day. Through further discussion we learn that *what she wants* is to be in a relationship with her partner where she is able to talk with him when she's angry. Thus, she will know that things are better when she is able to do this more times than not. This, then, becomes the goal of treatment—not working on "relationship problems" or "anger" or any other therapist-derived conceptualization.

Sometimes what young people, parents, and caregivers initially complain about is not their primary concern. Other times clients mention numerous concerns, and which ones take precedence is unclear. Often these clients just want their experiences and views to be acknowledged and heard. They will then move on to concerns that are more significant for them. For this reason, we always check with clients to be sure that we clearly understand what it is that they want to see change. When there are multiple complaints, we summarize and acknowledge them all, and learn which ones are most pressing.

In the event that a client indicates that all complaints or concerns are of equal weight, we are sure to acknowledge that view. We then work with clients to determine which one or two concerns should be addressed first. This conveys to clients that all of their concerns are important and will be addressed and that we are just learning which ones are most troublesome and should be focused on initially.

The following brief case example illustrates how to use action-talk to clarify concerns and directions/goals.

JANET: "MY SON HAS FITS OF RAGE!"

A mother came to therapy to discuss her son's behavior. Early on in the initial session the woman stated that her son was "out of control" and that he was having "fits of rage." Although her frustration was evident, her description of her son's behavior was ambiguous. I therefore worked with her to clarify her concerns and to learn what she wanted to be different with her son.

Janet: *My son is out of control.*

Therapist: *Okay. What has your son done that's indicated to you that he's out of control?*

Janet: *He has fits of rage.*

Therapist: *So if I were to see him having a fit of rage, what would I see him doing?*

Janet: *He'd be yelling and using profanity.*

Therapist: *By yelling you mean . . .*

Janet: *He gets very loud. The neighbors can hear him.*

Therapist: *Okay. What do you mean by profanity?*

Janet: *You know, the "F" word and calling me a bitch.*

Therapist: *I see. Would he be yelling and using profanity with whoever was around?*

Janet: *No, just me.*

Therapist: *Mm, hmm. So if I were around he wouldn't yell or use profanity with me?*

Janet: *I highly doubt it.*

Therapist: *So does he do this mostly around you?*

Janet: *He only has his fits of rage around me . . . when he doesn't get his way. I mean, someone else might be around, but he wouldn't do it if I weren't there.*

Therapist: *I think I'm getting the picture. So he'd be yelling and using profanity with you. Is there anything else he might be doing if I were to see him having a fit of rage?*

Janet: *I think that's it.*

Therapist: *Okay. So am I right in thinking that you want your son to refrain from yelling and using profanity when things don't go his way?*

Janet: *Yeah.*

Therapist: *So what would you like to see your son do instead when he doesn't get his way?*

Janet: *I want him to tell me what he wants or go into another room until he cools down.*

Therapist: *I see. So he might get upset, and that would be okay with you, but then he would talk with you or go into another room until he cools down. Is that right?*

Janet: *Exactly. He could just sit down or go in another room. I'd prefer that we talk, but he might not want to sometimes. So he could do something else until he's calm and then we could talk later.*

Therapist: *I see. So there are several options.*

Janet: *Yes.*

Therapist: *And so that I'm clear, is that what you would like to work on here—finding ways of helping your son to talk to you, sit down, leave the room, or do something else acceptable that we haven't yet explored, when he doesn't get his way?*

Janet: *Yes. That's what I want.*

Therapist: *Great. And when he does this on more of a regular basis, what will be different?*

Janet: *Things will be calmer for sure!*

Therapist: *Ok, calmer. How so?*

Janet: *I'll actually be able to get some things done because we won't be fighting.*

Here, action-talk assisted the practitioner in learning from the parent what the son had done in the past to indicate he was out of control or had fits of rage. The questions prompted the parent to list very specific behaviors that indicated that the son was having a fit of rage. The concern then becomes one of yelling and using profanity, as opposed to being "out of control" or having a "fit of rage." Regardless of the model employed, therapists increase their chances of being effective when they work with clients to change clearly delineated behaviors rather than vague ones.

Further, this brief interchange offered information that might be helpful to promote future change. The therapist learned that the son only had fits of rage when the parent was around. Next, even if others were around, he only directed his yelling and profanity toward the parent. Just a few moments of conversation revealed that there were situations when the unwanted behaviors did and did not occur. Therefore, these indicate possible areas for creating positive change.

When young people and others describe what they don't want, it's important to respect and follow their conversational processes and not steer toward immediate solutions. People choose to talk about their situations in ways that are most comfortable for them. Practitioners can view client conversations as an invitation to learn about their perspectives and problem descriptions as well as patterns of action and interaction associated with those problems or concerns. This can help therapists match, honor, and learn more about clients' personal orientations and provide possible future areas of intervention.

In addition to learning what is not wanted, it is important that the therapist get a clear description of what the young person or other wants *instead* (Bertolino & O'Hanlon, 2002). In the previous example, we learned from the parent that the change being sought was for the son to talk with the parent or leave the room instead of yelling and using profanity. This becomes a goal for therapy. We also learned from the parent what will be different when her son is behaving more the way she'd like. Following is another case example illustrating how to learn about young people and others' concerns and preferred directions by utilizing action-talk.

Matthew: "I'm Always Anxious"

Twenty-year-old Matthew came to see me because he was feeling anxious. According to Matthew, he spent much time "dwelling on things" and this was negatively influencing his sleep. During our initial session I learned from Matthew that his lack of sleep was in turn affecting his work. Through careful attention and questioning I was able to determine what he wanted different in his life.

Therapist: *It seems that you've got a lot going on. I'd like to ask, what's most concerning to you at this point?*

Matthew: *Things aren't going well for me.*

Therapist: *You say that things haven't been going well for you . . . what's specifically been happening?*

Matthew: *Well, I'm always feeling anxious. I mean . . . I used to go out a lot, now I don't. My friend says I need to just move on.*

Therapist: *Uh, huh. So you haven't been going out like you used to. That's part of it. And when you're feeling anxious, what else happens?*

Matthew: *Well, I think a lot. I think about everything I've done wrong—my past decisions. I just dwell on things.*

Therapist: *You tend to think a lot about your past decisions and dwell on what you think you've done wrong . . .*

Matthew: *Yeah, and I also have trouble sleeping.*

Therapist: *Mm, hmm, trouble sleeping. Tell me more about that.*

Matthew: *I can't get to sleep because I keep dwelling on things.*

Therapist: *So it's trouble getting to sleep. And when you finally do get to sleep do you stay asleep?*

Matthew: *Yeah. Once I fall asleep I stay asleep but it takes three or four hours to get there. Then it's two or three in the morning and I have to get up at 5:30. Then I feel hungover at work and can't concentrate on what I need to do.*

Therapist: *I see. So not getting to sleep early enough really affects your work and how you feel the next day.*

Matthew: *Right.*

Therapist: *Are there other things that you do or, in your case, don't do, when you feel anxious?*

Matthew: *It's really those things.*

Therapist: *Okay. So if I were to see you being anxious I'd see you staying at home and not going out, thinking about decisions you've made in the past, and not getting to sleep on time. Is that right?*

Matthew: *Exactly.*

Therapist: *Now I think I follow you, but for sake of clarity, I'd like to ask you another question if it's okay with you.*

Matthew: *Sure.*

Therapist: *You've mentioned a few things that seem to be troublesome to you. Which of the these—not going out, thinking about your past decisions, not getting to sleep, or something else—is most concerning for you right now?*

Matthew: *Definitely not getting to sleep.*

Therapist: *Okay . . . and as you said, when you don't get enough sleep it really affects you the next day at work.*

Matthew: *That's right.*

Therapist: *So am I right in thinking that you'd like to find a way to get to sleep quicker and feel more rested in the morning?*

Matthew: *No doubt.*

Therapist: *And so what's a reasonable amount of time for you to lie in bed before falling asleep?*

Matthew: *If I could get to sleep within a half hour of lying down I'd be thrilled!*

Therapist: *So getting to sleep within a half hour would allow you to get a full night's sleep and perhaps be better rested for work.*
Matthew: *Uh, huh ... that's what I need.*
Therapist: *What will be different when you're getting to sleep earlier and getting a full night's sleep?*
Matthew: *My head will be clearer.*
Therapist: *How so?*
Matthew: *I'll be better rested and won't be obsessing so much.*
Therapist: *What difference will that make for you?*
Matthew: *If I'm not obsessing then I'll be getting things done and going out more.*

In this case example, Matthew used vague words and statements such as "Things just aren't going well for me," "I'm always feeling anxious," and "I think a lot." These statements tend to activate therapists' personal and theoretical views and guide therapy in ways that may be unhelpful to clients. For example, just hearing the word "anxious" causes some to immediately begin asking questions about anxiety-provoking situations and to consider an anxiety disorder. Others may gravitate toward a sleep disorder. Although these may seem to be legitimate directions, they are based more on therapists' ideas about what to focus on and ask questions about, not clients'. To remedy this, practitioners are encouraged to check with clients to see if the conversations that are taking place are in line with what they want and are helpful to them.

Matthew's statements also give little indication of what he was concerned about. Although he mentioned many concerns, he ultimately wanted to find a way of getting to sleep more quickly. Unless we orient toward clients' goals, we risk working in ways that are inconsistent with their preferences. In turn, when we learn about clients' goals, what will be different as a result of achieving the sought-after change becomes clear.

Are You Getting the Picture?
Using Videotalk

Another process that can be helpful in gaining clear, action-based descriptions is *videotalk* (Bertolino, 1999; Bertolino & O'Hanlon, 2002; Hudson & O'Hanlon, 1991; O'Hanlon & Bertolino, 2002; O'Hanlon & Wilk, 1987). This involves getting clients to describe the problem or goal as if it can be seen or heard on videotape. This again involves the use of action-talk. To use videotalk we ask, "If I were to videotape you being..., what would I see you doing on the videotape that would indicate to me that you were...?" The following case example illustrates the use of videotalk.

JOHN: "I HAVE A FEAR OF FAILURE"

John came to see me when his "obsessing" had started to affect his life both at home and work. As I worked with him, through clarifying questions I was able to learn more about his concern, what he wanted to see change in his life, and what would be different as a result of those changes taking place.

John: The main thing for me is to get over my fear of failure, but that's easier said than done.

Therapist: Mm, hmm. Tell me more about your fear of failure.

John: Well, I keep finding myself going into situations and thinking the worst. Like everything is going to go bad.

Therapist: You've found yourself in situations where you've thought that the worst was going to happen....

John: Right.... over and over again.

Therapist: So, if we were to catch you, on videotape, going into a situation where you were thinking the worst, what would we see happening on that tape?

John: I'd be pacing around a lot . . . and probably not doing my work, because I'd be obsessing about what might happen.

Therapist: Mm, hmm, you would be pacing. And one of the ways that an outsider like me would know that you were obsessing would be because you wouldn't be doing your work. Is that right?

John: Yes.

Therapist: Is there anything else that you would be doing that might indicate to me or others that you were obsessing?

John: I would go home and think about it more.

Therapist: I see. What would you be doing at home while you were thinking about it?

John: Just sitting. Not eating or doing anything else that's important. Just obsessing.

Therapist: Okay, just sitting and not doing other things that you sense are important. And if we were able to see inside your mind and videotape your obsessing, what might we see happening?

John: That's easy. You'd see me thinking about the same thing over and over and thinking the worst. My only thoughts would be about failing.

Therapist: So let me see if I understand you. When you've experienced thoughts about failure, you've paced and sat around obsessing. And the way you typically obsess is to think about the same thing over and over again—usually about failing.

John: That's right.

Therapist: And from what you've said, this has affected you because you haven't done the amount of work you'd liked to have done at work or at home.

John: Exactly.

Therapist: Are there other ways that this has affected your life?

John: *I don't want to be so lazy and unproductive at home, but the main thing is not getting my work done at my job. I don't want to get fired. I can't afford to. I've got to stop obsessing and get things done.*

Therapist: *Okay. Let me see if I understand you. So you don't want to be what you call lazy and unproductive at home; you'd like to get things done. But your main concern at this time is getting your work done on the job. Is that right?*

John: *Yes.*

Therapist: *And if we were to videotape you in the future when things are going better for you what would we see on that tape that would indicate that things were better? What would you be doing?*

John: *I would be turning my work in on schedule and keeping up on assignments . . . not falling behind.*

Therapist: *What kind of work?*

John: *Documentation and billing.*

Therapist: *Okay. So you'd like to find ways of getting your work done, specifically, documentation and billing, in a timely manner and keeping up on assignments.*

John: *That's what I want.*

Therapist: *What difference will that make for you when that's happening?*

John: *A ton! If I'm getting my work done then my boss will be off my case and I can keep my job.*

The young adult in this case example used many vague, nondescriptive words and statements that could have led the therapist in any number of directions. The aim was for the therapist to learn from John what he does when he's experiencing a "fear of failure" and "obsessing"— the specific ways that he went about "doing" his problem. In this way, the focus is on actions and how they affect the client negatively. Thus, it is not John's "fear of failure" that is of concern; it is his actions, such as not doing his work, that are a result of viewing himself and situations the way he does. Many people experience feelings and thoughts that they would rather not experience. However, not everyone succumbs to fear of failure. It is ultimately what people actually do or don't do in their lives as *a result of their perspectives* that affects their lives adversely.

John's therapist also learned what John wanted as opposed to what he did not want. What he wanted turned out to be getting work completed. This specifically meant getting documentation and billing done in a timely manner. This gives direction to therapy and helps practitioners and clients to better understand when progress has been made and sufficient positive change has occurred.

In addition to gaining direction in therapy with John, the therapist used dissolving impossibility talk and future talk. For example, the word *finding* was changed to *found,* thereby putting it into the past tense. This introduced the notion that John's experience was in the past and that the future might be different. The therapist also took problem statements and worked with John to turn them into goals. Although these changes in language were small, they offered possibilities into otherwise closed-down statements.

Along with being clear, directions and goals should be realistic, attainable, ethical, and legal. For example, it is not unreasonable for a young person who has lost someone close to him or her to want that person to return. Even though this is not possible, it may be possible for the person to experience a caring relationship with another person. By acknowledging clients' internal experiences and views we can cut through many unrealistic expectations and cocreate solvable problems. Here is an example of how to do this:

Tory: "I Miss My Dad"
An adolescent who had lost his father was brought to see me. Through conversation with him I learned that there were certain qualities about his relationship with his father that were dear to him. I also learned that these types of qualities were things he hoped for in future relationships.

Tory: My dad died last year. I wish he were still here. I really miss him. That's really want I want . . . him to be back.

Therapist: I'm sorry for your loss. What do you miss most about him?

Tory: He used to listen to me . . . really listen to me.

Therapist: How did you know when he was really listening to you?

Tory: He would look me in the eyes and not judge me.

Therapist: What did he do to let you know that he wasn't judging you?

Tory: Well, he didn't make comments like "You should have . . ." or "That was stupid to do that."

Therapist: I see. And how did that help you?

Tory: I knew he valued me and I haven't had that since.

Therapist: Is that something you would like to experience again in a relationship with someone—that sense of being listened to, not judged, and valued?

Tory: I would love to have that again.

Therapist: What would be different for you as a result of having that again?

Tory: I'd feel great. I'd feel better about going through each day knowing that I could talk with somebody who understood me.

Although it is not possible to bring back the adolescent's deceased father, it is possible for her to be in a relationship where she feels listened to, not judged, and valued. Thus, presented with a goal that was not possible, the therapist put forth the possibility of achieving what the goal symbolized.

Clear descriptions of young people and others' concerns, can also help therapists learn more about clients' orientations and potential ways to facilitate change. For example, if a client speaks about "feeling" a certain way, we would acknowledge and validate more, focusing on internal experience and affect. If a client talks about "seeing" or "doing" things in certain ways, we would focus more on views and behaviors. This is discussed further in the next chapter.

In addition to action-talk and videotalk, several other methods can be used to learn what young people and others want to see different in their lives and help them to gain a sense of the future: *the crystal ball, the question, the miracle question,* and *the time machine.* Although these are creative methods, they should not overshadow the importance of gaining clarity and a sense of direction.

The Crystal Ball

Based on Milton Erickson's (1954) "pseudo-orientation in time," this approach involves having clients peer into an imaginary crystal ball that represents the future and suggesting that they are able to achieve the change they desire—to see a time when their problems are no longer problems. First, have the client imagine peering into an imaginary crystal ball or window that represents the future. Then suggest to the client that he or she envision a time in the future when the problem he or she came to therapy for is gone. Follow this with questions such as "How did your problem get solved/resolved?"; "What did you do?"; "What did others do?"; and "How is your life different as a result?"

The Question

Alfred Adler (1956), the creator of individual psychology, developed the "question," a strategy that was later popularized by Rudolf Dreikurs. Dreikurs would ask, "Let us imagine I gave you a pill and you would be completely well as soon as you left this office. What would be different in your life; what would you do differently than before?" (1954, p. 132). With adolescents and young adults, this question can be helpful in learning what they want to be different in their lives in the future.

The Miracle Question

Steve de Shazer and colleagues at the Brief Family Therapy Center (BFTC) in Milwaukee, Wisconsin, developed the "miracle question" as a way of helping clients envision their lives in the future when the problem has been solved. Prior asking the miracle question, therapists usually inform clients that the question will require them to use their imagination. Clients are then asked, "Suppose you were to go home tonight, and while you were asleep, a miracle happened and this problem was solved. How will you know the miracle happened? What will be different?" (de Shazer 1988, p. 5).

An alternative for adolescents and young adults is the "dream method." With this method the young person is asked, "Let's suppose that tonight, while you were sleeping, you have a dream. In this dream the problem you have is resolved. Tell me about what happened in that dream that led to your problem no longer being a problem. What happened?"

The Time Machine

With younger clients it can helpful to use a more age-sensitive approach to determine what they want in the future. One way to do this is through the "time machine" (Bertolino, 1999). To use the time machine, say to the young person: "Let's say there is a time machine sitting here in the office. Let's say that you climb in and it propels you into the future, to a time when things are going the way you want them to go. After arriving at your future destination the first thing you notice is that the problems that brought you to therapy have disappeared." This pitch is then followed by questions such as: "Where are you?"; "Who is with you?"; "What is happening?"; "What are you doing?"; "How is your life different than before?"; "Where did your problems go?"; and "How did they go away?"

Whether using basic questions or creative methods, therapists want to help clients to gain clarity and answer the question "How will you know when things are better?" Action-talk and videotalk provide the foundation for this process. Once therapists are clear on what young people and others want, they can begin to collaborate with them on steps to make those positive changes occur.

The "No-Talk" Adolescent

If you work with children, adolescents, or young adults you have probably encountered several (hopefully not too many!) who speak very little or not at all in therapy. Although their caregivers or referrers have goals it can be difficult to determine what the young person wants to have different in his or her life or situation. In such cases it is important that we remain patient and maintain a change orientation. Therapy tends to be much more interesting when there is dialogue; however, young people can still benefit and make positive change when they choose not to speak.

By maintaining a change orientation, we are able to assume that the young person wants something better—something that is an improvement of their current situation (e.g., a caregiver complaining about them, trouble at school). For many adolescents, an improvement is not to have to come back to therapy again the future. Although there may be a lack of verbal exchange, this does not mean that they do not want things to change. If we fall into the trap of viewing young people as resistant, noncompliant, or as not wanting to change, we close down the possibilities for change. Additionally, a change orientation allows us to continue to look for ways to invite young people to make positive changes and move toward the futures they prefer.

When working with young people who talk very little or not at all, it is essential that we give permission not to have to speak. This can be done by saying, "It's okay if you don't want to talk. Sometimes I feel that way." We might also add, "And if you want to talk later that's fine. If you don't, that's okay, too." Simply giving permission can help to create a context where the young person will hopefully experience a sense of comfort and safety.

I've also found it helpful to use storytelling and self-disclosure to invite young people into conversation. One of the ways I've done this is by first giving permission not to have to speak and then telling the young person that I have a few things I would like to share with him or her. Following is an example of what I have said to several young people who were not speaking:

> I just wanted to let you know that it's okay if you don't want or feel like talking. I've felt that way at times. And, if you want or feel like talking later, that's okay, too—but there's no pressure to have to say anything. And you know, today might be a good day to not talk. You know why? Because I have a lot to say! You see, I wanted to tell you about this television show I saw last night....

I follow this introduction by sharing some experience about television, movies, sports, or some other topic that will increase the level of comfort for the young person and *might* spark some interest. If a youth smiles and gives some sort of verbal or nonverbal response I'll often say something like, "You know what I mean. But hang on, I'm not finished yet . . ." Even if a young person offers a response, I typically continue on a bit longer. I genuinely want young people to know that they do not have to speak until they are absolutely ready.

Despite our best efforts, some young people will not speak. Once again, a change orientation helps us by assuming the possibility of an improved future. The moment we see a situation as impossible is the moment we become unhelpful to young people and their families. The following case example illustrates the importance of maintaining a belief that positive change exists on the horizon and that youth who do not speak in therapy can still benefit.

ALEX: BACK TO SCHOOL

Alex, a 14-year-old young man, was brought to therapy by his mother because he had missed over 30 days of school since his Christmas break. Throughout the initial meeting Alex did not speak. I met with him both alone and with his mother and his response was the same. He did not talk. His mother spoke and expressed her concern that the family court would take Alex and place him residentially. I wanted to assure Alex that I believed in his ability to make choices and was not there to lecture him. So I said to him, "If you think you should let the court process take its course that's your choice. I'm not here to tell you otherwise. I'm just not convinced that you're convinced that that's what you should do."

His mother believed that Alex had not gone back to school because some classmates had been picking on him. Alex did not respond when he was asked about this. It would have been easy to view Alex as a youth who was resistant, noncompliant, or delinquent. Yet none of those descriptions offered me possibilities for working with him. Therefore, based on what I knew about Alex (which I had learned from his mother), I chose to explore various possibilities that might invite him back into school. I wanted to do this in ways that helped him to eliminate any shame or guilt and ultimately allowed him to save face. Furthermore, I hoped that the decision to return to school would be his and one that he made because it was right for him, not because he was forced.

One of the ways I did this was to tell him a story about a star college football player who had made the decision to stay in school for his senior year. He had forgone a lucrative contract and promise of immediate stardom. He did this because his parents told him that he could always be a professional football player but he would never have another senior year and he'd never know what he might miss if he decided to leave school early. When Alex did not seem to respond the story I simply moved on.

My sense was that I did not really know what might touch Alex in some way and it was my responsibility to continue to explore other possibilities that might invite him back to school. I did this by reminding him that it could be hard to return to school following lengthy vacations. Despite having experienced many vacations, he had always found a way to get back to school. I also tried to evoke from within Alex a sense of competency. I did this by reminding Alex that he had been a "routine" student during his school career. He had never missed more than two days in a row and a few days overall in any school year. He was a ninth grader with an excellent record of attendance. My reminder was an attempt to let him know that he already knew something about attending school regularly.

I offered other stories and anecdotes during that initial session, which was on a Friday. At the end of the meeting, I told the mother to call me on Monday. Although I had a full evening schedule I could see her and Alex in the morning if he had not gone back to school. On Monday the mother called to say that Alex had not returned to school. She and Alex came in that morning for a second session. Just as in the first session, Alex did not speak. So I continued to explore ways of inviting him back to school.

At the end of the second session I told the mother that I would be gone for the remainder of the week but would be available to see them the following Monday morning if Alex had not gone back to school. Once again, I asked the mother to call me on Monday.

When the mother called she stated that Alex had returned to school. When I asked her what had happened, she said she didn't know. However, she said that something very strange had happened. On Sunday evening, Alex approached his mother and told her the story of the college football player who had remained in school for his senior year. The mother related that she was confused because she knew the story and could not figure out why he was telling her about it. It was odd that Alex was telling her the story as if she had never heard it. It then became clear to her that Alex did not recall that it was a story that had been told in therapy. According to the mother, when Alex finished his story, he told her, "You never know what you might be missing." The next day he retuned to school.

A third session was scheduled with Alex and his mother. Amazingly, from the moment Alex came into the room he began talking. He spoke about returning to school and the reactions of his classmates. Although he certainly was not excited, he persevered. We never learned "why" Alex missed so many days of school. For the remainder of his school career he did not miss more than his usual few days a year due to illness. Alex graduated a few years later, on schedule.

Our views of young people directly affect how we work with them. Even when youth are less verbal or do not speak at all in therapy, there is no way of knowing what might resonate with them. Part of what we want to do is maintain a philosophy that positive change is possible. We then work to facilitate positive change by exploring different ways of inviting young people into futures they prefer.

ARE WE THERE YET?
DETERMINING PROGRESS

An interesting phenomenon occurs at Walt Disney World and Universal Studios: Although the "goal" at these parks is to get on the rides, the entertainment begins once you get in line. There are television monitors showing videos, music coming out of speakers, things to look at and read along the way, and often refreshments are within reach. Furthermore, many of the rides have multiple parts. For example, a ride may begin by standing in a room to view a video, continue with a walk through a forest, and end by getting on the ride itself. In other words, park visitors are entertained throughout even though the lines to get on rides are often very long.

Another interesting addition to the Disney theme parks is the "fast pass." Originally offered for an additional fee, it now is available at no extra cost to all park visitors. The fast pass allows visitors to go to the front of the line, one time per day, on each of the major attractions. Despite certain restrictions (e.g., you must go on the attractions during assigned time frames, you can hold only one fast pass at a time, etc.), visitors know that they will have the opportunity to significantly cut down on their wait in line and get on each major attraction at least once per park visit. If they want to go on these rides again they have to wait in line the same length of time as other park patrons do.

What the people at Disney and Universal learned is that when people get the sense that they are moving and making progress toward their destinations—getting on the ride—they are less likely to become irritated, frustrated, angry, and drop out of line. So even though it still takes a long time to get on a ride, people at these amusement parks get the sense that they are progressing.

So what do amusement parks have to do with therapy? More than first meets the eye. Clients who attend therapy sometimes respond similarly to patrons waiting a long time to get on an amusement park ride. When clients get the sense that they are making progress they are less likely to become frustrated and give up. Therefore, once directions and goals have been clearly delineated, we also work to identify what will indicate that progress is being made toward the established goals. This can be referred to as identifying "signs" of change. The following questions assist with this process.

- What will be the first sign or indication that things have begun to turn the corner with your problem?
- What will be the first sign or indication to you that you have taken a solid step on the road to improvement even though you might not yet be out of the woods?
- What's one thing that might indicate to you that things are on the upswing?
- What will you see happening when things are beginning to go more the way you'd like them to go?
- What would have to happen that would indicate to you that things are changing in the direction you'd like them to change?

- How will you know when the change you are looking for has started?
- What is happening right now with your situation that you would like to have continue?

The following case example illustrates the importance of identifying progress with young people.

NANCY AND STEPHEN: "I'D FALL OVER "

Nancy brought her 15-year-old son, Stephen, to see me because, in her words, he needed to "get his act together." I asked Nancy several action-talk questions to clarify what that meant to her and she responded by saying that she wanted her son to get to school on time, talk to her "nicely" when he became angry, and improve his grades. When asked what would be the smallest indicator to her that Stephen was beginning to turn the corner, she said, "If he brought a book home from school I'd fall over!"

The next day, perhaps as a joke, Stephen brought a book home. He tossed it on the table and Nancy laughed, "Oh that's funny. I said if you brought a book home I'd fall over. You're funny." Following the brief exchange, the evening went well between Stephen and his mother.

Stephen later remarked that he liked the fact that his mother showed a sense of humor when he first brought a book home. He also stated that they had gotten along better. Consequently, Stephen continued to bring at least one book home from school each day. Then, one evening, Stephen and his mother were watching television. When his mother began watching a program that Stephen didn't care for, he began thumbing through his world history book. Several days later he was shocked when he knew the answers to several questions on his history exam. Although he narrowly missed passing the exam, Stephen thrived on the feeling he had when he realized he knew several of the answers—he enjoyed it and wanted more of it. He also realized that had he done more than thumb through the book, he might have known more and passed the exam.

Stephen continued to bring his world history book home and over time added others. He also began getting to school on time and reading at night. Over the course of a semester he raised his grades to passing in all but one of his classes. The following semester he passed all of his classes. In addition, the relationship between Stephen and his mother continued to improve and he stopped yelling and began talking in a calmer voice. His mother recognized the efforts Stephen had made and regularly encouraged him.

By focusing on in-between change, therapists can help young people and others to identify progress toward goals. This can both counter client frustration and help orient them toward exceptions and differences with regard to their described problems. In this way, young people and others notice when what they want—as opposed to what they do not—is happening.

ONGOING ASSESSMENT WITH
MULTIPLE CLIENTS

When working with young people in families or couples it is important that therapists attend to each person's conversational preferences,
goals, and ideas about progress toward end points. Because there will be
different ideas about how therapy ought to proceed, what the concerns
are, what needs to change, and what will indicate success, it is common
to have separate complaints and goals for each client. Even when this
is the case, there usually are common threads between complaints and
goals that we can work to identify.

It can be helpful to coordinate these complaints and goals through the
use of acknowledgment, tracking, and linking. To do this, each person's
perspective is acknowledged and restated in the least inflammatory way
possible, while still acknowledging and imparting the intended feeling
and meaning (Bertolino, 1999; Bertolino & O'Hanlon, 2002; O'Hanlon &
O'Hanlon, 1999). These statements are linked by the word "and," as it
builds on a common concern rather than opposing or competing needs
or goals. The following case example illustrates one way of using acknowledgment, tracking, and linking.

Tara and Tricia: Finding a Way Back

*A mother and daughter who came to see me seemed to be at significant odds
with one another. It appeared that they both wanted things to be different in the
future but were finding little common ground. I therefore helped to identify the
general direction in which each person wanted to head and then began to link
those preferences together.*

Tara: *I just want my daughter to return to school. It's ridiculous for her to be
out. And besides, if she doesn't go she'll never get the kind of job she wants.*

Therapist: *Okay. So you're concerned because your sense is that there's really
no reason for a 16-year-old to be out of school and that it could negatively
affect her future.*

Tara: *Right.*

Tricia: *What's the point? I can't stand school. Besides, if you're gonna continue to be on my case, then I'll never go back!*

Tara: *See, that's what I get every day!*

Therapist: *I can see that it's been rough on the both of you. And for you,
Tricia, you haven't found a reason to go to school and to tolerate it yet.*

Tricia: *Yeah. School is boring and if she doesn't back off... then forget it.*

Therapist: *And what do you mean by your mom being on your case?*

Tricia: *She constantly says, "You better go. You better go. You can't miss
another day!" It's like she thinks that I don't have a clue! I know that I need
to graduate to get a good job. Duh!*

Therapist: *Okay, and the ways that she's tried so far to get you to go haven't work so well for you?*
Tricia: *Nope.*
Therapist: *I see. So let me see if I'm following the two of you. Tara, you'd really like Tricia to return to school, finish her education, and have a better chance of reaching her dreams. And Tricia, you seem to have some dreams for yourself as well, and even though I haven't heard about them yet, it seems that school is a part of that in some way. So you'd like to find a way of tolerating school so that you can graduate and work toward the career you want. And maybe there are other ways that your mom can be helpful to you with that—ways that don't involve her telling you to go, because you already know that—but ways that you see as being supportive with school.*

In this example acknowledgment, tracking, and linking were used, particularly in the last therapist response. It's important to acknowledge each person and his or her perspective. Whether working with couples, families, or other multiple-client variations, clients should be free to clarify any misperceptions or areas of discomfort until a mutually agreeable description emerges. Once this occurs, therapists can begin to flesh out the direction and goals of therapy. This process can be done with all members present or in sessions with individuals.

COLLABORATION AS A CORNERSTONE WITH OUTSIDE HELPERS

Therapists working with adolescents and young adults often find themselves working with other mental health, health system, juvenile or adult-correctional system, or social service providers. This can be a challenging task when there are varying perspectives regarding what should happen with a particular young person or family. Whether working with other mental health practitioners or helpers outside the profession, it is important to maintain a collaborative stance. This involves having conversations with outside helpers to learn about their expectations and goals. The following case example illustrates how to do this.

EDDIE AND SHEILA: "I'D BE SHOCKED"
A Deputy Juvenile Officer (DJO), Sheila, was consulted about an adolescent, Eddie, who was on probation. Although Eddie was still living at home, Sheila was in the process of securing a placement for him in a residential facility. Through the conversation, the therapist was able to, learn from the DJO what specifically she needed to see Eddie doing that would indicate to her that he was doing better and, perhaps, would no longer need to be placed residentially.

Therapist: *So that I'm clear, what specifically are you wanting to be addressed in therapy?*

Sheila (deputy juvenile officer):   *Definitely Eddie's attitude about things. He thinks he's invincible.*

Therapist: *So what has he done that's given you the idea that he thinks he's invincible?*

Sheila: *He's assaulted people. He's stolen and he keeps thinking that he won't get caught even though he has been caught many times.*

Therapist: *So what would start to convince you that he wasn't seeing himself as being invincible any longer and was making effort to do better?*

Sheila: *He'd have to stop assaulting people and quit stealing. He'd also have to talk more respectfully to me. He tries to intimidate me.*

Therapist: *Okay. You mentioned that he'll be talking more respectfully to you. What else will he be doing instead of assaulting people and stealing?*

Sheila: *He'll be making it to school on time, getting passing grades, and, instead of fighting, he'll walk away from conflict.*

Therapist: *And when he's started to do those things you'll have to wonder if maybe he's turned the corner?*

Sheila: *Oh, yeah! But I can't see those things happening.*

Therapist: *So it would be surprising to you?*

Sheila: *That's putting it mildly. I'd be shocked.*

Therapist: *And for the sake of clarity, when he does those things, will you reconsider whether long-term residential placement is the right place for him or not?*

Sheila: *That's right.*

The presence or involvement of outside helpers is then incorporated into therapy sessions. One way of doing this is to first ask young people and others involved, "Did your teacher/juvenile officer/social worker etc. tell you what he/she expects us to focus on here?" If the young person or other knows, we proceed by incorporating those goals or directions into the therapy. If the young person or other does not know, we consider using speculation: "What do you think he/she will say when I talk with him/her?" We want to invite all parties involved to share with us their perceptions and understanding of what others may have conveyed to them.

When adolescents, young adults, or others involved truly do not know what outside helpers' concerns are or when their perceptions are inconsistent with what we have been told by outside helpers, we can gently introduce our own understandings. For example, we might say, "My understanding after talking with your juvenile officer is that she will have the sense that you're moving in the right direction when you're attending school more regularly." We then follow with, "How does that sound to you?" As with working with multiple clients, we acknowledge each perspective and search for continuity between the respective goals.

It can also be helpful to invite outside helpers to attend therapy sessions. By welcoming multiple perspectives and expanding the system, new possibilities and potential solutions may be generated. When outside helpers join therapy sessions, we must remember that there are multiple ways of viewing situations, with no one view being more correct than another. At the same time, we want to challenge perspectives that close down possibilities and promote those that can facilitate positive change.

This chapter explored how both formal and ongoing assessment procedures are important in determining what young people and others involved want to have change in their lives. The next chapter introduces ways of learning and matching young people and others' orientations to their concerns and problems and how to facilitate positive change.

Chapter 5

Invitations to Change: Exploring Pathways with Possibilities

THIS CHAPTER DELVES INTO PROCESSES AND PRACTICES THAT ASSIST young people and others involved in achieving positive change. It begins by exploring young people and others' orientations to change, the influences of context, and theories of change. By attending closely to and matching clients' ideas we increase our chances of successful outcomes.

Several case examples illustrate an array of ways to promote change through respectful processes and practices. Instead of focusing on how techniques and methods drive therapy, the chapter explores how young people and others inform therapy processes and how the techniques and methods that evolve out of these processor can be offered into therapeutic conversations, complementing young people and others' orientations to change.

CLIENTS AS TEACHERS: YOUNG PEOPLE'S AND OTHERS' ORIENTATIONS AS GUIDES TO CHANGE

To learn about young people and the lives of others involved, we tune into their stories and ask, "Who are you?" and "What's your story?" and "What's it like to be you?" These questions privilege the voices of young people over normative theoretical positions. They allow us to learn from young people how they've experienced the world and about the different influences that have shaped their lives. A change-oriented approach is based on the premise that young people and families are engineers of change.

As discussed in Chapter 1, client orientations include *influences of context*—what young people and others attribute their concerns and problems to as well what they view as resources—and *theories of change*—their ideas about how positive change will come about. Young people and others involved may not always have well-formed theories about their concerns and problems (and how such influences can contribute to change); however, they do typically have ideas regarding influences that can be identified through careful attention to language. Our role, then, becomes one of *inviting, learning, honoring,* and *matching* young people and others' orientations. To summarize what we learned in Chapter 1:

- *Inviting* involves creating a context where adolescents, young adults, and family members feel understood, thereby creating space where their ideas, stories, and narratives can be shared.
- *Learning* relates to an openness and commitment on the part of therapists to understand, as much as possible, how young people and others associated with therapy view their situations. This includes learning about the influences of context, preferences about who should be involved with therapy, and so on.
- *Honoring* clients' orientations speaks to the importance of acknowledgment and validation. It's important that the perceptions, ideas, beliefs, and so on of young people, parents, caregivers, and others are respected and validated. This does not mean that therapists must agree with such perspectives. Acknowledgment and validation simply let people know that we don't blame them or see them as crazy, maimed, bizarre, having bad intentions.
- *Matching* involves therapists' using processes and practices that are respectful of and consistent with clients' ideas about their concerns and problems, possibilities for attaining solutions, and the means and methods for achieving those hoped-for changes.

These processes help us to better understand how young people and others involved have constructed their worlds. We can then help them to achieve the change they desire within the orientations or worldviews they have established. When their orientations seem to contribute to stuckness, we collaborate with young people and others in finding valid alternative perspectives that open up possibilities for positive change.

THE INFLUENCES OF CONTEXT

All problems are influenced by context. In working with young people and families it is important to note that a multitude of influences on concerns and problems as well as possibilities for solutions, exist.

These include but are not limited to culture, family history and background, social relationships, genetics and biology, religion/spirituality, gender, sexual orientation, nutrition, and economics (Bertolino, 1999; Bertolino & O'Hanlon, 2002; Bertolino & Schultheis, 2002). Aspects of context do not *cause* concerns and problems or solutions; they *influence* them. Furthermore, we must accept that we can never truly know the contribution of any one influence to a concern, problem, or solution. All problems and solutions can have multiple influences.

Part of our challenge is to learn how contextual influences simultaneously affect concerns and problems *and* can serve as resources to open up possibilities for change. Young people, caregivers, and others involved in therapy continue to demonstrate that they are motivated primarily by what they believe influences their problems and what they see as viable possibilities for solution. To learn about contextual influences in the lives of young people and others we can do the following: Listen closely to the words young people and others use to describe themselves, their situations, concerns, problems, and resources; and ask specific questions.

Our clients are our best teachers. By inviting young people and others to share their experiences and stories, we can begin to learn what they see as influences in their lives. Although we do not have to agree with their perspectives, we acknowledge and honor them. We also strive to match their perspectives by using language and asking questions that are consistent with their worldviews. The following case example illustrates this idea.

JOAN: "HE'S JUST LIKE HIS FATHER"

Joan, a mother of three, came to see me because her 14-year-old son had been getting into trouble at home and school. Through careful listening and close attention to her use of language, I was able to learn from her what she saw as influencing her son's behavior.

Joan: My son is a chip off the old block. He's just like his father.

Therapist: *Can you say more about that?*

Joan: Yes. He acts just like his father.

Therapist: *Do you think it has more to do with genetics, or from watching his father, or . . .*

Joan: Well, of course he's got his father's genes—but genes don't make a person. He's the way he is because he's learned it from watching his father.

Therapist: *So you see his father as being a big influence in his life?*

Joan: The biggest. What his father says he does. It's as simple as that.

Therapist: *So how has that been helpful or unhelpful?*

Joan: His father lets him get away with everything and I don't. Since he only listens to his father, that's a problem.

Therapist: *It seems he only listens to his father and less to you.*

Joan: *Exactly. He even listens to his friends more than me.*
Therapist: *So his friends are also a big influence?*
Joan: *Definitely . . . and it's rarely good!*

In this particular example, we learned that two of the influences that the mother views as affecting the situation with her son are his father (family) and friends (social relationships). Although the therapist may see things differently, clients are more likely to feel we understand them when we stick to their explanations as opposed to imposing our own. If young people and others feel heard and understood and that their perspectives are valid, they are more likely to be open in the future to considering other perspectives.

The next case example illustrates this idea further.

Patty: "They Told Me . . . "

Patty, a 19-year-old mother, was referred to me because she was having some difficulty with her son's behavior. At one point during the therapy she discussed how she disciplined her son. She stated that she had recently started to spank him. She prefaced this by commenting that for the first two years of his life she did not spank him but that "people" had told her she had better get control of him or he would "become a terror" or "end up in jail." When asked which people she was referring to, she related that her friends had given her the advice.

In the previous example the young mother's friends played a significant role in her child-rearing practices. It can therefore be said that social relationships are a contextual influence for her. In the event that clients do not offer much in terms of their descriptions, we can ask questions. The following questions can assist therapists in learning from young people and others what they view as influences on their concerns and problems as well as what resources have been or could be helpful in the future:

- What do you see as being the most significant influences (e.g., family, culture, religion, social relationships) in your life/concern/ problem/situation?
- What do you see as contributing most/in any way to the concern/ problem/situation you've been facing?
- How have those influences affected you?
- How have they been helpful to you? How have they been unhelpful?
- What would others say have been the most significant influences in your life/concern/problem/situation? Would you agree or disagree with them?
- What thoughts/ideas/theories have you been considering about how this problem has come about and what might put it to rest?

- Given the ideas that you have about the problem you're facing, what do you think would be the first step in addressing it?
- What might you do differently as a result of the thought/idea/theory you've developed?
- What have you considered trying that is consistent with your ideas about what's influencing this problem?
- If you had this thought/idea/theory about someone else, what would you suggest that he or she do to resolve it?

Although we strive to be as informed as possible, our views as therapists are limited. Therefore, we learn from young people and others involved what it is like to be them. We claim no preconceived knowledge about their experiences in and with the world. We assume a "not knowing" position whereby we are always learning from clients what we still don't know about them and their experiences (Anderson & Goolishian, 1992). William Madsen (1999) stated:

Just as anthropologists (or more accurately ethnographers) immerse themselves in a foreign culture to learn about it, therapy from an anthropological stance can begin with immersing ourselves in a family's phenomenological reality in order to fully understand their experience. (p. 41)

Whether speaking of family, culture, religion, or some other influence, it can be said that we practice from a position of "curiosity." In this way we challenge our own values and beliefs and work with clients to do the same in ways that are respectful and open up possibilities. To do this we listen to young people and others' stories. Clients are our best teachers and their first-hand experiences can help us to understand the influence of context.

There are times when contextual influences become constraints for people and contribute to their problem situations. Thus, we ask young people and others involved to teach us how these influences may be restrictive in any way and how they may be strengths or resources. To learn more, we can ask questions about specific areas of context. Here are some examples of such questions:

Family history/background:
- Has your family influenced your life?
- What have been the positive influences?
- In what ways has the influence of your family been challenging for you?
- What qualities do you think you/your son/daughter have inherited from your family?
- What do those qualities say about the kind of person you are?
- How are they an asset to you?

- (if young person or other does not know one or both parents) Given the type of person that you are (caring/kind/honest, etc.), what do you think your father/mother/parents might have been like?
- What qualities do you think they've passed along to you that help you to move through life?
- What qualities would you like to pass on to your children? Why?
- How have you or other family members kept this problem from completely taking over your lives?
- How are you dealing with this problem differently than your father/sister/uncle, etc. did?
- Who in your family has successfully dealt (to any degree) with this problem? How did they do that?
- What qualities do your family members possess that have allowed them to stand up to problems/adversity? What does that tell you about your family?
- What qualities or traits do you think you've inherited from your family of origin that can help you to face this problem in your life? What does that tell you about yourself?
- As changes occur, what will be different in your family a week/a month/a year, etc. from now?
- What do you think all of this might say about your family?

Culture/ethnicity/religion spirituality:
- Has your culture/ethnicity/religion/spirituality influenced your life? What is most important for me to understand about that?
- What can you tell me about your cultural/ethnic/religious/spiritual background that will help me to better understand you/who you are/your concern/problem/situation?
- What has it been like for you to grow up with that background?
- What has it been like to grow up black/Columbian/Jewish, etc.?
- In what ways has your cultural/ethnic/religious/spiritual background been a strength? How could it be in the future?
- In what ways has that background presented a challenge for you? How have you dealt with that challenge thus far?
- What do people like me need to know about you to better understand the influence of that background in your life?
- What has been your most profound cultural/ethnic/religious/spiritual experience, if any?
- What kind of cultural/ethnic/religious/spiritual activities would you like to do in the future, if any?

Social relationships/community:
- How do you connect with other people?
- How have you typically met other people you have felt a connection with?

- Who is/has been helpful to you in your day-to-day life?
- How or what does that person or people do to be of help to you?
- Who has been helpful to you in the past in facing daily challenges? How have they been helpful?
- What did the assistance of these people allow you to do that you might not have otherwise done?
- Who have you met in your life that knew or knows exactly what you've been going through? How do they know that about you? How has that been helpful to you, knowing that they understood?
- Who do you look up to? Why?
- Who has helped you through tough times? How so?
- Whom do you feel you can count on?
- When you're struggling, who knows just what to say/do to help you to get back on track?
- Who has the right idea about you?
- (to another family member) Who in your son's/daughter's/ mother's, etc. life seems to be able to get through to him or her? How do they do that?
- Who seems to get through to or is able to have an impact on your son/daughter/mother, etc.? How so?
- Whom do you know that your son/daughter/mother, etc. responds to would be willing to help out?

The aforementioned areas are not inclusive of every possible contextual influence. They merely underscore the importance of tuning into the plethora of influences that exist and can affect problems and possibilities. In addition, by learning about the influences in young people's and others' lives, we are tapping into client factors such as internal strengths (including resiliency, protective factors, and coping skills) and external support systems (including individual and community resources). The idea is to have young people and others involved teach us what we need to know about their experiences. We want to understand, as much as possible, how young people and others have constructed their worldviews. We can then work with them to make changes in their views, actions, or interactions.

THEORIES OF CHANGE

A significant part of clients' orientations is their ideas about how positive change might occur in their situations or lives. This has been referred to as clients' *theories of change* (Duncan & Miller, 2000; Duncan & Sparks, 2001). Clients' theories of change represent their ideas, attitudes, and speculations regarding how they situate themselves in relation to problems, what might bring about change, at what rate and when change might occur, who might be involved, and what factors, including contextual influences, might be involved in facilitating change.

As mentioned previously, client theories are filtered through contextual influences and help us to better understand clients' worldviews and how to help them. Recall that young people and others involved won't necessarily enter therapy with clear-cut ideas, but will give indications of how they view themselves and their situations by the words they use. Through careful listening, questioning, and direct inquiries, we invite clients into conversations where we can learn details about how they expect change to occur.

These conversations involve asking adolescents, young adults, and others about how they feel their problems developed, how they have tried to resolve them, to what degree those efforts have or haven't worked, what they've considered but haven't tried, and what they might consider in the future to attain the change they desire.

One way of learning young people's and others' theories of change is to ask questions such as:

- How do things usually change in your life?
- What prompts or initiates change in your life?
- How do you usually go about trying to resolve your concerns/ problems?
- What have you done in the past to resolve your concerns/problems?
- What ideas do you have about how change is going to take place with your concern/problem/situation?
- What ideas have you considered that might assist with your concern/problem/situation?
- If you had this idea about someone else, what would you suggest he or she do to resolve it?
- What has to happen before the change you are seeking occurs?
- At what rate (e.g., slow, fast) do you think change will occur?
- Will change likely be in big amounts, small amounts, incrementally, etc?
- Do you expect change to occur by viewing things differently? By doing something different? By others' doing something different?

When working with young people and others it is very easy to be drawn to certain influences and not to others. It is also easy to believe that change occurs only at certain times, with specific people, or at certain rates. The problem is when practitioners' ideas take precedence over those of clients. A mission of ours, then, is to remain client-informed by letting young people and others involved determine the influences in their lives.

LEARNING YOUNG PEOPLE'S AND
OTHERS' RELATIONSHIPS TO
CONCERNS AND PROBLEMS

Learning how clients situate themselves in relation to their concerns and problems is particularly important with adolescents and young adults, as negative outcomes can often be traced to a mismatch between practitioners' and clients' views regarding who is involved and the degree of their involvement. To learn about how young people and others view themselves in relation to their concerns and problems, we tune into their use of pronouns—*I, me, myself, we, he/she, him/her*, and *they/them*. When adolescents, young adults, caregivers, or others use *I* or *we* they are probably accepting some level of involvement and accountability with their concerns or problems. Conversely, a lack of the presence of *I, me,* or *we* often indicates that they are removing or distancing themselves from involvement with problems. Although this is generally the case, it is important to note that same pronouns may have different meanings in different languages.

Another way of learning how young people and others situate themselves is to ask specific questions such as:

- Who would you say is involved with this concern/problem?
- What would you say is your part, if any, in all of this?
- What is our role, if any, in what's going on in your family?
- On a scale of one to ten, how involved would you say you are with the concern/problem?

Therapists who attempt to get adolescents, young adults, caregivers, or others to change their behaviors or take action when they do not see themselves as directly involved may be unknowingly creating a mismatch. A change-oriented approach emphasizes the importance of working with young people and others in ways that are consistent with the manner in which they view their lives, concerns, problems, and situations.

Furthermore, clients often change the way they see their situations. Because we want young people, family members, and others to be accountable in their lives, we want to be sure to acknowledge any efforts to accept responsibility. For example, if an adolescent says, "She hit me first; then I hit her," we would want to acknowledge the *I* part of the statement, perhaps by saying, "I'm glad to hear that you are owning up to hitting your sister."

Knowing how young people and others situate themselves with regard to concerns and problems is part of the matrix of clients' orientations. As we move into various processes and practices to help promote positive change, we want to remain focused on the importance of continuing to tune in to each client's orientation. We also want to maintain flexibility, recognizing that young people and their views, concerns, and problems are not static. Therefore the only consistent, accurate way of knowing whether or not we are working in ways that are helpful is by having ongoing conversations with clients to learn about their experiences in therapy.

PROMOTING CHANGE THROUGH
COLLABORATIVE, CLIENT-INFORMED
PROCESSES AND PRACTICES

Most models of psychotherapy focus on one or two domains (e.g., affect, cognition, behavior, interactions) to explain problems and help young people and families to change. A change-oriented approach emphasizes clients' orientations to concerns and problems. As stated throughout, we recognize that concerns and problems as well as solutions are influenced by context. Whether speaking of views, actions, or interactions, we work with young people and others to promote change in any and all areas, recognizing that young people and others are the most significant contributors to change processes.

We are always searching for ways of facilitating change processes by working with young people and others in identifying the "not so obvious" as well as creating new perspectives on influences that have not been viewed as helpful in the past. This can include their families, social support systems and relationships, community, ethnic and cultural propensities, spiritual supports, and so on.

Many publications have offered various ways of promoting change, and a multitude of techniques, methods, and interventions associated with collaborative, competency-based, change-oriented, and client-informed therapy have been explored in depth (see Bertolino, 1999; Bertolino & O'Hanlon, 2002; Bertolino & Schultheis, 2002; Bertolino & Thomson, 1999; O'Hanlon & Bertolino, 2002). This book takes a different direction by illustrating how the orientations of young people and others involved drive therapy and how techniques and methods evolve out of and match those orientations. Although numerous ideas are outlined in tables and illustrated in case examples, we must recognize that in order for these specific actions or "techniques," "methods," and "interventions" to be successful, they must:

- Build on or create hope;
- Enhance the effects of other common factors/general effects;

- Be believable to clients and practitioners;
- Fit with clients' orientations to their concerns and problems;
- Fit with clients' orientations regarding potential possibilities and solutions;
- Fit with clients' goals and preferences;
- Fit with clients' ideas about how to accomplish goals.

Following are a variety of ways of matching young people's and other's orientations and promoting change through therapeutic processes and practices.

CHANGING VIEWS AND PERSPECTIVES

Many young people and most adolescents who enter therapy do not identify themselves as having problems or even being related to problems. It is others who are concerned about something. In such cases prompting a young person to do anything differently is very difficult. So when it is clear that young people or others are not identifying themselves as involved with problems or if they indicate that problems are psychological or related to thinking (i.e., they use phrases such as "I *think* the problem is . . . " or "The way I *see* it"), we: (1) learn about what they see as contextual influences, and (2) orient toward helping them to change their views and perspectives.

Table 5.1 has been designed to provide multiple ways of helping young people and others to alter or change their perspectives in ways that remain consistent with and respectful of their orientations. This table is not inclusive of the myriad ways to facilitate a change in perspective. It is merely a template of possibilities. What is most important is learning from young people and others their ideas about how change will occur. Practitioners are the facilitators and clients are the engineers. The table offers ways of helping young people and others to notice "what else" may be happening and, ultimately, to create new ways of viewing themselves, others, events, and situations. For many, a new perspective can lead to a change in actions or interactions and ultimately to problem resolution.

The following case examples illustrate several ways of working with clients' orientations to help them change their views of their concerns, problems, situations, and selves.

RACHEL, KEVIN, AND KRIS: WHAT IS A MAN?

A colleague, Nick, asked me (Bob) to assist him as a cotherapist in working with a family of three. The family included a single mother, Rachel, and two teenage sons, Kevin and Kris. Rachel brought her two sons to see Nick because both had

TABLE 5.1
POSSIBILITIES FOR CHANGING VIEWS AND PERSPECTIVES

1. Search for counterevidence, exceptions, and unique outcomes. Acknowledge the internal experiences of young people and others while simultaneously exploring aspects of their lives, events, or situations to identify evidence or facts that don't fit with their problem descriptions or stories.

2. Search for alternative stories or explanations. Offer alternative explanations or interpretations to the ones subscribed to by young people and others. These alternative perspectives are not imposed on clients or stated as facts or truths. Instead, they are offered as possibilities, with young people and others having the space to accept or reject all or part of therapists' interpretations.

3. Search for resilient qualities. Explore the lives of young people or family members for qualities they possess that allow them, to any degree, to stand up to adversity and manage very difficult situations.

4. Use externalizing language. Help adolescents, young adults, family members, and others to separate from their problems. Assist young people and others to "step outside" of their current views and look at their situations and lives differently.

5. Search for counterexamples that indicate choice or accountability. When young people have been viewed as not accepting responsibility for their actions or behaviors, search for times when they were accountable to any degree. Sometimes it's helpful to start in the present and work backward, looking for times when they made good choices and accepted responsibility for their actions and behaviors.

6. Use the word "and" to link internal experience and accountability. Acknowledge and extend permission for internal experience and simultaneously hold young people and others accountable for their actions and behavior.

7. Identify a valuing witness. Identify others in the lives of young people who have witnessed them behaving well and demonstrating accountability and responsibility.

continued

Table 5.1, continued

8. Normalize and destigmatize. Let young people and others involved know that they are not alone and that others have gone through the same or similar experiences and challenges.

9. Use metaphor, stories, music, movies, etc. Use mediums that are familiar and compelling to young people to offer alternative ways of viewing their situations and lives. Such mediums can strengthen the therapeutic relationship and alliance, normalize, acknowledge, instill hope, offer new possibilities and perspectives, bypass everyday conscious ways of processing information, and remind clients of previous solutions and resources.

10. Create or rehabilitate a compelling vision for the future. Help young people and others involved to create some vision, however small, of a future preferred future. Then help them to identify perceived barriers and create a plan to move toward that preferred future.

11. Suggest that young people and others change their sensory attention. Suggest that young people and others shift from seeing things to listening; or from listening to touching, or from talking to oneself to smelling. A change is sensory attention can help them to alter unhelpful patterns of attention.

12. Suggest that young people and others recall other aspects of the situation they are remembering. This can help young people and others to notice aspects of a situation that they had not noticed previously, thereby bringing about a shift in perspective.

13. Suggest to young people and others that they think of one thing that would challenge their thoughts or get them to doubt them. Have young people and others challenge their own thoughts so they can create new perspectives for themselves.

14. Suggest that young people and others shift from focusing on the past to focusing on the present. Suggest that young people and others shift their attention from the past to the present so they can change a pattern of viewing and perhaps gain a new perspective.

15. Suggest that young people and others shift from focusing on the present or the past to focusing on the future. Suggest that young people or others shift their attention from the present to the future—they can change a pattern of viewing and perhaps gain a new perspective.

16. Suggest that young people and others shift from focusing on their internal experience to focusing on the external environment or other people. Suggest that young people and others orient their attention elsewhere—old patterns can be changed, and new perspectives can result.

17. Suggest that young people and others shift from focusing on the external environment or other people to focusing on their inner worlds. Suggest that young people or others orient their attention elsewhere—old patterns can be changed, and new perspectives can result.

18. Suggest that young people and others focus on what has worked rather than what has not. Suggest that young people or others focus on what they have done with regard to their problems that is worked to any degree.

been violent with schoolmates and each other. During the initial session Nick also learned that the boys had been physically aggressive toward their mother on multiple occasions, yet no reports or charges had been filed. The reason, according Rachel, was that she did not want her sons to "get in trouble with the law." Nick then learned that Rachel herself was a police officer, assigned to desk duty. Further discussion with the family found that the boys' father, two uncles, and grandfather were also police officers.

The boys appeared to be very agitated, arguing with their mother, calling her names, and denying responsibility for their actions by saying things such as, "She needs to shut her mouth and everything will be fine" and "I warned her. She knew what was coming." On several occasions, because of their behavior, Nick had to separate the boys from their mother and from each other.

I joined the therapy in the third session. One of the first things I did was ask Rachel what she had hoped to see happen as a result of coming to therapy. She said that she wanted the boys to stop hitting her and to learn to be respectful of people. The boys were each asked the same question. Kevin, the older at 14 years, stated, "I don't care. This sucks." Kris, who was 13 years old, pointed at his mother and answered, "That lady needs to get a life and get out of mine." I then asked Rachel, "Where do you think the boys got the idea that violence and aggression are the way to handle things?" The following dialogue then took place.

Rachel: *I know where they got it. That's what they've been told for years by their father.*

Bob: *What have they been told by their father?*

Rachel: *To stand up to people. Don't let anyone walk over you. You have to be a real man.*

Kevin: *[raising his voice] Shut up!*

Bob: *Kevin, you can be upset and you don't have to agree with your mom and it's not okay to tell her to shut up or to be mean to her. Now, I'd like to ask you how you learned to deal with anger?*

Kevin: *[silence]*

Bob: *It's okay if you don't feel like talking right now. I sometimes feel that way. [to Kris] Kris, do you have any ideas about that?*

Kris: *You've got to take care of yourself and don't let anybody walk on you. Especially girls.*

Nick: *Where did you learn that?*

Kris: *My dad always says that.*

Bob: *I see. And what do you think he meant by that?*

Kris: *He meant you have to be tough.*

Bob: *What does that mean to you?*

Kris: *If people say stuff or make you mad you have to stand up. So that means fighting back.*

Bob: *Okay. If you had to guess, where do you think your dad got the idea about having to be tough?*

Kris: *He's a cop. They have to be tough.*

Nick: *So he learned it through his training to be a cop?*

Kris: *Yeah, but my uncles are cops too and my grandpa was one. I think they told him to be tough.*

Kevin: *[interjecting] Cops have to stand up.*

Nick: *Sometimes they do.*

Bob: *Kris, you mentioned that it's especially important to not let girls walk on you. What did you mean by that?*

Kris: *Men are in charge. Girls can't tell you what to do.*

Bob: *Did you hear that from your dad as well?*

Kris: *My dad, my uncle Vic, and my grandpa.*

Bob: *So there are several men in your family that believe that to be true.*

Kris: *Yep.*

Kevin: *Yeah, they're right, too.*

Bob: *I'm curious about a few things. Can you teach me some more about your family?*

Kris: *What do you want to know?*

Bob: *Well, you mentioned that you have two uncles who are police officers. One is your uncle Vic. Who's the other?*

Kris: *Steve. He's cool.*

Bob: *What does Steve think about the idea that you have to be tough and stand up to people, especially women?*

Kris: *I don't know. He doesn't talk about it.*

Kevin: *I don't know either.*

Rachel: *He's a very nice man and always treats his wife, Sharon, great and his kids, too. He's got two girls.*

Kevin: *Yeah, Katy and Diane. They're nice.*

Nick: *So do you get along with your aunt Sharon and Katy and Diane?*

Kevin: *Yeah.*

Nick: *What would you do if you didn't agree with them about something?*

Kris: *I know I would just talk to them.*

Kevin: *Yeah, because Uncle Steve would get mad at us if we argued with them.*

Bob: *So your uncle Steve would step in. What do you think he would say?*

Kevin: *Don't fight. You don't need to fight.*

Bob: *I have to admit that I'm really confused here. It really sounds like your uncle Steve believes that girls and women should be treated with respect.*

Kris: *He told me that everyone should be treated with respect.*

Bob: *Really?*

Kris: *Yep.*

Bob: *Help us to understand here. It sounds like even though some members of your family think that you should stand up to people, particularly girls and women, some of them don't believe that. How is it that some of your family members have been able to stand up to aggression and disrespect?*

Kris: *Well, I think they just don't like it.*

Bob: *I agree, and I'm getting the sense that part of you doesn't like it and doesn't really believe that you should be aggressive and disrespectful to girls and women. Is that right?*

Kris: *I don't want to be mean.*

Bob: *What do you want your mom to know about how you feel about her?*

Kris: *I love her.*

Kevin: *So do I!*

Bob: *Well, help me to understand how assaulting, threatening, and verbally abusing her lets her know that you love her.*

Kris: *[crying] I'm sorry, Mom.*

Rachel: *[crying] I know . . . but it really hurts me when you're mean to me.*

Kevin: *[tearful] We do love you. I'm sorry.*

Bob: *You know, we all inherit different things from our families. I'm getting the sense that maybe you've inherited some of that compassion for others that your uncle Steve has. Now is the time to bring that out and use it and stand up to the other ideas that have been hurting you and your family. What do you think?*

Rachel: *I've always known that the boys had it in them. I've seen traces of it here and there.*

Bob: *So how can you two begin to make use of those inherited family qualities of being respectful and kind more often in the future?*
Kevin: *I just have to be nice. I know I can be.*
Kris: *I can be nice, too.*

Following the session, the boys' violence and aggression toward Rachel ceased, and over the course of five more sessions, both boys improved their relationships with others. The most dramatic change occurred with Kris, whose relationship with his female teachers changed dramatically. In fact, Rachel was contacted by one of his teachers, who said to her, "I don't know what has happened with Kris, but he has become quite a gentleman." The mother said it was the first time she had pictured Kris as a "gentleman." Her story about him had begun to change.

With this particular family, multiple contextual influences—including family background, gender roles, and social relationships—were operative. In particular, Kevin and Kris were able to use their family background, which had significantly influenced the problem, as a resource for learning to be respectful to others. It was important to understand the influences within the family in order to work within their orientation. It was then possible to search for exceptions, alternative stories, and resilient qualities, thereby helping all involved to shift their views.

The previous case example illustrated how contextual influences can contribute to problems as well as strengths, resources, and solutions that affect positive change. Whereas the first example demonstrated this with families, the next shows how these influences can play a role with individuals.

NAOMI: "THE BEST OF BOTH WORLDS"
Naomi, a 19-year-old single mother came to see me. She had been adopted at the age of three months. During her second session Naomi stated, "I don't want to turn out like my mom. She was a bad mother. She was an alcoholic, she was promiscuous, and she died young. I mean, it was good that she gave up her children because she knew couldn't care for them, but she was bad otherwise."

I inquired, "You don't want to be like your mom in that way—battling alcoholism and promiscuity—and yet there seemed to be this redeeming quality your mother had—she cared about you and knew she needed to have someone else care for you when she couldn't. Do you think that you've inherited the quality of being willing to do anything for your children?"

"Absolutely. I know I have. I would do anything for my children, so I guess I got that from my mom."

I then asked, "And what else has contributed to you becoming the terrific mom that you are?"

"My adoptive mom has taught me a lot. She's had to deal with a lot and isn't perfect, but she's a great mom," Naomi replied.

I followed, "So you've had the benefit of drawing on the qualities of two mothers."

"I sure have."

I then asked, "What does that say about the type of person you are?"

"I'd have to say that I've taken the best of both worlds and I left the rest behind," She replied. Over the course of therapy, we explored what Naomi had learned about being a mother that might hinder as well as help her in becoming the mother she wanted to be.

This client had family influences from both her biological and adoptive mothers. Although it would have been easy to let theory take over and assume the extent of these or other influences, I instead tuned in to Naomi's orientation. She was able to identify qualities from her biological and adoptive mother that contributed to who she was as a person. The identification and amplification of such qualities can contribute to a change in perspective—one that increases hope and possibilities.

Like Naomi, young people sometimes know or have heard negative things about their families. They may make comments such as "My mother was an alcoholic," "My father was a drug dealer and a womanizer," or "My family was full of crazy people." The implication of these stories is that young people are predisposed to or have inherited these negative qualities. Other times young people know little or nothing at all about their families of origin. Some spend their lives trying to find out something about their families or establish a connection with them. In many cases they never find them. This does not stop them, however, from forming views about their parents and other family members. Many times, despite a lack of evidence, these views are negative.

When young people or others have made generalizations about themselves or their families—whether based on personal experience, little information, or no information—we can help them to identify qualities within themselves or their families that are valuable or redeeming (resilience, coping skills, etc.) or explore other influences (culture, spirituality, etc.) that may counter such negativity. This can be particularly therapeutic with children and adolescents who are in residential treatment centers, foster homes, runaway shelters, and other placements (Bertolino, 1999; Bertolino & O'Hanlon, 2002; Bertolino & Thompson, 1999).

Although some youth have never known their parents and never will, they continue to wonder and speculate about them, searching for a connection. Because they are already creating their own stories, which are sometimes problematic, we explore with them the possibility that their personal characteristics and qualities might be related to something positive that their parents passed on (or some other contextual influence).

This can help to diffuse anger and negative feelings that youth have carried around in their stories about their parents.

SEAN: "I'D BE HAPPY TO"

Several years ago I was doing contract work for a local community mental health agency. Many of the youth I saw had been labeled severely emotionally disturbed and given up on by other providers. This was the case with a 14-year-old named Sean. His family had moved three times to three different states over a period of two years. At each place of residence they sought mental health services (individual and family therapy, psychiatric services) because Sean's behavior had been so poor. They had been through traditional office-based family therapy and intensive home-based services and case management. Not even contacts with local law enforcement and the family (juvenile) court made a difference.

According to his mother, each time Sean entered a new school he would "have enemies within five minutes." He had been in numerous fights with classmates and with neighborhood youth, argued with his teachers, had poor grades, had been caught stealing, and would frequently come in late, after curfew. Sean had been suspended from school eleven times in two years, and his parents felt hopeless that things would change.

While working with the family, I explored many different avenues. At times, Sean appeared to have turned the corner and would do better. However, these changes were generally short-lived. Progress seemed to be one step forward and two steps backward, as just when things had improved, Sean would get into a fight or some other type of serious trouble.

Then, in the matter of one day, things changed dramatically. On a warm spring afternoon, Sean and I were sitting on the front porch of his home when a purple truck pulled into the driveway across the street. This clearly sparked Sean's attention. As a man stepped out of the truck, Sean yelled, "Hey, Mark, what's up?" The man turned, waved, and replied, "Not much. Come on by later." When I asked Sean who the man was, he answered, "He's cool. He helps me out sometimes. I just like hanging out at his house."

After my meeting with Sean, I asked his mother about Mark. She said that Mark was in his mid-thirties, was married, and had a young child. "He spends a lot of time over there and Mark doesn't seem to mind," she said. "It's weird, but Sean really listens to him and respects him." I then asked the mother if I could have permission to talk with Mark. I made it clear that Mark did not have to know the details of Sean's trouble but suggested that because Sean seemed to respond well to Mark, he might be a good resource. Sean's mother readily agreed and signed a consent form giving me permission to talk with Mark.

I felt as if I needed to act quickly, so the next day I met Mark as he arrived home from work. I introduced myself and said, "I've been working with Sean and his family because things haven't been going so well lately. And the reason I've come to you is because I understand that Sean really looks up to you."

Mark smiled and added, "Well, he does spent a lot of time over here and we like having him here."

I continued, "It seems to me that he really gets something from his relationship with you, and even though I have no idea what that is, I think it could be a calming resource for Sean. And what I'd like to know is, would you be willing to continue to spend time with him and perhaps teach him what you know about dealing with trouble and conflict?" I did not need to be any more specific. Almost telepathically, Mark seemed to know what was I getting at. He smiled and replied, "I'd be happy to."

The events that transpired over the course of the next few weeks were truly remarkable. Sean's behavior changed dramatically. His fighting stopped completely. He also made more of an effort at school. He began helping out with his younger sister. He came home on time. Six weeks following the conversation with Mark, Sean transitioned out of therapy.

Relationships can be amazing resources. With this in mind, one way of maximizing the general effects and helping to change perspectives is to learn about those individuals or groups who have made or could make positive contributions to young people through their relationships. The preceding case example illustrated the importance of social support systems in the lives of adolescents and young adults.

General effects contribute significantly more to therapeutic outcome than any model, method, or technique. Part of what enhances the effectiveness of models, methods, and techniques is the degree to which they tap into or build on general effects. One of these is the client's world outside of therapy, including social support systems (family, partners, friends, spiritual advisors, teachers, coworkers, classmates, scout leaders, coaches, etc.) and community resources. With young people it is crucial that we search for ways of tapping into support systems. Sometimes this means inviting such individuals, with the permission of clients, to participate in therapy or connecting young people or others with further community-based resources. People and relationships are the best resource we have for helping young people and their families.

Many young people can identify at least one person who they felt accepted them unconditionally. At times, these people are not physically available as a resource. This need not be a deterrent. In these cases we focus on what the relationship symbolized for the young person. It may be possible to find another way of replicating what that relationship symbolized for the young person. In other words, there may be another person who can offer the same relational and supportive qualities that were important to the young person.

SALLY: "A GOD THING"
Upon beginning therapy, 20-year-old Sally had several concerns. These included becoming sober, healing from a breakup with her boyfriend, and securing

employment. In my second session with Sally, she said, "A God thing happened to me today. You know, I lost my job a few weeks ago and today I got a call from a temp agency that I applied at five months ago. At AA [Alcoholics Anonymous] they say 'give it to God,' and I did and look at what happened."

I replied, "That's terrific. And I wonder, some people would say, 'God helps those who help themselves.' Do you think that's true for you?"

"I hope so," answered Sally.

"If that is true for you, what is the next step?" I inquired.

Sally quickly responded, "Well, I think it's to go to the interview and see what happens."

Once again, influences of context do not cause problems, they influence them. Further, it is the young person or other's belief in an influence, not the therapist's, that is most important. In this case, I learned from Sally that her faith was a resource—one that strengthened and elevated her spirit. Ultimately, it helped her to achieve and maintain sobriety and allowed her to move forward toward her goal of securing employment.

In the case of Sally, we learned how a change in an adolescent, young adult, parent, or other's view can contribute to positive movement in the direction of a goal or preferred future. Next we'll see how a shift in attention can help to alleviate pain and suffering, thereby creating hope for the future.

JEVON: FROM INSIDE TO OUTSIDE

A 15-year-old young man, Jevon, was referred to me because he had been sexually abused by a male adult while in foster care. Jevon was experiencing severe anxiety that seemed to be triggered by flashbacks. During the therapy I learned from Jevon that just prior to his flashbacks he became extremely internally focused. He stated that he became "stuck" in a place that was "hard to get out of." Jevon wanted to be able to "feel better" and reduce the intensity of the flashbacks. As we talked about his flashbacks, I learned that they varied significantly from being very intense (causing him to hyperventilate) to less intense (causing him to experience only mild agitation). Jevon remarked that the intensity seemed to increase when he was "really stuck, focusing inside." He further stated, the intensity goes down, "When I can get out of my mind." Through learning Jevon's orientation to his concern, I was able to collaborate with him to help him shift his attention from an internal focus to an external focus. He was able to do this by recognizing the first signs that he was beginning to "go inside." These included becoming very quiet and still and a subsequent increase in breathing rate. Jevon had learned that in the past he was able to reduce the level of intensity by recognizing these signs and then deliberately looking at the things in the physical environment around him to remind himself that he was in the present, not the past.

Depending on the theory held, there are many possible ways that a therapist could have worked with Jevon to alleviate his flashbacks. Yet Jevon's orientation to his concern was very specific. He recognized that a shift in attention had worked for him in the past. In addition, Jevon's having already found something that had been successful for him in the past increased the chance that he would try it again in the future.

Some clients are particularly prone to a specific fixation of attention. As therapists, we become similar to anthropologists, investigating where their attention has been stuck at problem times and where it goes when things have gone differently. We can help young people become unstuck by encouraging them to shift attention regarding time (past, present, or future), sensory perceptions (visual, kinesthetic, auditory, gustatory, olfactory), internal or external focus, what they do well rather than mistakes or problems, and actions instead of explanations. In collaborating with young people we want to employ a position of conjecture. This involves asking questions, making interpretations, and offering new perspectives from a position of curiosity or wonderment. This allows therapists to offer alternative views as possibilities as opposed to truths or facts. For example, we might say to a young adult, "The next time you notice yourself drifting back to the time of the abuse, I was wondering if you might consider noticing what else was happening at that time in your life." In this way, young people can accept or reject what has been offered. Therefore we merely suggest possibilities that they can try as a way of changing their attentional focus. We then learn from them whether these suggestions help them to solve the problems at hand or start to make changes in the direction of goals and preferred futures.

MILES AND JENNIFER: "SHE NEVER GOES BY THE RULES"

A 13-year-old teenager, Jennifer, was brought to therapy by her father, Miles, who had said of Jennifer "she never goes by the rules." Upon further conversation, I learned that Miles wanted his daughter to complete her chores. In the initial session, the following dialogue occurred between Miles, Jennifer, and me.

Miles: *Jennifer never goes by the rules. In fact, I don't know why we even have rules. She doesn't think they to apply to her.*

Bob: *It seems that Jennifer really hasn't been up to par with the rules. Tell me a little about the particular rules that she's broken that have been most bothersome.*

Miles: *Well, she doesn't do her chores. That's the main problem. I just can't get her to lift a finger.*

Bob: *I see. And it seems like she hasn't helped out as much as maybe she should.*

Miles: *Not at all. I'd settle for any effort at this point.*

Bob: *Okay, and when was the last time you can remember her pitching in?*

Miles: *I don't know. Maybe a month ago she helped her mother with the dishes.*
Jennifer: *A month ago?! I did them yesterday! Are you blind?*
Miles: *Wonders never cease! You should have done them anyway.*
Bob: *[to Jennifer] Was that a fluke? Or do you sometimes do other things too and pitch in more?*
Jennifer: *My room is always clean.*
Bob: *Really? How do you manage to keep it clean?*
Jennifer: *It's easy, I just make sure I have it straight before I go to bed.*
Bob: *Terrific. What else do you sometimes do?*
Jennifer: *I take out the dog every morning.*
Bob: *[to Miles] Is that accurate?*
Miles: *Well, yeah, she does. But she's responsible for doing those things.*
Bob: *Right. There are some things that she's responsible for and it's been frustrating to you when she hasn't done them all. Is it safe to say that with some rules she shows more responsibility than others?*
Miles: *Yeah, that's true.*

The preceding case illustrates the importance of acknowledging each person's perspective. This is essential to promoting a change in view or perspective. If at a basic level young people, parents, or others involved do not feel acknowledged and understood, the likelihood of any kind of a shift decreases. Additionally, a search for exceptions (counterevidence) in the case revealed times when things went differently. In searching for counterevidence it is usually helpful to start in the present and work backward (Bertolino & O'Hanlon, 2002), because the more recent the counterevidence is, the more powerful it tends to be.

Sometimes we have to go back a few weeks, months, or even years to find evidence. The idea is to be persistent and work toward evoking and eliciting exceptions that represent abilities that have been covered up or have gone unnoticed. These abilities and competencies are important because clients are generally more apt to do what has worked for them in the past than they are to try something completely new.

Another way of exploring exceptions and counterevidence is to use metaphors and stories. These mediums offer an excellent way of strengthening the therapeutic relationship and alliance. Metaphors and stories also help to normalize, acknowledge, offer hope, and evoke previous solutions and resources. For example, a therapist working with a young person experiencing school problems might say:

When you were very young, maybe in early grades like third, fourth, and fifth, I'm willing to bet that you did well in school. One thing that I know about you is that you've been learning for many years. If that weren't true you never would have learned your left hand from your right, or the alphabet—upper and lower case. You wouldn't have learned how to form words, to make sentences, to read and write. Somehow you learned these things even when you thought they were so hard that you'd never figure them out.

The story can be followed with questions such as "How far back would you have to go to a time when you were doing better in school?"; "What do you remember doing that helped you to learn things that you didn't think you would ever learn?"; and "How did you manage to learn things that you didn't think you would be able to learn?" It's even okay if these questions go unanswered. We simply want to reorient young people to times when they noticed things going differently and they had some influence over the problem. They can be followed up with inquiries about what the person *did* differently at those times. This can help to identify actions that the young person undertook as a result of a different view.

KELLY AND ALISON: "MY MOTHER DOESN'T HAVE A CLUE"

Kelly came to therapy because of "conflict" between her and her daughter Alison. Both the mother and daughter had firm, incompatible views about the other. These views kept them stuck and seemingly at war with one another.

Alison: My mother doesn't have a clue about what's going on. She thinks she does. What a joke! All she does is ground me and make rules and try to make my life miserable. If she wants me to hate her she's doing a good job.

Bob: It seems to you that your mother's mission is to put restrictions on you and make your life miserable.

Kelly: I've tried to raise her to be respectful of others and look at the result! It's a rare day when she goes by the rules. All she does is fight with me. I'm very bitter about it.

Bob: You've tried hard and it seems that your efforts to teach her so far haven't been as successful as you'd like—things haven't gone the way you'd like yet. I can see how that might make you bitter.

Kelly: I am.

Bob: [to Alison] You know, your mom hasn't raised a 15-year-old daughter before, and you haven't been a 15-year-old before. I wonder if your mom is doing what she thinks is best for you, and that maybe she will need some further education about what it's like to be a teenager in this day and age. No matter our age, we keep on learning. [to Kelly] You mentioned before that you have an 18-year-old son who is doing well. Perhaps you're finding out that it can be different to raise daughters and sons. Some of the things you've tried haven't worked and some have—because on those rare days sometimes you get through to her. So I'm wondering if you're still making adjustments in raising a 15-year-old daughter versus a 15-year-old son.

Following this segment, I saw Kelly and Alison separately. Alison did not respond verbally to the new interpretation, but Kelly did. She stated, "I never thought about that. I have raised Alison the same way I've raised my son, and he's fine. I wondered, 'Why should I have any problems with Kelly?' But I have three brothers, and if my parents had raised me the exact same way they raised them, there would have been a lot more trouble than there was! So I want to go home and think more about what you said."

Kelly later reported that she had started to communicate differently with Alison. Specifically; she stated that she had "taken a step back" and made sure to let her daughter say what she had to say before responding. Kelly stated that her merely being "a better listener" had reduced much of the conflict between them.

When young people and others involved feel acknowledged and understood, they are more likely to be open to other ways of viewing themselves and their situations. This is crucial when offering new interpretations. In the previous case example, a new interpretation of the same evidence or facts was offered to both Alison and Kelly. For Alison, the new interpretation seemed to make little or no difference. However, it helped Kelly in that she was able to gain a new perspective of her situation. What followed was a change in how she approached her daughter and her situation. Before offering an alternative perspective, we want to be sure to invite, learn, honor, and match others' orientations and views.

If young people or others change their frames of reference, their actions are more likely to be in accordance with those views. For example, if a father believes that his son's behavior is a result of the son's trying to manipulate him, he may express anger and resentment toward the son. However, if the same father sees his son's behavior as plea for more affection, he will probably respond quite differently. Therefore, we want to help young people and others to subscribe to views that will generate creativity, change, and possibilities.

BRETT: STANDING UP TO ADVERSITY

Twelve-year-old Brett was referred to me after seeing a total of 17 psychiatrists, psychologists, and psychotherapists over a period of six years. He had displayed aggression toward parents, teachers, and classmates. Due to this behavior, Brett had been psychiatrically hospitalized seven times. He had been given multiple diagnoses and was deemed a "chronic" case. Brett's mother, Eileen, also had been diagnosed with several psychiatric disorders and was emotionally unstable. Additionally, his father, Luke, was a severe alcoholic with an assortment of ongoing health problems. The family also faced housing and financial stressors.

Early on in my work with Brett it became clear that he had a remarkable ability to take care of himself. Furthermore, there were times when he took care of others in the family. Part of what Brett did to care for himself was to seek out people he knew he could count on for support and help. These included teachers, neighbors, friends, and mental health professionals. He reminded his mother of his appointments and dealt with her erratic behavior on a daily basis. He helped his father even though he was frequently embarrassed by his episodes of drinking. As if growing up weren't hard enough, the young boy took on the day-to-day challenges that life presented to him.

Two of the ways that Brett's internal abilities and external resources were evoked were by building on his resilience and by tapping into his social support systems. In each session, Brett was asked questions such as, "What have you already learned about how to make it through a day of school?, "How have you managed to go so many days in a row at school without having a tantrum?" and "How will you let people know when you become angry without hurting yourself or anyone else?" To utilize his support systems, Brett was asked, "Who will you want to be sure to talk to this week at school?" and "Until we meet again next week, who can you depend on to help you if you start to feel trouble coming on?" He was able to use these resources to help make it through the ups and downs he faced in the classroom and at home.

Brett's behavior changed dramatically over the year-long course of our 37 sessions. Through externalizing language, he was able to stand up to "Mr. Tantrum," the playful name given to his aggression. He also followed directions better at home and school, and his comprehension increased at school. He repeatedly stood up to adversity and survived conditions that were unimaginable to most people. He somehow mined his own resourcefulness to survive, and in doing so taught his parents how to do the same.

Children, adolescents, young adults, parents, and others routinely defy the odds and move from day to day. It's not easy, yet they persevere. One of the resources that allows them to do this is the resilient qualities they possess as individuals and families. Resilience, coping skills, and protective factors are client factors that can contribute largely to the general effects discussed throughout this book.

As practitioners, we also want to help young people and others to notice what qualities and associated actions enable them to stay afloat, manage adversity, and move from day to day. We do not try to convince young people or others of anything. We don't want to say, "Don't you see all the wonderful qualities that you have?" Such a statement invalidates people who are suffering and in pain. We want young people and others to *convince us* by telling us "what" about themselves contributed to change and "how" they did it. In other words, as practitioners we ask questions that help clients to tap into their own personal and familial resources. This can contribute to a change in views.

We also want young people and others to attribute the majority of change or "control" to their personal qualities, internal abilities and resources, and actions as opposed to some external factor (medication, diagnosis, change of season, therapists, etc.). This is crucial to lasting change. Although many influences may contribute to positive change, *all* change is *self change*. When young people and others are able to "blame" themselves for positive changes and accept responsibility for them, the likelihood that they will become more accountable in the future increases. In addition, orienting young people and others toward these aspects of themselves helps them to change the views they have of themselves and their situations and to use those resources to deal with future adversity.

JEREMY: MAKING A DIFFERENCE IN THE WORLD

Twenty-one-year-old Jeremy entered therapy after spending most of his childhood and adolescent years in residential facilities. He had been living with friends and keeping odd jobs since being released from the custody of the state at age 18. Jeremy stated that he did not think about the future because "it wasn't worth thinking about." As I talked with Jeremy I asked him how he made it from one day to the next. He remarked that he had a dog that he loved and needed to take care of. As Jeremy talked further he stated that what he wanted more than anything was to eventually have a job working with animals. About four sessions into therapy, Jeremy brought in a brochure from the Humane Society. He stated that he would love to work there. As our conversation progressed it became clear that Jeremy's vision was to make a difference in the world, and he was willing to deal with any barriers that went along with that. As a result, we were able to research opportunities available for Jeremy at the Human Society. We then identified possible barriers (e.g., work schedule) and how he would manage them. Jeremy made a plan of action. After completing training as a volunteer and working one weekend day for 6 months, Jeremy was hired full-time by the Humane Society, fulfilling one of the many dreams he had for himself.

For Jeremy, the dream of working with animals and making a difference in the world originally seemed out of reach. It was, however, very much within his reach. He simply had to negotiate a few perceived barriers and make a plan of action to achieve what he wanted. This is precisely what he did.

For many young people the lack of a future vision can have extremely debilitating effects. For example, many clients experiencing suicidal ideation have a distinct absence of a vision of a future without pain and suffering. The same can be true for clients who have been sexually abused or traumatized in some way.

One way to help young people and others to recognize the importance of a future vision is by asking questions and using methods that encourage a focus on the future. We can also help young people to connect with and articulate a preferred future vision or sense, as well as negotiate any barriers, either internal (stories, beliefs, fears, self-imposed limitations, restricted views of one's identity, etc.) or external (lack of money or transportation, prejudices or biases, etc.). Finally, a plan can be made to overcome such barriers and to begin to move toward that future.

By changing their views, many young people, families, and others achieve resolution to their concerns and problems. Some young people and families, however, seem to develop amnesia in times of pain and suffering. They forget about their resources. Often it isn't that these resources have disappeared; they just haven't been utilized. Therefore, as therapists, we help young people and others to reorient toward those resources and reconnect with them or identify new ones that may fulfill the same needs.

CHANGING ACTIONS AND INTERACTIONS

Whereas for some adolescents, young adults, family members, and others involved making changes in perspectives is sufficient, for others more deliberate action is needed. Once again we want to be sure to invite, learn, honor, and match the orientations of those involved in therapy. We must tune in to hear how young people and others situate themselves in relation to concerns and problems. As noted earlier, if clients use pronouns such as *I, me, myself* or *we* it is likely that they are identifying themselves as have at least some level of involvement with concerns and problems.

Next, we must listen for clues that indicate to us that there may be some action or interactional components. For example, if a parent says, "He does this, then I do that," the parent is identifying him- or herself as having a role in the interaction. This is in contrast to a parent who might say, "He does it. It's all on him." We must also continue to tune in to what influences are being attributed to concerns and problems. In a previous publication with Bill O'Hanlon (O'Hanlon & Bertolino, 2002), I discussed the role of therapists in identifying clients' problematic patterns:

> We explore with clients the negative problem patterns that seem to be inhibiting or intruding in their lives. We seek to be geographers, exploring the topography and the coastline of Problem-Land. We want to know the details of the problem or symptom, *and* help the client to find ways of escaping it. (p. 66)

There is a saying that states, "Insanity is doing the same thing over and over again and expecting different results." This could be the credo for many young adults and family members who have become stuck in perpetual patterns. In a metaphorical sense, it's as if some logs get jammed up in a bend in the river. Our goal is help remove the fewest number of logs possible to break up the logjam. It's not necessary to take every log out of the river. Nor do we need to get into the water and push the logs down the river every week. We merely need to help break up the pattern that keeps the logs stuck.

Often it is only necessary to alter one aspect of a pattern for the problem to change. We want to collaborate with our clients to find out what makes the most sense for them and what they are willing to do. This differs significantly from many traditional approaches that require therapists to create interventions and then "deliver" or "assign" them to young people and families. This kind of philosophy assumes that therapists are the experts and therefore know what is best. It also treats people as if they aren't intelligent enough to understand the logic of doing something different. A change-oriented approach is based on a different philosophy. We believe that young people and others do have the ability to resolve their concerns and problems. They are merely stuck in their thinking or ways of acting or interacting. Therefore, we want to collaborate with young people and others involved not only to help them come up with what will work for them, but also to think more creatively in the future. Education is paramount.

As practitioners we want to create a context of warmth and trust where ideas are generated and clients can choose those that make the most sense to them given their concerns and situations. We recognize and communicate to young people and others that there are no correct methods. There are only possibilities. The best methods are the ones that work for clients. Therefore we strive to be creative with young people and others. In order to learn what clients think will work best for them, we need to know how they've tried to solve or resolve their concern in the past. We also want to know what they feel might work before giving any suggestions. We don't want to suggest things that clients have already tried or are completely out of the question in terms of their orientations and theories of change. Many times clients provide little or no information as to why they are stuck. This is okay. We simply collaborate with them to generate possibilities that fit with them.

As described earlier, action-talk and videotalk can be helpful in gaining clear, observable descriptions. We want to listen to the descriptions young people and others involved give and search for any aspect of the problem that repeats, indicating a pattern. We can then help young people and families to *alter their repetitive patterns* or *identify and encourage the use of solution patterns*. Table 5.2 outlines these two processes and offers several different ways of changing patterns. Again, this table is not inclusive of all the different ways of helping young people and others

TABLE 5.2
POSSIBILITIES FOR CHANGING ACTIONS AND INTERACTIONS

1. Depatterning. *Alter repetitive patterns of action and interaction involved in problems. To do this, collaborate with young people and others to learn any or all of the following information:*

- How often does the problem typically happen (once an hour, once a day, once a week)?
- What is the typical timing (time of day/week/month/year) of the problem?
- What is the usual duration of the problem?
- Where does the problem typically happen?
- What does the young person, caregiver, or others who are around usually do when the problem is happening?

Then, collaborate with young people and others involved in changing one aspect of their actions or interactions through one or more of the following:

- Change the frequency/rate of the complaint or the pattern around the complaint.
- Change the location of the performance of the complaint.
- Change the duration of the complaint or the pattern around the complaint.
- Change the time (hour/time of day/week/month/year) of the complaint or the pattern around the complaint.
- Change the sequence of events involved in or around the complaint.
- Interrupt or otherwise prevent the occurrence of the complaint.
- Break up any previously whole element of the complaint into smaller elements.
- Reverse the direction of striving in the performance of the problem [paradox].
- Link the occurrence of the complaint to another pattern that is a burdensome activity [ordeal].
- Change the body behavior/performance of the complaint.

2. Repatterning. *Establish new patterns in place of problems by identifying and encouraging the use of solution patterns of action*

continued

Table 5.2, continued

and interaction through one or more of the following:

- Find out about previous solutions to the problem including partial solutions and partial successes.
- Find out what happens when the problem ends or starts to end.
- Find out about any helpful changes that happened before treatment began [pretreatment change].
- Search for contexts in which the young person or other feels competent and had good problem-solving or creative skills.
- Find out why the problem isn't worse.
- Use rituals of continuity, stability, and connection.

---

to act and interact differently; it simply suggests some possibilities for practitioners and clients.

The following case examples illustrate some possibilities for changing patterns of action and interaction.

FRAN: "DO YOU WANT TO DANCE?"

Fran came to see me because of a concern she had with her 11-year-old son, Benji. When the boy did not get his way, he would grab onto her clothes and yell at her. She reported that he would not let go of her clothes until she gave in. She was extremely frustrated because, not knowing what else to do, she gave in to him every time. In addition, her clothes were getting ruined from Benji's hanging onto them, stretching and occasionally tearing them. During our conversation, Fran and I talked about many different things. One was her position in a symphony orchestra and her love of music.

I asked Fran, "What does your family think about your being in the symphony?"

"My husband loves it, but my son can't stand classical music," she replied.

"That must make it hard to practice at home," I followed.

The woman smiled and said, "No, it doesn't, because I don't practice at home. I practice at our rehearsal site."

Confused, I inquired, "Well how do you know that he doesn't like classical music?"

"Because every time I turn it on at home he leaves the room. I should say, he runs out of the room," she answered.

As the mother spoke those words, she began to smile and laugh. It was as if the proverbial "lightbulb" went on. She said, "I know what to do. The next time he grabs my clothes I'll just run into the living room and turn on classical music."

I encouraged her, "Sounds great!"

The next session with Fran was scheduled for two weeks later. She began by describing how, after telling her he could not go to a friend's house after dark, Benji reached for her clothes. However, with Benji following close behind, Fran managed to get into the living room and turned off the stereo. When the classical music came on, Benji yelled at her, "Turn that crap off!" After a brief delay, he lunged toward her in an attempt to grab her clothing again. This time, however, Fran responded differently. Whereas in the past she had moved away from his attempts to grab her clothes, this time she moved toward her son and said, "Do you want to dance? I love to dance and your father's not here. . . . " She proceeded to grab his arms as if to dance with him. Benji immediately pulled his arms back and said, "What are you doing? You're a freak!" and ran out of the room.

Fran then turned off the music and proceeded to leave the room. As she did, her son came back around the corner and went after her. She again pursued him and said, "I don't need music to dance. Common!" Once again, Benji ran from her and stood behind the kitchen table where she could not reach him. From that point the pattern of him grabbing onto her clothes had been altered.

Of course, the best ideas are the ones that work. But it is important to encourage young people and others to consider *any* new ideas and not worry about finding "right" ones. In general, people are usually more invested trying something new if they feel like they have made a contribution to the development of the idea. So when we hear ideas from clients we try to draw those out further by saying, "Tell me more about that idea," and asking, "How might that work for you?"; "What do you need to do to make that happen?"; "What will be your first step in putting this idea in motion?"; and "What, if anything, can others do to help to put this idea into motion?"

As discussed previously, many clients do not have specific ideas about what to do differently. In these cases we want to continue to collaborate with young people and others to see what ideas might be generated. We can also tell stories, offering metaphorical possibilities and solutions, offer straightforward anecdotes about how other clients solved similar problems, or make suggestions based on how clients understand their patterns. The ideas generated are only *ideas*—that is, clients can accept or reject them. And we always bear in mind that if what we are doing isn't working, we need to try something else.

KEITH: "LONGER, PLEASE"

A young boy, Keith, was brought to see me because he screamed very loudly when he did not get his way. His mother, Louise, had grown tired of this behavior and was at her wits' end. I explored with Louise the pattern of interaction and the sequence of events that seemed to occur between her and her son. I learned that the longest Keith had screamed was about 30 seconds (with short breaks to breathe) because Louise would give in every time. She said, "I just can't take it so I give him what he wants."

Although there were several areas to explore regarding changing the pattern, Louise continued to go back to the length of the screaming. Therefore, I asked her if we could spend some time exploring that aspect of the concern. She agreed. When I asked if she had any specific ideas about what might work, she stated that she did not. She did, however, say that she was "open to any and all suggestions." I then encouraged her to consider the possibility of changing the length of the time that Keith spent screaming.

I said, "This may sound weird, so please bear with me. You said that the longest Keith has screamed for is about 30 seconds. It becomes too much for you and you give in. What do you think would happen if you encouraged him to scream for a longer period of time?"

Louise's first reaction was to say, "I couldn't do that. I couldn't take it."

I followed, "I certainly can understand that. But do you really think he would?"

Louise smiled. "I see what you're saying. He wouldn't expect me to tell him to scream longer because I always tell him to stop."

"That's what I was thinking," I replied.

As we continued to talk, I reminded Louise that we wanted to think as creatively as we could without trying to find the correct answer. Further, whatever was tried needed to be something she agreed with and would actually follow through on. Finally, if something didn't work, we would modify or abandon it. We came up with a plan where the next time Keith did not get his way and began to scream, she would wait him out. To do this she would focus on her watch and time the length of his scream. When he quit, she would encourage him to scream longer, perhaps for two or three minutes.

The evening following the session Louise told Keith "no" and he began to scream. At first she felt herself drifting back into her old pattern of trying to get him to stop. She quickly caught herself, sat down in a chair, and glanced down at her watch to keep time. Surprised by this, Keith looked at his mom, tried to distract her, and then stopped screaming. Louise immediately responded to the silence, "Twenty seconds of screaming isn't enough. You need to scream for at least two minutes to make sure you got it all out. You owe me another minute and forty seconds." Keith was shocked by his mother's reaction. He grunted and left the room. A short while later, Louise told Keith "no" for something else and as he took a deep breath to scream, she looked down at her watch. Keith stopped and again left the room. The pattern had been disrupted.

In the next session, I explained to Keith that it was perfectly fine for him to get upset. However, there were better ways of letting his mom know how he felt. We then proceeded to work on ways that he could let her know how he was feeling and what he needed.

In the previous case example, a small change was enough to alter the problem pattern. Other situations may require more action on the part of one or more people involved. The following case illustrates this.

Maria: "My Friends"

A family of four came to therapy because the oldest daughter, Maria, had been staying out all night, partying with her friends. Maria was 18 years old, and her parents were considering throwing her out of the home but wanted to try to "salvage" things before it reached that point. As the parents described their situation, they stated that, on an average, Maria would stay out late at least four times a week. I explored with Maria and the family what happened on those evenings when she made the choice to remain out all night. The parents stated that her friends were a negative influence her. Maria disagreed. I then talked with all involved about what was different on the nights that she chose to stay home or came in early.

Maria made it clear that when she didn't go out it was because she didn't feel like it. When I asked her how she got herself to stay home or come in early she said, "I don't know." Staying with the influence of social relationships and friends, in particular, I then asked her in what ways her friends had been part of her life. Maria stated that her friends were very important to her and helped her to stay out of trouble. I followed, "Tell me more about how they help you to stay out of trouble, because I can see why your parents are having trouble seeing that." Maria explained that her friends supported her "at all costs."

When I questioned her about this further, she stated, "There have been plenty of times I came home early because they told me I needed to."

"Really?" I inquired. "How did you get yourself to follow their advice?"

"I just figured they were right and went home. They really didn't want me to get in trouble," she explained.

Curious, I asked, "Do your friends know how serious things are right now? That your parents have about had it with you and are considering having you leave home?"

After a brief pause, she responded, "No. They would be mad at me. They pretty much think my parents let me do what I want because that's what I told them."

"So if they really knew what was going on and how your parents felt, what would they do?" I asked.

"They would tell me to listen to my parents," Maria stated.

"Those do sound like friends who care about you and your parents," I re-marked. "Have your parents met your friends?"

Maria's father then chimed in, "No, she never brings them to the house. We wish she would."

We developed a plan where Maria's friends would come to her house so her parents could meet and get to know them. We also explored how at times Maria herself had taken the initiative to come home on time or stay home more frequently. The family transitioned out of therapy after seven sessions. At that point the parents had met Maria's friends. They liked Maria's friends and let them know that they appreciated them looking after Maria. However, it was also made clear that Maria was not to stay out all night while living at home— which was a point that all her friends agreed with. The concern with Maria staying out all night was resolved.

In the preceding case example the influence of family and social rela-tionships was apparent. In fact, what could have been seen as a negative influence—friendships and social relationships—turned out to be a pos-itive influence. In addition, exploration revealed that there were times when Maria's behavior had been different—when she had stayed home all night or come in early. We want elicit and evoke such solution pat-terns, including abilities, competencies, and strengths. The idea is not to convince young people and others that they have solutions and compe-tencies, but rather to ask questions and gather information in a way that highlights for them what they do. For example, we would not say, "You can do it! Look at all your strengths!" This would invalidate clients who are experiencing difficulty and pain. Instead, we ask questions such as "How were you able to do that?" and "What did you do differently at that time?"

A position of curiosity can be helpful in learning about times when young people or others have had some sort of influence over the problem at hand. Even when they appear to be stuck, there *are* times when they haven't experienced their problems in full force or when they expected to. These are exceptions. In our explorations with clients, we *presuppose* the existence of exceptions and aim to gain clear, action descriptions of them. For example, a therapist might ask, "From what I understand, usually you would have just backed down in the face of intimidation like that, but you didn't that one time. What did you do that was different that time? How did you get yourself to do it?" The goal is to find out what happened, when it happened, and what needs to happen in the future so that the solution pattern occurs more deliberately and with more frequency.

To reiterate, it is not uncommon for clients to have difficulty identify-ing what they did differently or what worked for them. Asking questions about exceptions helps clients to at least temporarily reorient their attention toward the influence they have over problems rather than the influence problem has had on them in the past. It also can be helpful for therapists to offer multiple-choice options to see if something that came out of a conversation resonates with them, as well as to offer other possibilities for future situations. For example, a therapist might say, "I'm curious as to whether it was thinking of your family, or friends, or something else that made a difference for you." Clients often affirm one of the choices or respond, "No, what really helped me was...."

Finally, we aim for small changes. We don't say, "Tell me about a time recently when you didn't have the problem" or "When were things better?" The responses of young people and others to such inquiries are not surprising: "I always have the problem," or "It's never better!" That's too big a leap for most clients. Because their orientation is generally toward the problem and what is not working, it is too much for them to turn 180 degrees and look at when the problem is completely absent. Therefore, we might inquire, for example, "Tell me about a time recently when things went a little better" or "What's been different about the times when the problem has been a little less dominating in your life?" Smaller increments of change are typically more palatable for clients and easier to identify.

In the event that young people, parents, caregivers, or others continue to struggle to notice *any* solutions, including partial ones, consider the following:

- Whether they feel acknowledged and validated. Are we hearing what they want us to hear? Do they feel understood?
- Whether we understand their orientations and influences on their concerns as well as potential solutions.
- Whether we are working with them in ways that they consider to be helpful and consistent with their ideas about how change might come about.
- Whether we are trying to work from worst to best. Start with understanding how "bad" the problem is before exploring any shades of difference regarding its intensity (Bertolino & O'Hanlon, 2002).

SARA: "PICTURES OF YOU"

Sara, a young woman who had been raped suffered from repeated flashbacks. During these flashbacks she experienced body memories and cried uncontrollably. When I asked Sara what brought the flashbacks to an end, she stated that she would have a vision of her mother, who had been the one to discover her following the rape. Even though her mother had passed away, Sara found her a continuing source of comfort. I asked her how the picture comforted her, and she explained that when she looked at it, it reminded her of her mother's comforting voice.

I told Sara I had an idea and wanted to know if she would like to hear it. She said she did. I then told her that it seemed that if her mother was a source of comfort, maybe there was a way to have her mother "around more often." The young woman liked the idea. So I asked her if she had a small picture of her mother. She acknowledged that she did. I asked her if she would be willing to make multiple copies of it. She agreed. I then asked her to place copies of the picture in her purse, the glove compartment in her car, on her desk at work, and in other places where she was more amenable to flashbacks. When she started to notice herself experiencing a flashback, she could look at the picture of her mother and bring the flashback to an end. Sara did this and it helped her to change a problem pattern around the flashbacks. By knowing what helped to bring her flashbacks to an end, we could work to deliberately import a solution.

All problems have beginnings and endings. By exploring these moments in time solution patterns may be identified. To further learn about beginnings and endings we ask questions such as "How do you know when the problem is coming to an end?"; "What is the first sign that the problem is going away or subsiding?"; "How can the your friends, family, coworkers, etc., tell when the problem has subsided or started to subside?"; and "How do these problem-free activities differ from what you do when the problem is happening or present?"

KARIM: "WHAT'S YOUR JOB?"

Karim, a 16-year-old young man, was brought to see me due to fighting at school. Interestingly, although he had numerous problems at school, none of them were replicated when he played organized sports. Further, Karim had a vision of the future—to play college football. The following dialogue was taken from the second session of therapy with Karim.

Bob: *How's it been going at home?*

Karim: *Bad. . . .*

Bob: *How so?*

Karim: *My parents won't get off my case about the fights. They just need to leave it alone and everything would be fine.*

Bob: *They've been on your case a lot lately . . . mostly about the fights at school.*

Karim: *Yep. They don't get it. If people say stuff to me at school I'm gonna stand up to it. That's the way it is.*

Bob: *I can see how that might get to you.*

Karim: *It does.*

Bob: *And so that's what happens in school. What about on the football field?*

Karim: *What do you mean?*

Bob: *Well, I haven't heard about you getting ejected from a football game for fighting. In fact, have you ever even had a personal foul called on you?*

Karim: *No way.*

Bob: *How come?*

Karim: *I can't get kicked out of the game—that's what happens when you get a personal foul in high school sports.*

Bob: *So what? Haven't you been so mad that you felt like going after another player?*

Karim: *Oh yeah, all the time.*

Bob: *What do you do when there's an opposing player talking trash or one that shoves you after a play?*

Karim: *I just ignore it and get back to business.*

Bob: *How do you do that?*

Karim: *I just focus on the next play and getting it done and I let it go.*

Bob: *That's interesting. Tell me more about how you focus.*

Karim: *I just focus in on the game and eliminate everything else.*

Bob: *It sounds a bit similar to what I used to do when I was in high school. I played baseball and hockey, and on the days that I was pitching, people would say that it was like I was in a trance or something because I was sort of like a zombie. I was just focusing.*

Karim: *Exactly! I do that too—it's kind of hard to do anything on game days.*

Bob: *That's actually a very good skill that serves you well on the field. And it also raises my curiosity about you. What if you were to get suspended from school for fighting during football season—what would happen?*

Karim: *I'd miss a game—at least.*

Bob: *Are you willing to risk that?*

Karim: *No way.*

Bob: *OK, so what I'm wondering is how do you get yourself to focus on the field in those moments when you really need it?*

Karim: *It's the bigger picture. I've got a job to do—to help my team to win.*

Bob: *What about at school—what's your job there?*

Karim: *I guess to get an education.*

Bob: *So fighting hasn't interfered with your job on the field but it has with your job in the classroom.*

Karim: *Yeah.*

Bob: *So how can that ability that you have to focus on the field be helpful to you when you're in school?*

Karim: *I see what you mean. Yeah, I think I just have to keep remembering what my job is on and off the field.*

Bob: *Your dad told me that you want to play college ball. Is that right?*

Karim: Yeah, I've got some colleges looking at me.

Bob: That's terrific. And adding a new element to your overall game wouldn't hurt—showing the ability to focus in and out of school—on different things. That's why we have academic All-American athletes each year in college sports. They do well in academics and in sports. I bet many coaches would find the ability of being able to focus a wonderful quality in a player—and perhaps a sign of maturity.

Karim: That's what my dad would say. I know I can focus better in school and I'm not going to ruin going to college because of some idiot who knows he can get me riled up.

Bob: It's not worth losing your dream is it?

Karim: No way.

Karim's behavior improved at school. He had no further fights and was able to maintain passing grades. A year later he was offered a full scholarship to play football for a university that was nationally ranked.

Although young people or others may be experiencing difficulties in specific areas of their lives, they often have competencies including strengths and abilities in other areas of their lives that can be helpful in solving the problem at hand. These different contexts include employment, school, hobbies, sports, clubs, or other areas where clients have special knowledge or abilities that can be a tapped into as resources for solving problems. These are *contexts of competence.*

Although abilities often exist, we may forget to inquire about them. For example, many parents say things such as, "He's horrible at home, but the neighbors think he's the most wonderful kid!" or "I don't get it, he's fine here but at school all he does is get in trouble." One of our tasks as therapists is to *assume* that young people have some abilities. It's a matter of asking questions to identify and evoke those competencies and then linking them to problem contexts.

ED AND CAMERON: "WE'RE A LOT ALIKE"

A family of four came to therapy with the concern that the oldest son, Cameron, 19, and his father, Ed, had been having repeated arguments. In the first session, I asked both Ed and Cameron how they had managed to keep things from completely bottoming out. Both seemed genuinely surprised at the question. Ed went first: "I think it's because we both realize that we're a lot alike. Maybe too alike." To this, Cameron replied, "So we butt heads constantly. We work together and we argue about most things."

After I obtained some clear descriptions regarding each person's concern, I returned to the initial question: "When it's really heading downhill, what prevents things from getting worse?"

Cameron was the first to reply. "We know when enough is enough and when we need to come together again."

I asked, "How much is enough?"

"When we start yelling at one another—arguing is one thing—yelling is another. When we start yelling it's time to stop," offered Ed.

"When it reaches that point, what do you do to stop it and not let it deteriorate further?" I inquired.

Ed answered, "One of us apologizes. Then the other does the same and we hug. We can then sit down and start working in a civil way again." The remainder of the therapy was spent on finding ways that Ed and Cameron could come together prior to reaching the point of yelling, thereby changing the pattern.

Problems are not static; they get better, then worse, then better again, and so on. Sometimes when problem situations don't seem to be improving, clients have mechanisms in place to keep them from completely bottoming out. These mechanisms are other kinds of abilities, strengths, and resources and can be useful in altering the direction of change. One way to explore this idea is to have the client think of the worst possible state that a young person or other could be in and explain why their problem isn't that severe. This normalizes and helps put things in perspective. It also gives you information about how clients keep themselves from getting into worse trouble. Another way to do this is to ask the young person or other to compare any incident of the problem to its worst manifestation and explain what is different about the times the problem is less severe.

I often tell my supervisees and students, "The clients you're working with have had experiences in life dealing with all sorts of concerns and conditions. Some of those things were present before you got involved and some will occur later. Consider asking your clients, 'How have you managed to keep things from getting worse when they could have? How have you stayed afloat and what will allow you to keep going when we're finished meeting?'" These and the questions offered earlier can orient young people and others involved to whatever aspects of themselves, others, or their situations, however small, have worked to any degree. The preventative mechanisms can help to build hope for clients when they feel or think that nothing is going right.

DAVID: THE OLD BALL GAME

David, a teenager, was brought to therapy by his father. David and his father had been very close since he was about 7 years old. He would follow his father around the house and they would spends lots if time together. One of their favorite activities was to attend baseball games together. As time passed, David began to spend more and more time with his friends. This meant less time with his father. Around the age of 16, David began getting into trouble. Initially he was charged with breaking and entering. Finally, he was charged with a felony, stealing, and sentenced to residential placement in a juvenile facility.

Over the course of a year, David was able to earn the right to go on weekend passes with his father. One August weekend, David's father picked him up from the juvenile facility. As they were driving along, David's father pulled out a pair of baseball tickets. He said to his son, I'm sure you want to go see your friends because you don't come home much, but I figured I'd ask anyway. Do you want to go to this game?" David began to cry and said, "I didn't think you'd ever want to be around me after what I'd done." His father responded, "I didn't think you would ever want to be around me because I wasn't cool anymore." The two went on to share a few laughs and tears together. Today, David and his father are committed season ticket holders.

Events such as attending baseball games together can be considered rituals. They occur daily, weekly, monthly, yearly, seasonally, or on holidays. Rituals are consistent activities that provide stability and promote connection between young people, family members, and others. In their research, Steve and Sybil Wolin (1993) found that children who had faced adversity in childhood but did not develop many dysfunctional patterns in adulthood had grown up in environments with no apparent disruption in family rituals. In other words, everyday routines and activities remained a constant in these children's lives. There included, daily, weekly, monthly, seasonal, and yearly rituals. The Wolins found that children whose rituals were disrupted didn't do as well. The following story from my own life illustrates the importance of rituals.

WILL: "I'M BACK"
When I was in the fifth grade I made friends with a boy named Will. We lived within a half-mile of each other and Will would visit me and my family frequently. In fact, Will's visits came to be routine and predictable. Most evenings he would show up at the back door of my home precisely as our family was beginning to have dinner. We gradually came to understand that while Will's home life was chaotic and unpredictable, at my home things tended to be routine and consistent. Each evening my mom would make enough food for a small army, which was necessary with seven children, and there was always plenty of food, conversation, and camaraderie. Will could just blend in as one of the family. Will's routine remained consistent for several years until our family moved to Massachusetts when I was in the eighth grade.

Years passed, and after I graduated from high school, our moved back to Missouri. Then coincidence happened. One day, Will spotted my sister Mary driving on the highway. Although approximately four years had passed, he recognized Mary, turned around, and followed her home. From that point, Will began to come around regularly again, and in fact lived in our home for a while. It seemed that Will had found his stability again.

Though rituals, Will found continuity and stability in his life and with others. He sought out consistency through social relationships. At my house Will knew he would not intentionally be made fun of, would have enough to eat, and would be around people who enjoyed his company. For many people from chaotic, abusive, alcoholic, or other detrimental environments, rituals that connect them to others and provide consistency can make a significant difference in helping them to deal with adversity in life.

Regardless of the context (home, residential, foster care, etc.), part of what we can do with young people who have experienced disruption is to help them to restore rituals that have been interrupted by their life changes, or help them to create new ones (Bertolino & Thompson, 1999). These are rituals of *continuity or stability*—habits that help establish some stability or connection to themselves or others in their lives.

Clearly, different families have different orientations to their concerns. Some respond better to changes in their views and perspectives, and some prefer to take action in their lives. Others opt for some combination of the two. What is essential is that practitioners collaborate with young people and others to maximize the general effects that account for the majority of change in psychotherapy outcomes.

Chapter 6

A Work in Progress: Building on Change

THIS CHAPTER EXPLORES NUMEROUS AVENUES FOR IDENTIFYING, amplifying, and building on changes in therapy with adolescents, young adults, and families. It also focuses on ways of collaborating with clients to evaluate progress and plan next steps. Last, because all mental health professionals encounter logjams in their work with young people and families, an array of possibilities to negotiate what seem to be therapeutic impasses are offered.

ARE YOU WITH ME? SUBSEQUENT SESSIONS AND BEYOND

With few exceptions (e.g., youth in residential placements), we never know for sure whether young people and others will return for future sessions. As discussed in Chapter 3, at the end of the session we can check in by using any of the following questions:

- How was the session/meeting for you?
- What was helpful or unhelpful?
- Did we talk about what you wanted to talk about?
- Did we work on what you wanted to work on?
- How was the pace of our conversation/session/meeting?
- Was there anything missing from our session?
- Is there anything I should have asked that I did not ask?
- Is the way we approached your concern/situation fitting with the way you expect change to occur?

- Are there any changes you would recommend if we were to meet again?
- Did you feel heard and understood?
- Is there anything you would need me to do differently if we were to meet again?
- How would you explain your experience in therapy today to others who might be curious?

Learning about young people's and other's perceptions of what transpired in therapy helps us should there be future sessions. Clients teach us what is working for them (to any degree) and what is not. Recall that most young people and others will not voluntarily tell us about their experiences in therapy. It is up to us to ask.

We do not want to assume that clients will make subsequent appointments and return to therapy. Therefore, it is generally a good idea to ask young people and others involved what they would like to do—that is, would they like to schedule another session? If so, when? Some will want to meet weekly; others will prefer every other week, and so on. If clients ask us for our opinions about how to proceed we can say, "My sense is that we should go with what makes most sense for you. Would you like to come back next week, or the week after, or...?" In many cases those involved already have an idea and may want to see if what they're thinking is okay. We also let them know that adjustments can be made at any time.

Spreading out sessions can be an excellent way of measuring change over time and of helping clients to feel connected. For example, we might meet with a young person or family for three consecutive weeks and then move into meeting in two- or three-week intervals. It is not unusual to see young people once a month or once every six or eight weeks.

Particularly when change has occurred in the direction of goals, lengthening times between sessions can be useful in observing changes over an extended period of time. It also helps young people and others to stay on track and hold course with the changes they've made, as they know they will be returning in the future. Chapter 2 stressed the importance of collaborating with clients to learn about their preferences for meeting arrangements. Because these preferences can change, we want to check in with clients at the end of every session.

Many young people do not *choose* to attend therapy. Thus, we must remember that they may voice displeasure with scheduling future appointments. If someone other than the young person is scheduling future appointments, we still need to acknowledge the young person. We can also ask, "What might make coming here again a little better for you?" Even if our questions are met with little or no response, or with sarcasm, it is important that we offer opportunities for every person involved to give his or her perspective.

GETTING STARTED IN
FUTURE SESSIONS

In working with young people and families, much can transpire in between sessions. With this in mind, we want to begin all sessions by extending permission to those involved to begin where they feel most comfortable. We continue to acknowledge and validate and help young people and others to feel heard and understood as they convey their stories. Furthermore, we continue to create a climate that promotes hope and possibilities for future change. Here are some possible questions to get things going:

- Can you tell me a little bit about how things are in relation to the last time we met?
- What's been different since the last time we met?
- What's your sense about how things are going now, compared to last time?
- The last time we met, you mentioned that on a scale of one to ten, things were at a five. Where would you say things are today?

The ways that young people and others respond in second and subsequent sessions are numerous. Some will report new concerns or problems. Others will express indifference, stating that their situations are "the same." Still others will identify changes that may have occurred. Regardless, we want to stay with them to learn what directions, old, new, or modified, they want to take in therapy.

For those clients, particularly parents and caregivers, who report new concerns or problems, what transpired between sessions is often looming large in their minds. Simply acknowledging those concerns helps many to move on. Other clients need more than acknowledgment. Additionally, sometimes it is unclear whether the concerns they are describing are more significant than the ones discussed in previous sessions. In these cases it is imperative that therapists talk with those involved to determine the weight of the present concerns. The only way to know is to check in with our clients. One way to do this is to summarize both the goals that were previously set and the current complaints and then ask clients which ones are most concerning. Following are some ways of entering into these types of conversations.

Would you say that the concerns you've been talking about today take precedence over the ones we discussed last week?

In out last session you mentioned that [a particular problem] was really concerning you and was something that you wanted to focus our attention on. Based on the concerns you've mentioned today, do you think our time might be best spent on what we discussed last week or this week?

If it's all right with you, I'd just like to make sure we're talking about what you want to talk about. I can see that you've got a few concerns. Would you rather spend this time talking about the concerns you're having now or the ones we discussed last week?

For some, acknowledgment of their current concerns is enough for them to return to previously established directions and goals. For example, a parent might say, "Well, I am concerned about my son's grades, but I'm more concerned about him staying out all night. Let's talk about that." Another might say, "I'm not as worried about his staying out all night as I am him flunking out of school. I think we should talk about that." Still another parent might say, "I want to work on them both."

Without feedback from those involved, therapists may gravitate toward what they think needs to change. With the exception of clients who are potentially putting themselves or others in danger, young people and others involved must be allowed to choose the directions of therapy.

It is natural for goals to change from session to session. But, whenever new concerns arise, we should, at some point, ask about what has transpired in relation to previously established goals. Otherwise positive change that may have occurred could go unnoticed. By identifying positive changes, however small, we can help young people and others to notice that change is always happening. We can also help them to learn more about the influence they have over their concerns and problems. This can serve as a source of empowerment for future change. What clients did to bring about the change may also be helpful with other concerns in the present or the future. The following case example illustrates the importance of exploring future change.

ROGER: A BRIEF UPDATE
Fifteen-year-old Roger had been staying out long after curfew, until 3:00 or 4:00 A.M. In the initial session, his father indicated that this is what brought

him and his son to therapy and what he wanted to see change. At the next session, the father related that Roger had been truant from school during the previous week. After acknowledging this concern and learning more about it, I asked the father if he was most concerned with Roger's staying out late or having been truant. To this the father responded that the truancy was a bigger concern.

Before proceeding, I inquired, "Before we talk about this further, could you give me a brief update on what's happened with the situation of Roger coming in late?"

To this the father replied, "Well, he didn't stay out late this past week, so that's better."

I followed, "Really? Were you surprised?"

"A little," answered the father. Before moving onto the concern of truancy, I was able to identify and amplify positive change by asking Roger and his father a series of questions, including: "Roger, what did you do differently? Even though you thought about coming in late a few times, how did you get yourself to come in when you were supposed to?" and "What did you do when you found that Roger was coming in on time each night?"

If there is no exploration of change in relation to previous goals, examples of positive change might be overlooked and those involved might become overwhelmed—feeling as if their lives are *only* problematic and unmanageable (Bertolino & O'Hanlon, 2002). The following case example illustrates this point.

JAKE: "A MIRACLE IN AND OF ITSELF"

A 17-year-old, Jake, was brought to therapy by his father and mother. The parents had divorced three years earlier, but both continued to be invested in the welfare and well-being of their son, and they attended all sessions together. The parents had several concerns regarding their son, including his failing grades, smoking marijuana, coming in very late every night, and not getting a job to help pay for his car insurance, which he had agreed to do months earlier.

Although there had been small indications of change over the course of about four months, I felt that our progress was generally very poor. It seemed that even when change occurred, it was minimal and often overridden by some sort of crisis that happened between sessions. Finally, I said aloud in a session, "I just wanted to share something with all of you. I've been thinking about it for a couple of weeks now. I don't really feel like I've been helpful to you. It seems to me that things seem to get a little better, but then they slip back. It feels to me like quicksand in some ways."

Following my statement, Jake's mother remarked, "I think you've been very helpful."

I inquired, "In what way?"

She responded, "Jake has been doing much better in English and math and it looks like he has a chance of graduating now. We couldn't have said that before."

Jake added, "Yeah, I am going to pass and I've got a job interview next week."

The father then followed, "And he does at least tell me when he's going to be late now. That's a miracle in and of itself."

It then became clear to me that the family members had different ideas about how the therapy had been proceeding and the changes that had occurred. This, in turn, taught me about what I needed to do more of to be helpful to the family. Had I not asked, I might have made changes that were unhelpful in the eyes of the family members.

Without the identification of progress and positive change, therapists can begin to feel hopeless and as if those involved cannot be helped. In contrast, by identifying change that may have occurred between sessions, therapists can promote hope and facilitate future change in other areas of young people and others' lives.

What's Different? Identifying and Amplifying Change

Whether changes have been reported by those involved or revealed though conversations with therapists, it is important to identify and amplify them. To assist with the processes of identifying change therapists can ask:

- What have you noticed that has changed with your concern/ problem/self/situation?
- What specifically seems to be going better?
- Who first noticed that things had changed?
- Who else noticed the change?
- When did you first notice that things had changed?
- What did you notice happening?

Amplifying change involves determining how the change occurred and what difference it makes in young people's and others' lives and in relation to their goals. To amplify change we ask:

- How did the change happen?
- What were the influences (family, culture, spirituality, etc.)?
- What did you find worked for you?
- What did you do?
- How did you do that?
- How did you get yourself to do that?

- How did you get that to happen?
- How was that different than before?
- How did that help you?
- Where did you get the idea to do it that way?
- What did you tell yourself?

All types of questions may bring about only vague answers. In such cases, therapists must work to translate vague descriptions into clear, observable ones. For example, if an adolescent responds to the question "How did the change happen?" with "I just acted different" or "It just did," it is important that the therapist ask him or her what specifically he or she did differently. Once again, ambiguity can lead to confusion for therapists *and* clients.

When young people, particularly, adolescents, respond with, "I don't know," we do not need to worry. There are instances when those involved are unable to identify specifics regarding what contributed to positive change. In such cases we can speculate aloud about what might have influenced the change. For example, we might ask, "If you had to guess and there were no wrong answers, what would you say made a difference for you?" or "If your mother/brother/teacher, etc., were here, what would he/she say has contributed to the change you've experienced?"

If young people or others involved struggle with this type of speculating, we can offer possibilities into the conversation. For example, we might say, "Do you think it's possible that [therapist's speculation] might have contributed to the change you've experienced?" What is most important is what those involved attribute the change to. If they attribute the significant portion of positive change to the therapist, the actions of others, medication, or some other external entity, the likelihood that the change will last long-term decreases. This is in part because accountability can be lost once external factors are removed or diminish as causal change agents in the eyes of clients (Bertolino & O'Hanlon, 2002).

Whether change happens before or during therapy, and whether it results from young people's or others' actions or from happenstance, we want to enhance the effects of change by helping clients to see change and the maintenance of it as a consequence of their own efforts (Duncan & Miller, 2000; Miller et al., 1997). We want young people and others involved to attribute the major part of the change to who they are as people and to their personal actions. We *blame* them for changing for the better. The following questions can assist with this process:

- Who are you such that you've been able to ... ?
- Who are you such that you've been able to stand up to ... ?

- Who are you such that you've been able to get the upper hand with . . . ?
- What does it say about you that you've been able to face up to adversity?
- What kind of person are you that you've been able to overcome . . . ?
- Where did the wherewithal come from to . . . ?
- What kinds of inner strengths do you draw on in moments of difficulty/adversity?
- What kinds of inner qualities do you possess that allow you to manage difficulty/adversity?
- What would others say are qualities that you possess that help you when you need them?

Even when young people or others have benefited from external factors we aim to help them attribute the major portion of change to themselves. This helps to promote accountability and self-efficacy. These questions can assist with this:

- You mentioned that you feel/think that medication/therapy, etc. is helping. How are you working with it to better your life?
- In your mind, what does medication/therapy, etc. allow you to do that you might not have otherwise done?
- What percentage of the change you've experienced is a result of medication/therapy, etc. and what percentage do you think is the result of your own doing?
- As a result of *feeling* better from medication/therapy, etc., what are *you* then able to *do*?

By helping clients to attribute change to internal qualities, we contribute to the idea that even though external factors may aid in producing change, it is clients who are in charge of their lives.

We can also use speculation as a way of attributing change to young people and others. We can speculate about internal changes that suggest that those involved might be changing their perspectives or behavior and evolving in ways that support new stories of growth, resiliency, and hope. To do this, we again use *conjecture,* and speculate from a position of curiosity. In this way clients have the space to either accept or reject the speculations, depending on whether or not they fit for them. Here are a few questions to assist with using speculation in this way:

- I'm wondering if perhaps part of the reason things are going better for you is because you are becoming more responsible/more mature/growing up, etc. Perhaps you are becoming the type of person you want to be and learning new ways of managing your life.

- Is it possible that the change you've experienced might be related to your ...?
- Is it possible that the change you've experienced might be related to your learning more about yourself?
- Is it possible that the change you've experienced might be related to your wanting to lead a different life?
- Is it possible that the change you've experienced might be related to your becoming more mature in dealing with life's circumstances?
- Is it possible that the change you've experienced might be an indication that you're taking back control of your life?
- Is it possible that the change you've experienced might be an indication that you've turned the corner with ...?
- Is it possible that the change you've experienced might be a sign of a new, preferred direction for you?

The benefits of speculation are numerous. First, it attributes change to young people's and others' own doing. Because our speculations are about positive qualities or actions, clients are less likely to reject them. Young people rarely say, "No, I'm not getting smarter and more mature. I'm getting dumber and more immature." Second, even if our speculations are off-target, because they highlight competencies, those involved will at least ponder them. Furthermore, for some, therapist speculations will trigger new ideas about what the change might be due to. Speculations can be a starting point that clients add on to. The following case example illustrates this point.

Tony: "I Also Think"
Fourteen-year-old Tony had been brought to therapy by his mother. Tony and a friend had stolen his friend's mother's ATM card and withdrawn $2000. Tony had also been failing his classes at school. Over the course of seven months of therapy, Tony made drastic changes in his life. First, he made amends and paid restitution for the theft. He also raised his grades in school by turning in his homework and doing extra credit. Finally, he began helping his mother out at home by mowing the lawn and cleaning. When I asked how he had made the changes, Tony remarked, "I'm not sure." I followed with speculation: "I wonder if it's because you are becoming more mature and responsible. Maybe you're also thinking more about others, like your mom, for example." Following my speculation, Tony stated, "Yeah, I think that's part of it. I also think I'm just seeing that things need to be done and no one can do them but me. I've done it and I'm proud."

The use of speculation we can help young people and others to reauthor new stories that run counter to the problem-saturated ones that brought them to therapy, thereby "anchoring" the change (Bertolino, 1999). *Anchoring* means that the more people are able to connect with their internal experiences, including feelings and sensory perceptions, the more profound change can become. To help young people and others to connect internally with change, we can ask questions such as:

- When you were able to . . . , what did that feel like?
- When you saw your son/daughter . . . , what did that feel like?
- How did you experience that change inside?
- How was that feeling similar or different than before?
- What does it feel like to know that others may also benefit from the changes you've made?

As stated previously, most young people have had some positive internal experience that once made them feel joy, comfort, reassurance, and hope. Another possibility, then, is to again evoke such feelings from the past as a way of reorienting them to previous positive experiences. The following case example illustrates this idea.

ALEX: "AN A FEELS BETTER THAN AN F"

I once worked with a 15-year-old adolescent, Alex, who had received very poor grades at school—five Fs and one D. As with most teenagers, he did well in school in his early years. Through the sixth grade he was an A and B student. When he hit seventh grade, however, his grades dropped dramatically, without any particular, identifiable reason.

At the start of therapy, Alex was in the ninth grade and, according to his mother, had only been allowed to advance in school because school officials thought it would be "detrimental socially" to hold him back. As Alex began the ninth grade he was once again receiving mostly failing grades. After several months of therapy, Alex gradually began to raise his grades. As he was doing so, I asked him what it was like for him to have raised his grades. Alex replied, "It's okay" I then reminded him that even though it had been a few years since he had received the type of grades he was capable of, he hadn't forgotten what it felt like to get As, Bs, and even Cs. The feelings associated with those grades were very different than the ones he experienced while getting Ds and Fs. I then suggested to Alex that he might even be able to remember those feelings now—what it was like to have his mother put one of his papers with a "smiley face" on it on the refrigerator or the favorable reactions of his teachers when he did well. After I finished, Alex smiled and said, "Yeah, I remember how proud of me my mom used to be. I liked that. I felt real happy. She can be proud of me again. I like getting good grades. It makes me and my mom feel better." Alex finished his final quarter of the ninth grade with two As, three Bs, and two Cs—enough to pass the grade.

Like a snowball traveling downhill or a domino pushed-over that causes the whole line of dominos to fall, change in one area of a client's life can lead to further changes. With this in mind, when positive change has been identified and amplified, it can helpful to inquire about other possible changes that may have occurred. Here are questions to assist with this:

- What else have you noticed that has changed?
- What else is different?
- What difference has that made for you?
- What difference has that made with employment/school/home life, etc.?
- Who else has benefited from these changes?
- What difference has that made for him/her/them?

Although certain goals may have been identified at various points of therapy, it is not uncommon for other informal or secondary goals or areas also to be affected in some way. In addition, concerns that may not have been addressed in treatment or discussed in terms of goals may have been resolved or lessened in severity. It is therefore a good idea to ask young people and others about other positive changes or benefits that may have occurred in their lives as a result of the initial change.

Are We There Yet? Situating Change in
Relation to Goals and Preferred Futures

The relative significance of positive change is dependent on those involved. So when positive change has been identified, we want to learn from young people and others how that change relates to the established goals—that is, to what degree does the change indicate progress toward established goals? Has the concern or problem been resolved? What else needs to happen for therapy to be considered successful or for goals to be met? The following questions can be of assistance in determining this:

- How are you benefiting from the change you've experienced?
- What difference has the change made in your life?
- What will be different in the future as these changes continue to occur?
- In the future, what kinds of other changes do you think might occur that might not have otherwise come about?
- Who else might benefit from these changes? How so?
- In the future, what will indicate to you that these changes are continuing to happen?
- How does the change that's happened relate to the goals that we set?

- What difference has this change made in relation to your goals for treatment?
- To what degree have things improved?
- Has the problem that brought you here been resolved?
- What else needs to happen to make this problem fade from your life?
- What else, if anything, needs to happen so that you'll feel/think that the problem you came here for is manageable without therapy?
- What else, if anything, needs to happen so that you'll be convinced that the problem is no longer a problem?
- Last time, you indicated that if you were able to . . . , you would know that things were better. Now that you have achieved this, how do you see things?
- At the start of therapy you told me that things were at a four on a scale of one to ten. You also mentioned that you would know that therapy had been successful when. . . . That would represent an eight. Now that those things have happened, does that indicate to you that things are at an eight? What else, if anything, needs to happen for you to feel like you have met your goals?

LOGJAMS AND PERCEIVED IMPASSES: NEGOTIATING STUCKNESS

Young people inevitably experience ups and downs. They do worse at times and better at times, and there are shades between these ends of the continuum. When clients report that things are so-so, the same, unchanged, worse, or some variation thereof, we acknowledge and validate their internal experiences and views. Those involved need to feel that therapists understand their pain and suffering. At the same time, it is also important that we recognize that these perspectives are changeable.

In those cases, we want learn what hasn't worked and what has worked, to any degree. When therapeutic logjams seem to permeate therapy, we do not abandon our clients in favor of our theories. We stick with them, checking in on those involved. This helps to us to learn whether we are working with them in ways that are helpful or whether changes need to be made. Here are some questions that can assist with this process:

- In terms of our work together, what has been helpful or unhelpful? In what ways?
- Are there other things that you feel/think we should be discussing instead?
- Is there anything I should have asked that I have not asked?
- Has anything been overlooked?

- How satisfied are you with how things are going so far on a scale from one to ten, ten meaning you are completely satisfied with things?
- Are there any changes we should make at this point?
- Is there anything I should be doing differently?
- Is the way we've approached your concern/situation fitting with the way you expect change to occur?
- Is there a way to approach your situation that we have not yet considered?
- Has anything been missing from our sessions?

By checking in with those involved we can work toward gaining a clearer understanding of how they are viewing the therapeutic relationship and any associated processes.

Altering Therapist Views and Patterns

Just as clients can become stuck, therapists are at risk of working in ways that may be unhelpful. We all repeat patterns that may be more or less helpful given a particular context. One way of identifying therapist patterns is to videotape sessions. Because therapists don't always recognize when they are working in ways that are helpful or unhelpful, taping can reveal aspects of sessions that therapists might not otherwise remember. Once a tape has been made, the therapist reviews the tape and considers some of the following questions:

- What did I do well?
- How do I know it was helpful to the client?
- What should I consider doing more of in the next session?
- What should I consider doing differently in the future?
- What changes should I consider making in the next session?
- What difference might that make?

By reviewing a videotaped session the therapist can watch the therapeutic discourse unfold from a different position. This can help to generate new ideas and possibilities for future sessions. Another tack that can be helpful is to get a "second perspective" from another colleague or supervisor (Bertolino & O'Hanlon, 2002). Using the same or a similar set of questions, the person offering the second perspective can help to generate other ideas about what might be helpful in future sessions.

The new ideas generated ought to be shared with the individual, couple, or family. This is important four two reasons. First, we do not want to privilege the ideas of mental health professionals over young people and others involved. We want those involved to decide for themselves what fits and what does not. Just because a mental health professional believes in an idea does not mean that clients will feel or think the same. Next, we want to share many different ideas with young people and others as opposed to one or two that the therapist has selected. In this way, those involved are not just hearing the idea that the therapist likes the best. Instead, they hear a number of ideas and can determine what makes most sense and fits best with them.

One way of offering ideas that have been generated to young people and others is to say, "I reviewed the videotape last week and had some new thoughts that I would like to share with you, if that's okay." If you consulted a colleague or supervisor, you might say, "I reviewed the tape from last week with a colleague/supervisor and he/she had a few ideas that I would like to share with you, if that's okay." The following questions can then assist therapists in offering to young people and others involved new ideas that were generated through the aforementioned processes:

- Do any of these ideas stand out for you?
- Which ones specifically seem to stand out the most for you?
- What thoughts or ideas do you have as a result of hearing those ideas?
- What else comes to mind?
- How might these ideas be helpful to you?
- Are there other ideas you have as a result of listening to those I offered?

Reflecting Consultations

Another way of generating new ideas and negotiating impasses is by forming a consultation team made up of two to four practitioners. The team listens to the primary therapist from a not-knowing position—they assume no prior knowledge about the client. The task of the team is to generate new ideas from their own experience as a way of helping to move the therapy along or get things unstuck.

After the case summary has been given, the consulting therapists converse with one another. During this process, the primary therapist listens to the conversation. This allows the therapist to choose which reflections fit best with him or her. Following this, another therapist who has not been involved to this point interviews the primary therapist and asks questions such as:

- What stuck out for you?
- What was new to you?
- What else was new for you?

- What did you hear?
- What else did you hear?
- What new ideas do you have as a result of listening to the conversation?
- What will you consider doing differently as a result of having these new ideas?

Change Is Change: Being Mindful of Small Changes and Efforts

When client reports are ambiguous or vague (e.g., so-so, the same) we assume that there have been times when things have gone differently. We therefore work with those involved to identify and amplify any positive change, however small or microscopic, that may have occurred. We are mindful to acknowledge the difficulties that young people and others face, yet want to do this in ways that keep open the possibilities for positive change. For clients who report that things are the same or worse, we want to acknowledge their concerns and simultaneously keep possibilities open for future change. We can do this in several ways.

Using Strengths as a Countermeasure

One way to acknowledge the social realities of young people and others while searching for possibilities for change is to consider that there are often qualities and actions that keep them going and from deteriorating further. The same can be said for young people, parents, and caregivers who seem more ambivalent or pessimistic about change and say, "Yes, but. . . ." As discussed in the previous chapter, it is often helpful to learn about why things aren't worse. Here are some questions that can assist with this process:

- Why aren't things worse with your situation?
- What have you done to keep things from getting worse?
- What steps have you taken to prevent things from heading downhill any further?
- What else has helped things from getting worse?
- How has that made a difference for you/with your situation?
- What is the smallest thing that you could do that might make a difference with your situation?
- What could others do?
- How could we get that to happen a little now?

The following case example illustrates how the aforementioned questions can help in shifting the direction of change.

JOLANDA: "GOING DOWN THE DRAIN"
A family, consisting of a father, his wife, a mother, her boyfriend, and two boys, 14- and 9-years-old, respectively, came to therapy because the 14-year-old had been stealing car stereos, breaking curfew, and doing poorly in school. Along with two other clinicians, I was part of a reflecting team that worked with the family at a stuck point. During the initial part of the session, the mother, Jolanda, stated that she felt as if things were "going down the drain." During the conversation between members of the reflecting team, I responded to this comment by saying, "You know those sticky things they put in bathtubs to keep people from slipping and falling? I wonder what those sticky things are in this family— what will keep them from going down the drain even though they fall down sometimes?" After the team finished and the family members were asked about their experiences Jolanda responded, "I know what keeps things from going down the drain. We love each other." To this the therapist responded, "That's so nice to hear. And I'm curious, what difference does that make that you love each other?" Jolanda replied, "We can't give up, "so we pull together when things get rough." The therapist was then able to explore with the family members how they pull together during rough times and what they do differently when things start to get slippery. Then, in a later session, they discussed how the family members could utilize that ability more in the future.

By using questions such as those offered, therapists can identify and amplify very small changes that represent what is working in clients' lives. These can then be used as starting points for changing the momentum of treatment and for working toward more significant changes.

Share Credit for Change

The importance of the quality of the client's participation in therapy has already been discussed. When young people and others involved are left out of therapy processes we begin to see what looks like noncompliance or resistance. Likewise, when positive change has occurred but is being negated in some way (e.g., "It won't last" or "He's done that before") by a young person, parent, caregiver, or other, or when situations seem to be deteriorating, sometimes it is because clients do not feel as if they have made a valued or positive contribution to the change.

For example, family members can become adept at blaming one another or feeling blamed by others for causing problems, but they don't always get credit for their individual contributions when things go better. Other times parents who bring their children or adolescents to therapy and experience success begin having feelings of inadequacy. They will say things to themselves such as "I raised my daughter for 15 years and couldn't help her. Then I take her to a therapist and things change in a week. I must be a lousy parent." In these types of scenarios family members often make comments such as, "Yeah it's been better, but it won't last" or "You haven't seen the *real* Ellen yet." Such people tend to experience a "double whammy" of negativity: First, they feel like a failure for not being to fix the problem that led to therapy. Second, they feel invalidated when a stranger "fixes" the situation. Therefore, we recommend that therapists identify the contributions that parents, caregivers, and others involved have made to the lives of young people and share the credit for change (Bertolino, 1999).

The idea of sharing credit for change is not in conflict with attributing change to the qualities and actions of individuals. It is a situation of "both/and" as opposed to "either/or." We continue to help young people and others involved to attribute the major portion of significant change to themselves. We all have qualities and take actions that improve our lives. At the same time, we have had many experiences in life that have shaped who we are as individuals. As discussed in the previous chapter, these include interactions and relationships with others.

In sharing credit for change, we help clients to identify their contributions. One way is to openly give the client credit by saying:

- I'm impressed with how you instilled in your son/daughter, etc. the value of....
- I've noticed that your son/daughter, etc. holds the same value of ... that you do and I can't help thinking that he/she learned it from you.
- It seems to me that your son/daughter, etc. has learned the value of ... from you.

A second way is to evoke from clients something that they feel contributed to the change process:

- What part of your parenting do you think contributed most to your son's/daughter's, etc. ability to ... ?
- In what ways do you think you have been able to help your son/daughter, etc. to stand up to adversity?
- In what ways do you think you were of assistance in helping your son/daughter, etc. to stand up to ... and get back on track?

A third possibility is to ask the primary client (most often a young person) what contributions others have made to his or her life then share those with others who are involved:

- What did you learn from your mother/father, etc. about how to overcome ... ?
- Who taught you the value of ... ?

When parents and caregivers, in particular, feel their efforts have been recognized and are valued, negativity can be neutralized. Additionally, families who share credit for change, often experience a new sense of togetherness or spirit of family.

SLIPS AND SLIDES: MANAGING SETBACKS

Adolescents and young adults continue to face challenges as they grow and mature. Many young people and their families experience temporary setbacks or challenges in maintaining changes. We want those involved to know they may experience some ups and downs and that these fluctuations do not have to knock them off course. When young people or others experience setbacks, we find out about those difficulties and help them to orient toward exceptions and differences.

Setbacks also provide opportunities to learn about what worked and what did not. They are simply part of the terrain, part and parcel of what some young people experience in achieving their goals and preferred futures.

TRACY: "EVERYTHING'S CHANGED"

At the start of our sixth session, 23-year-old Tracy told me, "I feel like my old self again. I'm doing so much better." At one time Tracy had been self-mutilating by cutting her arms with broken glass or scissors, putting herself down through self-talk such as "I'm no good," "I'll never amount to anything," and "I'm a failure," not attending her university classes, and lying to her parents about how she was doing. Now it seemed to her that things had finally turned the corner for the better.

Two weeks later, Tracy showed for her appointment with me in tears. As she sat down she struggled to tell me what she was experiencing.

Bob: *It's okay to cry, Tracy.*

Tracy: [sobbing] *I know. I just can't believe it.*

Bob: *Tell me about that.*

Tracy: *Everything's changed.*

Bob: *Something's changed....*

Tracy: *... Yeah, I was doing so good and now ... I'm back to where I was.*

Bob: *I don't understand, can you tell me what has given you the idea that you're back to where you were?*

Tracy: *Everything was going fine. Then yesterday I found out that there was no way to pass my communications class because I've missed too many classes. Why should I even bother?*

Bob: *So your professor told you that?*

Tracy: *Yeah.*

Bob: *I'm sorry to hear that. What did you do when you got the news?*

Tracy: *I had to go to my next class.*

Bob: *You went to your next class? How did you muster up the strength to do that after what you had been told?*

Tracy: *[wiping her tears] Well, I can still pass my other two classes.*

Bob: *Okay. And what's confusing to me is that before you would have just gone home and given up.*

Tracy: *I would have.*

Bob: *So after class what did you do?*

Tracy: *I went home and called my mom.*

Bob: *What happened?*

Tracy: *She told me not to worry about it. I was doing better and that I could retake the class. But it still hurts; I feel like I failed.*

Bob: *I can see how you might feel that way.*

Tracy: *I do.*

Bob: *Do you mind if I ask you another question?*

Tracy: *Go ahead.*

Bob: *When you called your mom, did you lie to her?*

Tracy: *No.*

Bob: *Really? Did you cut on your arms?*

Tracy: *No.*

Bob: *So as upset as you were, you went to class and called your mom and were honest with her. You took care of yourself in good ways and didn't cut on yourself.*

Tracy: *That's true. I did take care of myself and didn't slip back.*

Bob: *Right. Somehow, even though you were rightfully upset, you kept things from becoming worse. Can you tell me more about what you did that helped you?*

Tracy: *I went to bed early. I felt a little better this morning, but then got sad again later.*

Bob: *So sleep helped a little. What else?*

Tracy: *Just talking to my mom. I'm going to call her again after this.*

Bob: *It sounds like you and your mom have been getting along better lately.*

Tracy: *We have. I think because I'm more honest with her now.*

Bob: *Okay. So getting sleep and talking with your mom helped. If you were to face another obstacle what will you do?*

Tracy: *I guess call my mom and I know I can talk to my sister, too.*

When young people and their families experience setbacks we want to collaborate with them to learn what helped them during such times. Next are a number of different questions that can be helpful in learning about exceptions to setbacks:

- When you hit that rough spot, what kept things from going downhill any further?
- How did you manage to bring things to a halt?
- What did you do?
- What helped you to bring it to an end?
- Who helped you?
- How were they helpful to you?
- How might they be helpful to you in the future?
- What signs were present that things were beginning to slip?
- What can you do differently in the future if things begin to slip?
- What have you learned about this setback?
- What will you do differently in the future as a result of this knowledge?
- What do you suppose your mother/father/teacher, etc. would say that you will do differently as a result of this knowledge?
- What do you suppose will be different as a result of your doing things differently?
- What might be some signs that you are getting back on track?
- How will you know when you're out of the woods with this setback?

Sometimes change can be "three steps forward and two steps backward." Setbacks can provide opportunities to learn and practice new skills. We therefore work with young people and others to manage their setbacks and build their "muscles of resilience."

REWRITING YOUNG LIVES IN PROGRESS: EXPERIENCING NEW IDENTITY STORIES

As change occurs with young people, their stories about themselves and their lives also change. In a sense, they are rewritten. Young people begin to see themselves differently and others see them differently. These new, emerging identity stories can give birth to hope and possibilities. When young people experience themselves in new ways they can feel a renewed sense of self. The following questions can assist with helping young people in reauthoring their self-narratives:

- What does your decision to stand up to . . . tell you about yourself?
- Now that you've taken your life back from . . . , what does that say about the kind of person you are?
- How would you describe yourself now as opposed to when you began therapy?

- What's it like to hear you describe yourself as ...?
- What effect does knowing that you've put... to rest have on your view of yourself?
- Can you speculate about how this view of yourself as ... is changing how you're relating to me right now?
- What do you think your friends would say/think about you since you have come to think of yourself as able to stand up for yourself?
- How do you think my view of you has changed since hearing you describe yourself as ...?
- How do you think your mother/father/teacher, etc. will be able to treat you differently now that he/she knows that you see yourself as a person who is capable of getting the upper hand with ...?

In addition, we can invite others who may be involved in therapy to share their views regarding changes that young people have made. We can do this by asking the following questions:

- What do you think your son's/daughter's, etc. decision to stand up to... tells you about him/her that you wouldn't have otherwise known?
- What effect is hearing that your son/daughter, etc. views himself/herself as... having on your relationship with him/her?
- How do you think your son's/daughter's, etc. new sense of himself/herself as... will affect your relationship with him/her?

Another way of helping young people to reauthor new stories is to document changes they have made. This is a way of orienting young people and others toward what is working, tracking change over time, and extending those changes into the future (Bertolino, 1999). One way of doing this is to say to young people:

Down the road, others may be curious as to how you went about overcoming.... Some people write letters to themselves, others keep journals, diaries, or scrapbooks, or create new ways of keeping track of the changes they've made. What might help you to document this journey that you've been on?

The following case example illustrates how this might be utilized with clients.

TINA: "EVERYTHING THAT GLOWS"
I consulted with a therapist who had been seeing Tina, a young woman who had been severely physically abused as a child. The woman had come to therapy

because she had been feeling "depressed and isolated." She was also an aspiring musician who, according to her therapist, tended to write "deeply somber" songs. When Tina began to experience a lifting of her depression, her therapist stated that she saw "a side of herself that she did not know existed." She described her client as "warm and glowing." I suggested that the therapist talk with the woman about how this warm, glowing presence and new sense of self might be reflected in her music. About two weeks later, Tina brought her guitar to the session and played her new song, "Everything That Glows." She then went on to record the song so that it would be a "reminder" to her of "what can be."

By documenting change we can orient young people toward the changes they've made and can continue to make in the future. Many people had parents who kept scrapbooks or posted good grades on the refrigerator. Clients can do the same type of thing by writing therapeutic letters—therapeutic letters can be written by therapists to clients or clients to themselves. For example, a therapist might say in a letter to client, "As you continue to move toward the future I hope you'll take the time to notice and appreciate the changes you've made." Clients' letters to themselves might highlight certain changes that have been made, obstacles that have been overcome, or goals they have for the future—that can be reviewed when clients need to be reminded of what they've accomplished and where they're headed in the future. The following questions can be used to ask young people and others about how they might document progress:

• What have you done in the past to remind you of what's important in your life?
• What can you do to remind yourself of the progress that you've made?
• What will help to remind you of where you're heading in the future?
• What will help you to reorient toward what's worked for you should you hit some turbulence in the future?
• How will that help you?

Whether in the form of a scrapbook, diary, song, video, or something else, documentation of change can serve as a resource should young people need emotional boosts. These changes, documented or otherwise, can be shared with people outside of the young person's immediate family. In other words, as their stories change we can move toward sharing these new narratives of hope and possibility in larger contexts. This is a way of strengthening the valued stories that have been created.

Young people make extraordinary changes every day. They don't have to be famous or appear on *60 Minutes*, 20/20, or *Oprah Winfrey* to share their new stories. We can help them to share their stories in other ways. One way to do this is to ask clients some or all of the following questions:

- Who else needs to know about the changes that you've made?
- What difference do you think it would make in others' attitudes toward you if they had this news?
- Who else could benefit from these changes? How so?
- Would it be better to go along with others' old views about you or to update them on these new developments?
- What ideas do you have about letting others know about the changes that you've made?
- What might be a first step toward making this happen?

If young people, parents, caregivers, or others have identified ways of sharing change in larger social contexts, we can then investigate how to put those ideas into action. For example, parents might cofacilitate a parenting group. An adolescent might speak to a group of youth about his or her experiences. If clients don't have ideas we can give suggestions. With younger clients we might suggest that they show their scrapbooks to others—extended family, friends, teachers, and so on. Often younger adolescents, in particular, will be excited about showing their "collections of competence" to others.

When young people have experienced success and competence they can become consultants to others who have experienced similar difficulties. Freeman, Epston, and Lobovits wrote that when a child has taken significant steps toward revising his or her relationship with the problem, he or she "has gained knowledge and expertise that may assist others grappling with similar concerns" (1997, p. 126). Consistent with this idea, David Epston and Michael White (& "Ben," 1995) have discussed the idea of "consulting your consultant." They state:

> When persons are established as consultants to themselves, they experience themselves as more of an authority on their own lives, their problems, and the solution to these problems. This authority takes the form of a kind of knowledge or expertise which is recorded in a popular medium so that it is accessible to the consultant, therapist, and potential others. (pp. 282–283)

Another possibility is to ask young people to serve as consultants. We can heed their advice by asking some of the following questions:

- Periodically I meet with others who are experiencing the same or a similar problem to the one you've faced. From what you now know, what advice might I give them about facing their concerns?

- If new clients were to ask me to tell them how previous clients have solved similar problems in the past, what would you suggest that I say to them?
- What suggestions would you have for therapists or other mental health professionals who in the future might work with clients who have experienced the same or similar problems?

Young people can also be encouraged to share change and knowledge with larger social contexts through volunteer efforts with other organizations. I work for an agency that has both adult and youth volunteer programs. Former clients are often among those who use their personal experience and the training they received to help others. They provide conversation, companionship, and support to children, adolescents, and young adults.

TRANSITIONS: BEYOND THERAPY

From the start of therapy we work to maximize our effectiveness in each interaction and session. We also help young people and others to transition out of therapy. The length of therapy is dependent on conversations with those involved about what will constitute success, including the construction of goals, ways of accomplishing those goals, and recognizing when progress is being made (Bertolino & O'Hanlon, 2002). As change occurs and we work toward transitioning young people and others out of therapy we want to consider the ways that we can:

- Extend change into the future;
- Anticipate perceived hurdles and barriers;
- Use transition and celebratory rituals.

When young people and others have made positive changes, we want to work with them to *extend change into the future*. Because smaller changes can lead to bigger ones, we want to orient clients toward the possibilities of positive change in the future. We do this by inquiring about how new views and actions might assist them in reaching future goals and further positive change. To assist with this process, we ask young people and others involved questions including:

- How can you put your new learnings to work in the future?
- What have you been doing that you will continue to do once therapy has ended and in the future?
- How will you continue to solidify and build on the changes that you've made?

- What will you be doing differently that you might not have otherwise been able to do?
- After you leave here, what will you be doing to keep things going in the direction you prefer?
- What else?
- How will you keep things moving forward?
- How will you make sure that you will do that?
- How will you keep your eyes on the road ahead instead of staring into the rearview mirror?
- What do you need from others?
- How might they be of help to you?

As young people and families transition out of therapy we also want to *anticipate perceived hurdles and barriers* that may pose a threat to maintaining the changes they have made. We let people know that it is common to encounter turbulence and that they *may* experience challenges in the future. By discussing the idea that everyone faces challenges from time to time, some of the apprehension and fear that can accompany changes—such as transitioning out of therapy—can be neutralized. Further, by discussing possible future concerns, we can increase the likelihood that changes will continue.

One way to enter into conversations about possible hurdles or perceived barriers is to ask those involved, "Is there anything that might come up between now and the next time we meet that might pose a threat to the changes you've made?" or "Can you think of anything that might come up over the next few weeks/months that would present a challenge for you in staying on track?" If a young client answers "yes," we explore, in detail, what those challenges may be and how the client will handle these challenges. This is also another way of helping young people and others to manage any setbacks that result after transitioning out of therapy. The following questions can assist therapists in learning about any perceived hurdles or barriers. Several of these questions may be considered preventative, as they help young people and others to utilize their new learnings and skills in future contexts.

- What have you learned about your ability to stand up to ...?
- What might be an indication to you that the problem was attempting to resurface?
- What might be the first sign?
- What will you do differently in the future if faced with the same or a similar problem?
- How can what you've learned be of help to you in solving future problems?

- If you feel yourself slipping, what's one thing that can stop that slipping and get you heading again the direction you prefer?
- What's one thing that can bring a slippage under control or to an end?

To mark the achievement of goals or the ending of therapy it also can be helpful to accentuate the changes that have been made or assist in making the transition out of therapy a positive one. This can be done through *transition and celebratory rituals*. Rituals tend to represent a more personal message of "good luck" from therapists, but are not for everyone. In determining whether or not to use a ritual we might say to those involved:

> Often it helps people to mark the changes they've made or the ending of therapy with something symbolizes that they're moving on into the future. Is there anything that we might do here to put an exclamation point on the changes you've made or on your transition out of therapy?

The context of therapy (e.g., in home, office-based, residential) has an impact on how and to what degree transition and celebratory rituals are used. For example, transition rituals and rituals indicating rites of passage are more common in residential placement facilities (Bertolino & Thompson, 1999). What is important is engaging young people and others involved in conversations where they can determine if a ritual will be of help to them in transitioning.

WHAT DID YOU EXPERIENCE?
IMPROVING ON PROCESSES
AND PRACTICES

Throughout this book the importance of being collaborative, client-informed, and change-oriented has been discussed. We continue this path as young people and others involved transition out of therapy. To ensure quality and satisfaction, we ask those involved about their therapy experiences. Because research has demonstrated that clients' perceptions of therapists' attitudes are a better predictor of outcome than therapists' perceptions (Bachelor, 1991), we invite young people and others involved to share with us what worked and did not work for them. The following questions can assist practitioners in learning about clients' therapy experiences:

- Did you feel/think that you were heard and understood by me/our staff?

- Did you feel accepted for who you are as a person?
- Did you feel/think that your concerns were taken seriously?
- Did you feel/think that your strengths, resources, and wisdom were acknowledged and honored by our staff? If so, in what ways?
- Did you feel that you were an active participant in our work together?
- Were you given the opportunity to give feedback during the process of therapy?
- Did you feel/think that you were treated respectfully?
- Did you feel/think that an effort was made by our staff to understand your uniqueness?

The results of such questions, as well as those that may revealed through pencil and paper instruments, help us to monitor the quality and impact of services provided. This assists with maintaining accountability and in promoting respectful and effective methods.

A FINAL REMINDER

Relationships with young people, family members, and others involved often continue even after formal therapy has ended. We remain a part of clients' lives and, in turn, they remain a part of ours. As noted earlier, this does not mean that we continue being their therapists until the end of time. Instead, as discussed in Chapter 2, we maintain a "revolving door." We communicate to clients that if they need to contact us after therapy has ended they can do so, regardless of whether they are seeking additional services or just want to check in.

More and more people are coming to therapy to straighten a few things out and then move on. They then return in the future if necessary. They're not in it for the long haul. Therefore, we recognize the importance of brief trials of therapy as opposed to non-stop, ongoing, year after year treatment. Although some will need ongoing, long-term therapy, recall that research indicates that most the significant change in therapy typically occurs in the first handful of sessions.

SAVING GRACE: SMOTHERING THE
FLAMES OF BURNOUT

This book has been about promoting a change-oriented perspective with adolescents, young adults, and families. The benefits of a change-oriented perspective are far-reaching: First, clients get the benefit of working with practitioners who believe in them and the possibility of positive change. Second, young people and others involved are collaborated with in all aspects of therapy through respectful processes and practices. Finally, clients are allowed to make therapy work, as therapists emphasize their contributions to change.

It is my hope that the ideas offered throughout this book will not only be of professional benefit, but of personal benefit as well. Professionally, a change orientation can help mental health professionals to rekindle and promote hope in the lives of adolescents, young adults, and families. It can help us to search for possibilities for change in all aspects of their lives. In turn, it offers a way of countering burnout and extending our careers by orienting us toward what is possible. But a change-oriented perspective can also be seen as a perspective on life. In a sense, it is a way of "being." So let's begin "walking the talk" and letting people know that we believe in what we do in therapy and practice it in our lives as well.

References

Adler, A. (1956). *The individual psychology of Alfred Adler: A systematic presentation in selections from his writings.* [H. L. Ansbacher & R. R. Ansbacher, Trans.]. New York: Basic Books.

American Psychiatric Association. (1994). *Diagnostic and statistical manual of mental disorders* (4th ed.). Washington, DC: Author.

Andersen, T. (Ed.). (1991). *The reflecting team: Dialogues and dialogues about the dialogues.* New York: Norton.

Anderson, H., & Goolishian, H. (1992). The client is the expert: A not knowing approach to therapy. In S. McNamee & K. J. Gergen (Eds.), *Therapy as social construction* (pp. 25–39). Newbury Park, CA: Sage.

Arkowitz, H. (1992). Integrative theories of therapy. In D. K. Freedheim (Ed.), *History of psychotherapy: A century of change* (pp. 261–303). Washington, DC: American Psychological Association.

Asay, T. P., & Lambert, M. J. (1999). The empirical case for the common factors in therapy: Quantitative findings. In M. A. Hubble, B. L. Duncan, & S. D. Miller (Eds.), *The heart and soul of change: What works in therapy* (pp. 33–56). Washington, DC: APA Press.

Bachelor, A. (1991). Comparison and relationship to outcome of diverse dimensions of the helping alliance as seen by client and therapist. *Psychotherapy, 28,* 534–549.

Bailey, C. E. (Ed.). (2000). *Children in therapy: Using the family as a resource.* New York: Norton.

Barker, S. L., Funk, S. C., & Houston, B. K. (1988). Psychological treatment versus nonspecific factors: A meta-analysis of conditions that engender comparable expectations for improvement. *Clinical Psychology Review, 8,* 579–594.

Barrett, C. L., Hampe, I. E., & Miller, L. (1978). Research on psychotherapy with children. In S. L. Garfield & A. E. Bergin (Eds.), *Handbook of psychotherapy and behavior change* (2nd ed., pp. 411–436). New York: Wiley.

Berg, I. K., & Kelly, S. (2000). *Building solutions in child protective services.* New York: Norton.

Berger, P. L., & Luckmann, T. (1966). *The social construction of reality: A treatise in the sociology of knowledge.* New York: Doubleday/Anchor Books.

Bertolino, B. (1999). *Therapy with troubled teenagers: Rewriting young lives in progress.* New York: Wiley.

Bertolino, B., & O'Hanlon, B. (Eds.). (1998). *Invitation to possibility-land: An intensive teaching seminar with Bill O'Hanlon.* Bristol, PA: Brunner/Mazel.

Bertolino, B., & O'Hanlon, B. (2002). *Collaborative, competency-based counseling and therapy.* Boston: Allyn & Bacon.

Bertolino, B., & Schultheis, G. (2002). *The therapist's handbook for families: Solution-oriented exercises for working with children, youth, and families.* New York: The Haworth Press.

Bertolino, B., & Thompson, K. (1999). *The residential youth care worker in action: A collaborative, competency-based approach.* New York: The Haworth Press.

Beutler, L. E. (1989). Differential treatment selection: The role of diagnosis in psychotherapy. *Psychotherapy, 26,* 271–281.

Beutler, L. E., & Clarkin, J. (1990). Systematic treatment selection: Toward targeted therapeutic interventions. New York: Brunner/Mazel.

Beutler, L. E., Machado, P., & Neufeld, S. (1994). Therapist variables. In A. E. Bergin & S. L. Garfield (Eds.), *Handbook of psychotherapy and behavior change* (4th ed., pp. 229–269). New York: Wiley.

Bohart, A., & Tallman, K. (1999). *What clients do to make therapy work.* Washington, DC: American Psychological Association.

Bordin, E. S. (1979). The generalizability of the psychoanalytic concept of the working alliance. *Psychotherapy: Theory, Research, and Practice, 16,* 252–260.

Brown, J., Dreis, S., & Nace, D. K. (1999). What really makes a difference in psychotherapy outcome? Why does managed care want to know? In M. A. Hubble, B. L. Duncan, & S. D. Miller (Eds.), *The heart and soul of change: What works in therapy* (pp. 389–406). Washington, DC: American Psychological Association.

Cade, B., & O'Hanlon, W. H. (1993). *A brief guide to brief therapy.* New York: Norton.

Carr, A. (Ed.). (2000). *What works with children and adolescents: A critical review of psychological interventions with children, adolescents, and their families.* London: Routledge.

Carter, B., & McGoldrick, M. (Eds.). (1989). *The changing family life cycle: A framework for family therapy* (2nd ed.). Boston: Allyn & Bacon.

Carter, B., & McGoldrick, M. (Eds.). (1998). *The expanded family life cycle: Individual, family, and social perspectives* (3rd ed.). Boston: Allyn & Bacon.

Casey, R. J., & Berman, J. S. (1985). The outcome of psychotherapy with children. *Psychological Bulletin, 98,* 388–400.

Chambless, D. (1996). Identification of empirically supported psychological interventions. *Clinicians Research Digest, 14*(6), 1–2.

Chambless, D. L., & Hollon, S. D. (1998). Defining empirically supported therapies. *Journal of Consulting and Clinical Psychology, 66,* 7–18.

Chiles, J., Lambert, M. J., & Hatch, A. L. (1999). The impact of psychological interventions on medical cost offset: A meta-analytic review. *Clinical Psychology, 6*(2), 204–220.

Cohen, J. (1988). *Statistical power analysis for the behavioral sciences* (2nd ed.). Hillsdale, NJ: Erlbaum.

Cottone, R. R. (1992). *Theories and paradigms in counseling and psychotherapy.* Boston: Allyn & Bacon.

de Shazer, S, (1988). *Clues: Investigating solutions in brief therapy.* New York: Norton.

DeRubeis, R. J., & Crits-Christoph, P. (1998). Empirically supported individual and group psychological treatments for mental disorders. *Journal of Consulting and Clinical Psychology, 66,* 37–52.

Dreikurs, R. (1954). The psychological interview in medicine. *American Journal of Individual Psychology, 10,* 99–122.

Duncan, B. L., Hubble, M. A., & Miller, S. D. (1997a). Stepping off the throne. *Family Therapy Networker, 21*(4), 22–31, 33.

Duncan, B. L., Hubble, M. A., & Miller, S. D. (1997b). *Psychotherapy with "impossible" cases: The efficient treatment of therapy veterans.* New York: Norton.

Duncan, B. L., & Miller, S. D. (2000). *The heroic client: Doing client-centered, outcome-informed therapy.* San Francisco: Jossey-Bass.

Duncan, B., & Sparks, J. (Eds.). (2001). *Heroic clients, heroic agencies: Partners for change.* Florida: Nova Southeastern University Press.

Durak, J. A., Wells, A. M., Cotten, J. K., Johnson, S. (1995). Analysis of selected methodological issues in child psychotherapy research. *Journal of Clinical Child Psychology, 24,* 141–148.

Efran, J., & Lukens, M. D. (1985). The world according to Humberto Maturana. *Family Therapy Networker, 9*(3), 23–25, 27–28, 72–75.

Elkin, I. (1994). The NIMH treatment of depression collaborative research project: Where we began and where we are. In A. E. Bergin & S. L. Garfield (Eds.), *Handbook of psychotherapy and behavior change* (4th ed., pp. 114–142). New York: Wiley.

Epston, D., White, M., & "Ben." (1995). Consulting with your consultants: A means to the co-construction of alternative knowledges. In S. Friedman (Ed.), *The reflecting team in action: Collaborative practice in family therapy* (pp. 277–313). New York: Guilford.

Erickson, M. H. (1954). Pseudo-orientation in time as a hypnotherapeutic procedure. *Journal of Clinical and Experiential Hypnosis, 2,* 261–283.

Evans, I. M. (1991). Testing and diagnosis: A review and evaluation. In L. H. Meyer, C. A. Peck, & L. Brown (Eds.), *Critical issues in the lives of people with severe disabilities* (pp. 25–44). Baltimore, MD: Paul H. Brookes.

Fennell, M. J., & Teasdale, J. D. (1987). Cognitive therapy for depression: Individual differences and the process of change. *Cognitive Therapy and Research, 11,* 253–271.

Fonagy, P., & Target, M. (1996). A contemporary psychoanalytical perspective: Psychodynamic developmental therapy. In E. Hibbs & P. Jensen (Eds.), *Psychosocial treatments for child and adolescent disorders: Empirically based approaches* (pp. 619–638). Washington, DC: American Psychological Association and National Institutes of Health.

Fonagy, P., Target, M., Cottrell, D., Phillips, J., & Kurtz, Z. (2002). *What works for whom: A critical review of treatments for children and adolescents.* New York: Guilford.

Frank, J. D. (1973). *Persuasion and healing.* Baltimore: Johns Hopkins University Press.

Frank, J. D., & Frank, J. B. (1991). *Persuasion and healing: A comparative study of psychotherapy* (3rd ed.). Baltimore: Johns Hopkins University Press.

Frankl, V. (1963). *Man's search for meaning: An introduction to logotherapy.* New York: Pocket Books.

Frankl, V. (1969). *Will to meaning: Foundations and applications of logotherapy.* New York: World Publishing.

Freeman, J., Epston, D., & Lobovits, D. (1997). *Playful approaches to serious problems: Narrative therapy with children and their families.* New York: Norton.

Garfield, S. L. (1982). Eclecticism and integration in psychotherapy. *Behavior Therapy, 13,* 610–623.

Garfield, S. L. (1989). *The practice of brief psychotherapy.* New York: Pergamon.

Garfield, S. L. (1994). Research on client variables in psychotherapy. In A. E. Bergin & S. L. Garfield (Eds.), *Handbook of psychotherapy and behavior change* (4th ed., pp. 190–228). New York: Wiley.

Garfield, S. L., & Bergin, A. E. (1994). Introduction and historical overview. In A. E. Bergin & S. L. Garfield (Eds.), *Handbook of psychotherapy and behavior change* (pp. 3–18). New York: Wiley.

Gergen, K. J. (1982). *Toward transformation in social knowledge.* New York: Springer-Verlag.

Gergen, K. J. (1985). The social constructionist movement in modern psychology. *American Psychologist, 40,* 255–275.

Gergen, K. J. (1994). *Realities and relationships: Soundings in social construction.* Cambridge, MA: Harvard University Press.

Goldfried, M. R., & Newman, C. (1986). Psychotherapy integration: A historical perspective. In J. C. Norcross (Ed.), *Handbook of eclectic psychotherapy* (pp. 25–61). New York: Brunner/Mazel.

Greenberg, R. (2002, June). *Placebo, hope, and expectancy: Creating hope in psychotherapy.* Paper presented at the Heart and Soul of Change: What Works in Therapy Conference. Toronto, ON, Canada.

Grencavage, L. M., & Norcross, J. C. (1990). Where are the commonalities among therapeutic common factors? *Professional Psychology: Research and Practice, 21,* 372–378.

Gurman, A. S. (1977). The patient's perceptions of the therapeutic relationship. In A. S. Gurman & A. M. Razin (Eds.), *Effective psychotherapy* (pp. 503–545). New York: Pergamon.

Gurman, A. S., & Kniskern, D. P. (Eds.). (1981). *Handbook of family therapy* Volume 1. New York: Brunner Mazel.

Gurman, A. S., & Kniskern, D. P. (Eds.). (1991). *Handbook of family therapy* Volume II. New York: Brunner Mazel.

Guthrie, E., Moorey, J., Margison, F., Barker, H., Palmer, S., McGrath, G., Tomenson, B., & Creed, F. (1999). Cost-effectiveness of brief psychodynamic-interpersonal therapy in high utilizers of psychiatric services. *Archives of General Psychiatry, 56,* 19–26.

Haley, J. (1987). *Problem-solving therapy* (2nd ed.). San Francisco: Jossey-Bass.

Held, B. S. (1991). The process/content distinction in psychotherapy revisited. *Psychotherapy, 28*(2), 207–217.

Held, B. S. (1995). *Back to reality: A critique of postmodern theory in psychotherapy.* New York: Norton.

Herink, R. (Ed.). (1980). *The psychotherapy handbook: The A to Z guide to more than 250 different therapies in use today.* New York: New American Library.

Hoffman, L. (1981). *Foundations of family therapy: A conceptual framework for systems change.* New York: Basic Books.

Hoffman, L. (1990). Constructing realities: An art of lenses. *Family Process, 29,* 1–12.

Hoffman, L. (1995). Foreword. In S. Friedman (Ed.), *The reflecting team in action: Collaborative practice in family therapy* (pp. ix–xiv). New York: Guilford.

Horvath, A. O., & Luborsky, L. (1993). The role of the therapeutic alliance in psychotherapy. *Journal of Consulting and Clinical Psychology, 61,* 561–573.

Horvath, A. O., & Symonds, B. D. (1991). Relation between working alliance and outcome in psychotherapy: A meta-analysis. *Journal of Consulting and Clinical Psychology, 38,* 139–149.

Horvath, A. O., & Greenberg, L. S. (Eds.). (1994). *The working alliance: Theory, research, and practice.* New York: Wiley.

Howard, K. I., Kopta, S. M., Krause, M. S., & Orlinsky, D. E. (1986). The dose-effect relationship in psychotherapy. *American Psychologist, 41*(2), 159–164.

Howard, K. I., Lueger, R. J., Maling, M. S., & Martinovich, Z. (1993). A phase model of psychotherapy outcome: Causal mediation of change. *Journal of Consulting and Clinical Psychology, 61,* 678–685.

Howard, K. I., Moras, K., Brill, P. L., Martinovich, Z., & Lutz, W. (1996). Evaluation of psychotherapy: Efficacy, effectiveness, and patient progress. *American Psychologist, 51*(10), 1059–1064.

Hoyt, M. F. (Ed.). (1994). *Constructive therapies.* New York: Guilford.

Hoyt, M. F. (Ed.). (1996). *Constructive therapies 2.* New York: Guilford.

Hoyt, M. F. (Ed.). (1998). *The handbook of constructive therapies.* San Francisco: Jossey-Bass.

Hubble, M. A., Duncan, B. L., & Miller, S. D. (1999). Introduction. In M. A. Hubble, B. L. Duncan, & S. D. Miller (Eds.), *The heart and soul of change: What works in therapy* (pp. 1–19). Washington, DC.: American Psychological Association.

Hubble, M. A., Miller, S. D., & Duncan, B. L. (Eds.). (1999). *The heart and soul of change: What works in therapy.* Washington, DC: American Psychological Association.

Hubble, M. A., & O'Hanlon, W. H. (1992). Theory countertransference. *Dulwich Centre Newsletter, 1,* 25–30.

Hudson, P. O., & O'Hanlon, W. H. (1991). *Rewriting love stories: Brief marital therapy.* New York: Norton.

Ilardi, S. S., & Craighead, W. E. (1994). The role of nonspecific factors in cognitive-behavior therapy for depression. *Clinical Psychology: Science and Practice, 1,* 138–156.

Johnson, S. M., & Lee, A. C. (2000). Emotionally focused family therapy: Restructuring attachment. In C. E. Bailey (Ed.), *Children in therapy: Using the family as a resource* (pp. 112–133). New York: Norton.

Kaslow, F. W. (1996). (Ed.). *Handbook of relational diagnosis and dysfunctional family patterns.* New York: Wiley.

Kazdin, A. E. (1986). Comparative outcome studies of psychotherapy: Methodological issues and strategies. *Journal of Consulting and Clinical Psychology, 54,* 95–105.

Kazdin, A. E. (2000). *Psychotherapy for children and adolescents: Directions for research and practice.* New York: Oxford University Press.

Kazdin, A. E., Bass, D., Ayers, W. A., & Rodgers, A. (1990). Empirical and clinical focus of child and adolescent psychotherapy research. *Journal of Consulting and Clinical Psychology, 58,* 729–740.

Keat, D. B. (1996). Multimodal therapy with children: Anxious Ashley. *Psychotherapy in Private Practice, 15,* 63–79.

Keim, J. P. (2000). Oppositional behavior in children. In C. E. Bailey (Ed.), *Children in therapy: Using the family as a resource* (pp. 278–307). New York: Norton.

Klingberg, H. (2001). *When life calls out to us: The love and lifework of Viktor and Elly Frankl.* New York: Doubleday.

Kopp, S., Akhtarullah, S., Niazi, F., Duncan, B., & Sparks, J. (2001). The seamless use of measures: The nuts and bolts of accountability. In B. Duncan & J. Sparks (Eds.), *Heroic clients, heroic agencies: Partners for change* (pp. 88–94). Florida: Nova Southeastern University Press.

Koss, M. P., & Butcher, J. N. (1986). Research on brief psychotherapy. In A. E. Bergin & S. L. Garfield (Eds.), *Handbook of psychotherapy and behavior change* (3rd ed., pp. 627–663). New York: Wiley.

Lafferty, P., Beutler, L. E., & Crago, M. (1989). Differences between more and less effective psychotherapists: A study of select therapist variables. *Journal of Consulting and Clinical Psychology, 57,* 76–80.

Lambert, M. J. (1992). Implications of outcome research for psychotherapy integration. In J. C. Norcross & M. R. Goldfried (Eds.), *Handbook of psychotherapy integration.* (pp. 94–129). New York: Basic.

Lambert, M. J., & Bergin, A. E. (1994). The effectiveness of psychotherapy. In A. E. Bergin & S. L. Garfield (Eds.), *Handbook of psychotherapy and behavior change* (4th ed., pp. 143–189). New York: Wiley.

Lambert, M. J., Okiishi, J. C., Finch, A. E., & Johnson, L. D. (1998). Outcome assessment: From conceptualization to implementation. *Professional Psychology: Practice and Research, 29*(1), 63–70.

Lambert, M. J., Shapiro, D. A., & Bergin, A. E. (1986). The effectiveness of psychotherapy. In S. L. Garfield & A. E. Bergin (Eds.), *Handbook of psychotherapy and behavior change* (3rd ed., pp. 157–211). New York: Wiley.

Lambert, M. J. (2002, June). *Keynote: What works in therapy: Implications for therapists from outcome research.* Paper presented at the Heart and Soul of Change: What Works in Therapy Conference. Toronto, ON, Canada.

Lawson, D. (1994). Identifying pretreatment change. *Journal of Counseling and Development, 72,* 244–248.

Lawson, A., McElheran, N., & Slive, A. (1997). Single session walk-in therapy: A model for the 21st century. *Family Therapy News, 30*(4), 15, 25.

Lazarus, A. A. (1976). *Multimodal behavior therapy.* New York: Springer.

Lazarus, A. A. (1981). *The practice of multimodal therapy.* New York: McGraw-Hill. (Updated paperback edition, 1989, Johns Hopkins University Press).

Lazarus, A. A. (1992). Multimodal therapy: Technical eclecticism with minimal integration. In J. C. Norcross & M. R. Goldfried (Eds.), *Handbook of psychotherapy integration* (pp. 231–263). New York: Basic Books.

Lebow, J. (1997). New science for psychotherapy. *Family Therapy Networker, 21*(2), 85–91.

Lebow, J. (2001). From research to practice. *Psychotherapy Networker, 25*(2), 73–74, 76–77.

Levitt, E. E. (1966). Psychotherapy research and the expectation-reality discrepancy. *Psychotherapy, 3,* 163–166.

Liddle, H. A. (1988). Systemic supervision: Conceptual overlays and pragmatic guidelines. In H. Liddle, D. Breunlin, & R. Schwartz, (Eds.), *Handbook of family therapy training and supervision* (pp. 153–171).

Lipsey, M. W., & Wilson, D. B. (1993). The efficacy of psychological, educational, and behavioral treatment: Confirmation from meta-analysis. *American Psychologist, 48,* 1181–1209.

Loar, L. (2001). Eliciting cooperation from teenagers and their parents *Journal of Systemic Therapies, 20*(1), 59–78.

Luborsky, L., Diguer, L., Seligman, D. A., Rosenthal, R., Krause, E. D., Johnson, S., Halperin, G., Bishop, M., Berman, J. S., & Schweizer, E. (1999). The researcher's own therapy allegiances: A "wild card" in comparisons of treatment efficacy. *Clinical Psychology: Science and Practice, 6,* 95–106.

Luborsky, L., Singer, B., & Luborsky, L. (1975). Comparative studies of psychotherapies: Is it true that "everyone has won and all must have prizes"? *Archives of General Psychiatry, 32,* 995–1008.

Luborsky, L., McLellan, A. T., Diguer, L., Woody, G., & Seligman, D. A. (1997). The psychotherapist matters: Comparison of outcomes across twenty-two therapists and seven patient samples. *Clinical Psychology: Science and Practice, 4,* 53–65.

Madsen, W. C. (1999). *Collaborative therapy with multi-stressed families: From old problems to new futures.* New York: Guilford.

Maturana, H. R. (1978). Biology of language: Epistemology of reality. In G. Miller & E. Leneberg (Eds.), *Psychology and biology of language and thought* (pp. 27–63). New York: Academic.

McKeel, A. J., & Weiner-Davis, M. (1995). *Presuppostional questions and pre-treatment change: A further analysis.* Unpublished manuscript.

Miller, S. D. (1994). The solution conspiracy: A mystery in three installments. *Journal of Systemic Therapies, 13*(1), 18–37.

Miller, S. D., Duncan, B. L., & Hubble, M. A. (1997). *Escape from Babel: Toward a unifying language for psychotherapy practice.* New York: Norton.

Minuchin, S. (1974). *Families and family therapy.* Cambridge, MA: Harvard University Press.

Nathan, P., & Gorman, J. (1998). *A guide to treatments that work.* New York: Oxford University Press.

Norcross, J. C. (1986). Eclectic psychotherapy: An introduction and overview. In J. C. Norcross (Ed.), *Handbook of eclectic psychotherapy* (pp. 3–24). New York: Brunner/Mazel.

Norcross, J. C., & Goldfried, M. R. (Eds.). (1992). *Handbook of psychotherapy integration.* New York: Basic Books.

O'Hanlon, B. (1994). The third wave. *Family Therapy Networker, 18*(6),18–26, 28–29.

O'Hanlon, W. H. (1987). *Taproots: Underlying principles of Milton Erickson's therapy and hypnosis.* New York: Norton.

O'Hanlon, B. (1999). Possibility therapy: From iatrogenic injury to iatrogenic healing. In S. O'Hanlon & B. Bertolino (Eds.), *Evolving possibilities: Selected papers of Bill O'Hanlon* (pp. 143–157). Philadelphia, PA: Brunner/Mazel.

O'Hanlon, B., & Beadle, S. (1999). *A guide to possibility land: Fifty-one methods for doing brief, respectful therapy.* New York: Norton. (Originally published, 1994, as *A field guide to possibility land: Possibility therapy methods*).

O'Hanlon, S., & Bertolino, B. (Eds.). (1999). *Evolving possibilities: The selected papers of Bill O'Hanlon.* Philadelphia, PA: Brunner/Mazel.

O'Hanlon, B., & Bertolino, B. (2002). *Even from a broken web: Brief, respect-ful solution-oriented therapy for sexual abuse and trauma.* New York: Norton. (Originally published 1998)

O'Hanlon, W. H., & Weiner-Davis, M. (1989). *In search of solutions: A new direction in psychotherapy.* New York: Norton.

O'Hanlon, B., & Wilk, J. (1987). *Shifting contexts: The generation of effective psychotherapy.* New York: Guilford.

O'Hanlon, S., & O'Hanlon, B. (1999). Possibility therapy with families. In S. O'Hanlon & B. Bertolino (Eds.), *Evolving possibilities: Selected papers of Bill O'Hanlon* (pp. 185–204). Philadelphia, PA: Brunner/Mazel.

Orlinsky, D. E., Grawe, K., & Parks, B. K. (1994). Process and outcome in psychotherapy—noch einmal. In A. E. Bergin & S. L. Garfield (Eds.), *Handbook of psychotherapy and behavior change* (4th ed., pp. 270–378). New York: Wiley.

Patton, M., & Meara, N. (1982). The analysis of language in psychological treatment. In R. Russell (Ed.), *Spoken interaction in psychotherapy.* New York: Irving.

Paul, G. L. (1967). Outcome research in psychotherapy. *Journal of Consulting Psychology, 31,* 109–118.

Pearsall, D. F. (1997). Psychotherapy outcome research in child psychiatric disorders. *Canadian Journal of Psychiatry, 42*(6), 595–601.

Penn, P., & Sheinberg, M. (1991). Stories and conversations. *Journal of Strategic and Systemic Therapies, 10*, 30–37.

Petrocelli, J. V. (2002). Processes and stages of change: Counseling with the transtheoretical model of change. *Journal of Counseling and Development, 80*(1), 22–30.

Prioleau, L., Murdock, M., & Brody, N. (1983). An analysis of psychotherapy versus placebo studies. *The Behavioral and Brain Sciences, 6*, 275–310.

Prochaska, J. O., & DiClemente, C. C. (1982). Transtheoretical therapy: Toward a more integrative model of change. *Psychotherapy, 19*, 276–288.

Prochaska, J. O. (1995). Common problems: Common solutions. *Clinical Psychology: Science and Practice, 2*, 101–105.

Prochaska, J. O., & DiClemente, C. C. (1982). Transtheoretical therapy: Toward a more integrative model of change. *Psychotherapy Theory, Research, and Practice, 19*, 276–288.

Prochaska, J. O., & DiClemente, C. C. (1984). *The transtheoretical approach: Crossing traditional boundaries of therapy.* Homewood, IL: Dow Jones-Irwin.

Prochaska, J. O., & DiClemente, C. C. (1986). The transtheoretical approach. In J. C. Norcross (Ed.), *Handbook of eclectic psychotherapy* (pp. 163–200). New York: Brunner/Mazel.

Prochaska, J. O., DiClemente, C. C., & Norcross, J. C. (1992). In search of how people change: Applications to addictive behaviors. *American Psychologist, 47*, 1102–1114.

Prochaska, J. O., Norcross, J. C., & DiClemente, C. C. (1994). *Changing for good.* New York: Morrow.

Project MATCH Research Group. (1997). Matching alcoholism treatments to client heterogeneity: Project MATCH posttreatment drinking outcomes. *Journal of Studies on Alcohol, 58*, 7–29.

Prout, H. T., & Brown, D. T. (Eds.). (1999). *Counseling and psychotherapy with children and adolescents: Theory and practice for school and clinical settings.* New York: Wiley.

Prout, H. T., & DeMartino, R. A. (1986). A meta-analysis of school-based studies of psychotherapy. *Journal of School Psychology, 24*, 285–292.

Rogers, C. R. (1951). *Client-centered therapy.* Boston: Houghton Mifflin.

Rogers, C. R. (1961). *On becoming a person: A therapist's view of psychotherapy.* Boston: Houghton Mifflin.

Rosen, S. (1982). *My voice will go with you: The teaching tales of Milton H. Erickson.* New York: Norton.

Rosenzweig, S. (1936). Some implicit common factors in diverse methods of psychotherapy. *Journal of Orthopsychiatry, 6*, 412–415.

Rossi, E. L. (Ed.). (1980). *The collected papers of Milton H. Erickson on hypnosis* (Vol. 1–4). New York: Irvington.

Rossi, E. L., & Ryan, M. O. (Eds.). (1983). *Mind-body communication in hypnosis: The seminars, workshops, and lectures of Milton H. Erickson* (Volume III). New York: Irvington.

Safran, S., Heimberg, R., & Juster, H. (1997). Clients' expectancies and their relationship to pretreatment symptomatology and outcome of cognitive-behavioral group treatment for social phobia. *Journal of Consulting and Clinical Psychology, 65*, 694–698.

Schneider, W., & Klauer, T. (2001). Symptom level, treatment motivation, and the effects of inpatient psychotherapy. *Psychotherapy Research, 11*, 153–167.

Scotti, J. R., Morris, T. L., McNeil, C. B., & Hawkins, R. P. (1996). *DSM-IV* and disorders of childhood and adolescence: Can structural criteria be functional? *Journal of Consulting and Clinical Psychology, 64,* 1177–1191.

Selekman, M. D. (2002). *Living on the razor's edge: Solution-oriented brief family therapy with self-harming adolescents.* New York: Norton.

Seligman, M. E. P. (1995). Effectiveness of psychotherapy: The *Consumer Reports* study. *American Psychologist, 50,* 965–974.

Sells, S. P. (1998). *Treating the tough adolescent: A family-based, step-by-step guide.* New York: Guilford.

Shadish, W. R., Ragsdale, K., Glaser, R. R., & Montgomery, L. M. (1995). The efficacy and effectiveness of marital and family therapy: A perspective from meta-analysis. *Journal of Marital and Family Therapy, 21,* 345–360.

Shapiro, D. A., Firth-Cozens, J., & Stiles, W. B. (1989). The question of therapists' differential effectiveness: A Sheffield Psychotherapy Project addendum. *British Journal of Psychiatry, 154,* 383–385.

Shapiro, D. A., & Shapiro, D. (1982). Meta-analysis of comparative therapy outcome studies: A replication and refinement. *Psychological Bulletin, 92,* 581–604.

Shotter, J. (1993). *Conversational realities: Constructing life through language.* London: Sage.

Smith, M. L., Glass, G. V., & Miller, T. I. (1980). *The benefits of psychotherapy.* Englewood Cliffs, NJ: Prentice-Hall.

Steenbarger, B. N. (1992). Toward science-practice integration in brief counseling and therapy. *The Counseling Psychologist, 20,* 403–450.

Stricker, G., & Gold, J. R. (Eds.). (1983). *Comprehensive handbook of psychotherapy integration.* New York: Plenum.

Szapocznik, J., Kurtines, W., Foote, F., Perez-Vidal, A., & Hervis, O. (1986). Conjoint versus one person family therapy: Further evidence for the effectiveness of conducting family therapy through one person with drug-abusing adolescents. *Journal of Consulting and Clinical Psychology, 56,* 552–557.

Tallman, K., & Bohart, A. (1999). The client as a common factor: Clients as selfhealers. In M. A. Hubble, B. L. Duncan, & S. D. Miller (Eds.), *The heart and soul of change: What works in therapy* (pp. 91–132). Washington, DC: American Psychological Association.

Talmon, M. (1990). *Single session therapy: Maximizing the effect of the first (and often only) therapeutic encounter.* San Francisco: Jossey-Bass.

Talmon, M., Hoyt, M. F., & Rosenbaum, R. (1990). Effective single-session therapy: Step-by-step-guidelines. In. M. Talmon, *Single session therapy: Maximizing the effect of the first (and often only) therapeutic encounter* (pp. 34–56). San Francisco: Jossey-Bass.

Task Force on Promotion and Dissemination of Psychological Procedures. (1995). Training in and dissemination of empirically-validated psychological treatment: Report and recommendations. *The Clinical Psychologist, 48,* 2–23.

Tohn, S. L., & Oshlag, J. A. (1996). Solution-focused therapy with mandated clients: Cooperating with the uncooperative. In S. D. Miller, M. A. Hubble, & B. L. Duncan (Eds.), *Handbook of solution-focused brief therapy* (pp. 152–183). San Francisco: Jossey-Bass.

Tramontana, M. G. (1980). Critical review of research on psychotherapy with adolescents 1967–1977. *Psychological Bulletin, 88,* 429–450.

VandenBos, G. R., & Pino, C. D. (1980). Research on outcome of psychotherapy. In G. R. (Ed.), *Psychotherapy: Practice, research, and policy* (pp. 23–69). Beverly Hills, CA: Sage.

Vaughn, K., Cox Young, B., Webster, D. C., & Thomas, M. R. (1996). Solution-focused work in the hospital: A continuum-of-care model for inpatient psychiatric treatment. In S. D. Miller, M. A. Hubble, & B. L. Duncan (Eds.), *Handbook of solution-focused brief therapy* (pp. 99–127). San Francisco: Jossey-Bass.

von Foerster, H. (1984). On constructing a reality. In P. Watzlawick (Ed.), *The invented reality: How do we know what we believe we know? Contributions to constructivism* (pp. 41–61). New York: Norton.

von Glasersfeld, E. (1984). An introduction to radical constructivism. In P. Watzlawick (Ed.), *The invented reality: How do we know what we believe we know? Contributions to constructivism* (pp. 17–40). New York: Norton.

Wachtel, P. L. (1977). *Psychoanalysis, behavior therapy, and the relational word.* Washington, DC: American Psychological Association.

Wampold, B. E. (2001). *The great psychotherapy debate: Models, methods, and findings.* Mahwah, NJ: Erlbaum.

Wampold, B. E., Mondin, G. W., Moody, M., Stich, F., Benson, K., & Ahn, H. (1997). A meta-analysis of outcome studies comparing bona fide psychotherapies: Empirically, "all must have prizes." *Psychological Bulletin, 122,* 203–215.

Waters, D. B., & Lawrence, E. C. (1993). *Competence, courage, and change: An approach to family therapy.* New York: Norton.

Watzlawick, P. (Ed.). (1984). *The invented reality: How do we know what we believe we know? Contributions to constructivism.* New York: Norton.

Weiner-Davis, M., de Shazer, S., & Gingerich, W. J. (1987). Using pretreatment change to construct a therapeutic solution: An exploratory study. *Journal of Marital and Family Therapy, 13,* 359–363.

Weisz, J. R., Donenberg, G. R., Han, S. S., & Weiss, B. (1995). Bridging the gap between laboratory and clinic in child and adolescent psychotherapy. *Journal of Consulting and Clinical Psychology, 63,* 688–701.

Weisz, J. R., Weiss, B., Alicke, M. D., & Klotz, M. L. (1987). Effectiveness of psychotherapy with children and adolescents: A meta-analysis for clinicians. *Journal of Consulting and Clinical Psychology, 55,* 542–549.

Weisz, J. R., Weiss, B., & Donenberg, G. R. (1992). The lab versus the clinic: Effects of child and adolescent psychotherapy. *American Psychologist, 47,* 1578–1585.

Weisz, J. R., Weiss, B., Han, S. S., Granger, D. A., & Morton, T. (1995). Effects of psychotherapy with children and adolescents revisited: A meta-analysis of treatment outcome studies. *Psychological Bulletin, 117,* 450–468.

White, M. B., & Russell, C. S. (1997). Examining the multifaceted notion of isomorphism in marriage and family therapy supervision: A quest for conceptual clarity. *Journal of Marital and Family Therapy, 20*(3), 315–333.

Wolin, S., J., & Wolin, S. (1993). *The resilient self: How survivors of troubled families rise above adversity.* New York: Villard.

Index

accountability
   versus blame, 57–60
   and experience, 138
   as a goal of therapy, 135–36
   witnesses to, for changing views
      and perspectives, 138
acknowledgement
   combining with possibilities, 88–90
   of communication from clients, 86
   in honoring the client's orientation,
      34
   intervention through, 5–6
   by the therapist, 31
      of the client's perspective, 148–49
      linking goals in multiple-client
         sessions, 123–24
      in sessions after the first, 172
   see also validation
action-talk, for gaining clarity about
      concerns and complaints,
      107–12, 155–57
adjustments to the content of therapy,
      in response to client feedback,
      85–86
Adler, A. 116
adolescents
   defined, xi
   work with, need for flexibility and
      creativity, 1
alliance. see therapeutic alliance
allegiance effect, in evaluating the
      efficacy of therapies, 10, 41
all or nothing statements, validating,
      and translating into partial
      statements, 89
anchoring of changes, questions
      about, 178

anthropological stance, therapy from
      an, 131
assessment
   exceptions and, 101–4
   ongoing use of
      in determining directions for
         change, 105–20
      in work with multiple clients,
         123–24
   standardized methods for,
      respectful use of, 99–100
assumptions, theoretical, support for,
      28
attending, importance of, 86
attention, shifting the focus of, 139,
      147–48

barriers, that threaten changes, 193
behavioral therapies
   in the first wave of psychotherapy,
      5
   as the subjects of research, 9
beliefs of therapists, in the
      impossibility of change,
      26–27
believability, of therapeutic
      interventions, 137
Beutler, L., 11
BFTC. see Brief Family Therapy
      Center
bias, effect of, on clients, 46
bond, therapeutic, strength of and
      length of treatment, 31. see also
      therapeutic alliance
Brief Family Therapy Center (BFTC),
      116–17
brief therapy, 1

externalizing, for changing views
and perspectives, 138, 152
matching clients' preferences for
wording, about goals, 43
matching clients' linguistic styles,
effect on the therapeutic
relationship, 31
reflective of therapeutic rituals, 87
of systems therapy, 6
and the therapeutic relationship,
86–97
use of metaphor, in changing views
and perspectives, 139, 149–51
use of pronouns in clients'
descriptions of concerns, 135,
154
use of verb tense to acknowledge
clients while reflecting back
the problem, 88–89
words clients use in telling their
stories, 80–81, 129
see also action-talk
Lazarus, A., 13
learning
from setbacks, about what works,
186–88
by the therapist
about the client, 34, 46, 127–28
about the content of therapy, 170
life, reflection of, x
life cycle, family, 5–6
listening, importance of, 86
Loar, L., 52
location, of therapy, determining, as a
collaboration key, 65–66
logic, and human experience, 2
Logotherapy, 106

Madsen, W., 131
mandated therapy. see involuntary
therapy
matching, of clients' ideas with
possibilities for solutions, 34,
128, 137. see also language,
matching
maturation, attribution of meaning
in, 30
meaning, attribution of, to change, 30
means
as possibilities, 44–45
relevance of, 43–45

medical expenditures, relationship
with provision for
psychotherapy, 70
meta-analysis of psychotherapy
studies, from childhood
through young adulthood, 7
metaphor, use of, in changing views
and perspectives, 139,
149–51
methods, as possibilities, 44–45
miracle question, 116–17
motivation, as an issue of clinicians,
46–47
multimodal therapy, 13

narratives
rewriting, in young lives, 188–92
shared, 34, 128
normalization, for changing views
and perspectives, 139, 166
"no-talk" adolescent, 117–20
"not-knowing" position
for learning from clients, 131
in reflecting consultations,
182–83
"not so obvious" processes,
identifying in change-oriented
therapy, 136–37

"one model fits all" approach,
omissions in, 80
openings for change, creating in
therapy, 97. see also space
opinions, of clients about the
positions therapists ought to
take, 82
outcome-informed collaboration,
75–76
outcome-oriented therapy, 1
outcomes
defined, 42
factors that contribute to success,
15–16
findings from research, 20–23
identifying influences on and
contributions to, 3
relationship with early response in
treatment, 38, 74–75
see also success
outside helpers, collaborating with,
124–26